Hutcheson, Richard G.

God in the White House

$18.22

DATE			
SEP 13 1988			
MAR 12 1991			

GOD
IN THE
WHITE HOUSE

GOD IN THE WHITE HOUSE

How Religion Has Changed the Modern Presidency

Richard G. Hutcheson, Jr.

MACMILLAN PUBLISHING COMPANY · *New York*
COLLIER MACMILLAN PUBLISHERS · *London*

Macmillan Publishing Company
866 Third Avenue, New York, NY 10022
Collier Macmillan Canada, Inc.

Library of Congress Cataloging-in-Publication Data
Hutcheson, Richard G., 1921–
God in the White House: how religion has changed the modern presidency / Richard G. Hutcheson, Jr.
p. cm.
Includes index.
ISBN 0-02-557760-3
1. Freedom of religion—United States—History—20th century.
2. Presidents—United States—Religion.
3. Church and state—United States—History—20th century.
4. Conservatism—United States—History—20th century.
5. United States—Church history—20th century. I. Title.
BR516.H78 1988
322'.1'0973—dc19 88-2968
CIP

10 9 8 7 6 5 4 3 2 1

Printed in the United States of America

Contents

To my wife,

Ann Rivers Hutcheson

Preface

God in the White House is a presumptuous—some might even say sacrilegious—title for a book.

Yet there is a sense in which each of the three most recent presidents—Ford, Carter, and Reagan—has brought God into the White House in a unique way. Especially with born-again, Sunday School-teaching, Southern Baptist Jimmy Carter, and again with the anti-abortion, pro-school prayer program of the new religious right which has been promoted so vigorously by Ronald Reagan, religion has affected the presidency in ways previously unknown in American history.

To speak of these as "religious presidencies," as this book does from time to time, is inherently misleading. Religion is obviously only one of a multitude of factors affecting any president, no matter how devout. But seldom if ever before in the history of this nation, based as it is on separation of church and state, has religion played such a prominent role in the Oval Office. Why? What is it about recent presidents, and about our times, that has brought God into the White House in such a striking way?

The vigorous entry of religion into the councils of the presidency in our times has not been an accident. This book suggests that it has responded to the multidimensional moral crisis of the late twentieth century, compounded of Vietnam, Watergate, and the overturning of traditional values in the turmoil of the sixties. It has reflected a continuing American conviction, going all the way back to the founders of the nation, that public morality is rooted in religion. And it is a new manifestation of the traditional American expectation that presidents, as symbols of national unity, will exemplify the common underlying faith in God that holds a pluralistic society together.

Paradoxically, however, the ability of modern presidents to exemplify the public faith in such a way as to help fill the moral void is undermined by sharp polarization in the religious community. The liberal Protestant mainline denominations, long politically active, and the newly politicized religious right, are at loggerheads on every major public policy issue. Both the Carter and Reagan presidencies have reflected and suffered from this polarization.

After a look at the historical relationship of religion to the presidency and at the crises of the sixties and early seventies which turned traditional assumptions about religion and morality upside down, this book focuses on the place of religion in post-Watergate presidencies. It takes a brief look at Gerald Ford—squeaky clean and deeply religious, but a strong believer in the traditional truism that religion and politics don't mix. It then examines in some detail the place and importance of religion in the presidencies of Christian evangelicals Jimmy Carter and Ronald Reagan. It looks at the political role of the religious right, and at the pre-1988 candidacies of Jesse Jackson and Pat Robertson—the contemporary phenomenon of preachers seeking the presidency. In the final chapters the significance of the prominent place of religion in post-Watergate presidencies is probed: its effect on the historic principle of separation of church and state and its implications for American society.

Whether or not religion will continue to play so important a part in presidential politics and policy-making remains to be seen. But its prominence in recent times provides a fascinating chapter in the history of church and state in America, and a significant commentary on contemporary American culture.

Acknowledgments

Much of the material for this book comes from personal interviews with recent presidents, with persons close to the Oval Office who have observed the place of religion in the Ford, Carter, and Reagan presidencies, and with other observers of current religious and political trends and events.

I want to express my deep appreciation to each of the following, who gave me interviews:

President Jimmy Carter.

President Gerald R. Ford.

Mr. Carl A. Anderson, Reagan White House Special Assistant for Public Liaison (Catholic Religious Liaison).

Mr. Patrick J. Buchanan, Nixon White House speechwriter and Reagan White House Director of Communications.

Dr. Alberto R. Coll, Professor, U.S. Naval War College, Newport, Rhode Island, and writer on morality and public policy.

Mr. Michael Cromartie, Director of Protestant Studies, Ethics and Public Policy Center, Washington, D.C.

Secretary Donald Hodel, Reagan administration Secretary of the Interior, and Mrs. Hodel.

Ms. Carol Hornby, Reagan White House Special Assistant for Public Liaison (Protestant Religious Liaison).

Dr. John A. Huffman, Jr., President Nixon's pastor at Key Biscayne, Florida, Presbyterian Church, now pastor of St. Andrews Presbyterian Church, Newport Beach, California.

Ms. Diane Knippers, Deputy Director, Institute on Religion and Democracy, Washington, D.C.

Dr. Robert L. Maddox, Carter White House Special Assistant for Religious Liaison, now Executive Director of Americans United for Separation of Church and State.

Dr. Donn D. Moomaw, President Reagan's pastor at Bel Air Presbyterian Church, Los Angeles, California.

Pastor Richard John Neuhaus, Director, Center on Religion and Society, New York.

Mr. Joseph L. (Jody) Powell, Carter White House Press Secretary.

Dr. James M. Wall, Editor, *The Christian Century*, and former Chairman of the Carter election campaign in Illinois.

Congressman Frank R. Wolf, Republican, Tenth Congressional District, Virginia.

Without these interviews, this book would not have been possible.

The staffs of the Library of Congress, the Jimmy Carter and Gerald Ford Presidential Libraries, the Fairfax County, Virginia, Public Library, the Library of Virginia Theological Seminary, Alexandria, and the extension staff of the Library of Union Theological Seminary, Richmond, Virginia, have been consistently cooperative and helpful with documentary research.

I want to express my special appreciation to the Rockford Institute Center on Religion and Society, in New York, of which I am a Senior Fellow. The support and encouragement of the Center staff has undergirded all my work on this book. In particular, the Director of the Center, Pastor Richard John Neuhaus, in addition to an interview regarding his own involvement in certain aspects of the events covered, has spent countless hours with me in stimulating discussion of the subject matter, and has read successive drafts of the book, giving me invaluable comments and suggestions.

Special thanks are owed to the Earhart Foundation for the grant which funded the research for this book, and to the Rockford Institute for its efforts in obtaining and administering the grant.

I have deeply appreciated the support, help, and encouragement of my son, Richard G. Hutcheson, III, who discussed the concepts with me, helped me in obtaining important interviews, and read and commented on the manuscript. I am also grateful to Dr. Richard A. Ray, the publisher of my earlier books, who encouraged me in this project and read and commented on the manuscript.

Finally, I want to express my appreciation to my editor, Mr. Stephen S. Wilburn of the Macmillan Publishing Company, for his encouragement, his many positive suggestions, and his help at every stage of the writing of this book.

While I was assisted by many people, they are not, of course, in agreement with all my analyses and conclusions, and I bear full responsibility for the end product.

Richard G. Hutcheson, Jr.
November 1987

GOD
IN THE
WHITE HOUSE

1

Religion and the Modern Presidency

"We have a responsibility to try to shape government so that it does exemplify the will of God."

—JIMMY CARTER to reporters,
Plains Baptist Church, June 1976

IN SEPTEMBER 1984 former President Jimmy Carter and his wife, Rosalynn, along with forty other volunteers from his church in Georgia, spent a week in Manhattan's Lower East Side renovating an abandoned apartment building. Eating and sleeping camp-style at the Metro Baptist Church, the group replaced rotting beams and floors in the crumbling apartment house, helping to remodel it into twenty low-cost units to be owned cooperatively by the residents. In 1986 the Carters took part in a similar project in Chicago, and again in 1987 in Charlotte, North Carolina. All three projects were sponsored by Habitat for Humanity, a nonprofit ecumenical Christian organization based in Americus, Georgia, which has built with volunteer labor more than three thousand low-cost homes for the poor in Africa, South America, and the Caribbean, as well as the United States.

An ex-president of the United States? Sleeping in a sleeping bag on a church floor? Wielding a crowbar in work clothes? To provide housing for the poor? Improbable as it sounds, it was totally in character. Here was a lifelong Bible-reading, churchgoing, Sunday School-teaching Christian layman putting his faith into action. And similar attempts to put his Christian faith into action, in the conduct of the nation's business, had been characteristic of his years in the White House.

Nearly all American presidents have considered themselves Christians. Many have been conscientious Christians, some devout. But never before had the American public witnessed a born-again White House like that of Jimmy Carter, who taught a Sunday School class regularly at Washington's First Baptist Church during his White House years, who "witnessed" to the likes of South Korean President Chung Hee Park and Polish Communist leader Edward Gierek, and who daily read the Bible with his wife (in Spanish) in their White House family devotions.

Other presidents, while avoiding the public evidences which the Carter style made so obvious, may have been equally devout in personal devotions. But no one can be sure. Past American presidents have followed a long tradition of keeping private faith (whatever the nature of that private faith) separate from public performance of duty.

Many presidents have been churchgoers. Numerous churches in the Washington area point with pride to "Roosevelt's pew" or "Lincoln's pew" or "Washington's pew." Nixon brought "church" to the White House, with his much-publicized East Room religious services. American presidents have regularly called on God in public utterances on appropriate occasions. Divine blessings have been sought for national undertakings, and guidance asked in difficult times. Rare has been the inaugural address without a bow to the Almighty in the closing peroration.

But apart from lofty sentiments in ceremonial addresses, and churchgoing at decent if not regular intervals, the personal religion of most presidents has been confined to such devotions as might have been practiced in the privacy of the presidential living quarters. Indeed, the cherished principle of separation of church and state has, in the minds of most Americans (and presumably their presidents as well), translated into a taboo on allowing personal presidential religion to shape public policy.

From the beginning America has been an avowedly God-trusting but multifaith society. For nearly two centuries, as the doctrine of separation of church and state evolved, battles over the relationship of religion to public life were fought out in Congress and the courts. These institutions were themselves religiously pluralistic, always including representatives of a variety of religions. By general agreement the presidency was above the battle. Presidents, following the dominant pattern of the country itself, were usually conventional Protestants, adhering to one of the nation's many denominations. But their personal religion was kept separate from official duties. The president was a symbol of unity. As head of state in a religiously pluralistic society, he was president of all Americans. But he did, indeed, have an important religious function: that of symbolizing the common faith that bound all Americans together, the operative values on which the society was based. Sociologist Robert Bellah, adopting a term first used by Rousseau, has labeled this central core of religious belief, on which Americans have historically agreed, the "American civil religion." Whatever the label of this common faith, the president has been its symbolic head and spokesperson. Church-state battles have been left to the Congress and the courts.

There was always the potential, however, for a breach in this unwritten agreement. The presidency was the one place in the system that the religion of a single person, if vigorously practiced, could affect government in a significant way. Conceivably a Catholic, a Mormon, a Jew, or a sectarian Protestant president could base official actions on private convictions not shared by the people at large, thus upsetting the delicate balance of a multifaith society. So presidents, by unwritten law, drew a fairly clear line between private denominational religion and public responsibilities. It was the explicit promise of adherence to this line that cleared the way for the election of the first Roman Catholic president, John F. Kennedy.

The Carter Phenomenon

Jimmy Carter is both praised and damned for having crossed that line. Here was a president whose personal religion was a major element in his public persona. To secularists as well as those of more sedate and conventional religious traditions, his bubbling Baptist evangelicalism was all too painfully public. He talked openly about being born again, thereby establishing a born-again test for future presidential aspirants for the evangelical vote, who, in the years since, have felt obliged either to confess to a similar experience or explain away its absence. He insisted, against all advice, on teaching a Sunday School class in his Washington church. He found all sorts of occasions, not just with non-Christian foreign dignitaries, but with Americans of all kinds, even the press—for "witnessing."

Journalist James Wooten, White House correspondent for *The New York Times* during the Carter years, described it in his 1978 book, *Dasher*. The author of this treatment of "the roots and rising of Jimmy Carter" was clearly put off by "his rather simple religiosity":

> He seemed so comfortable with it, discussed it so easily. He had been "born again," he would say. Jesus had "come into" his "heart and cleansed it," he would explain. He would speak of the "Holy Ghost" and "justification by faith, not works" and "eternal salvation" and "everlasting life" and the need for Christians to "witness for the Lord daily" and of how he often taught a Sunday-school class back in the little village where he lived, and of how he once worked as a missionary for his church, spreading its gospel in Boston and Pennsylvania, and it was all so—so different, different enough to be odd, and odd enough, perhaps, to be downright peculiar. It was the sort of thing one expected to find on Sunday mornings on little southern radio stations, this fundamentalistic, "Brother, are you saved?" piety and zeal, but not from a man seeking such an office as he.

The secular intellectual establishment, and a good many liberal religious establishmentarians as well, found the whole thing acutely embarassing. Jimmy Carter's public piety, his corn-pone religiosity, and his born-again evangelicalism were sources of deep discomfort in Georgetown drawing rooms. It was one of the puzzles of his presidency that even though his policies and programs in many respects coincided with those of the liberal establishment, his establishment support was at best lukewarm. Surely this is part of the explanation.

But even so, an extraordinary degree of personal piety was not the factor that made Jimmy Carter's presidency a new phenomenon religiously. The truly remarkable thing was the extent to which his public policies, the goals and priorities of his administration, the imprint he left on American society (a deeper imprint, perhaps, than was recognized in the immediate aftermath) were a direct product of his religious convictions. The Jimmy Carter who put his faith into action wielding a hammer with Habitat for Humanity in New York and Chicago was the same Jimmy Carter who put his faith into action as he pressed for ratification of the highly unpopular Panama Canal treaties, sent the Reverend Andrew Young as his

Ambassador to the Third World-dominated United Nations, called for morality in foreign policy, made human rights a central theme, and exercised maddening restraint in the use of power when Iranian terrorists held American hostages. To see public policy drawn avowedly from Christian conviction was a new experience for the American people. It was an experience many of them found unpalatable, and one about which many more—even those who share his faith—have not yet made up their minds. More important, perhaps, it opened a new chapter in the nation's continuing battle over the relationship of church and state. The presidency, previously above the fray, became the new frontier in this long-standing struggle.

Ronald Reagan and the Religious Right

The Reagan presidency has presented a sharp contrast to the Carter religious style. An opaque curtain has been tightly drawn over the personal religious practices of the first family. Ronald Reagan, the son of a deeply religious evangelical mother and a conventionally Catholic father, grew up an active member of the Disciples of Christ church. Eureka College, his alma mater, was affiliated with that denomination, and he was a member of a Disciples of Christ church in Hollywood, though in the years immediately before his election to the presidency, he attended Bel Air Presbyterian Church with some regularity. He has referred to its pastor, the Reverend Donn D. Moomaw, as "my pastor."

After their arrival in the nation's capital, in an era of extremely tight security around all presidential appearances, the Reagans rarely attended church publicly. Perhaps in reaction to the highly visible religion of the Carters, the Reagans kept theirs invisible. Income-tax returns made public early in the presidency showed relatively little in the way of charitable contributions, and practically none to churches or religious organizations, though gifts to charity grew in later years.

But despite the near-total privacy enveloping personal religion, the religious impact on the Reagan presidency was, in a different way, as striking as that of the Carter years. Certain religious constituency groups—those known generally as the "new religious right"—wielded influence unmatched in any previous presidency. The political agenda of the religious right became, to a considerable extent, the social agenda of the administration. At the 1984 Republican National Convention, Jerry Falwell's presence was far more pervasive than his invocation, delivered on the night of Reagan's renomination, might have indicated, though that in itself was no insignificant signal. Platform deliberations were largely dominated by the religious right. And while many platform planks faded quickly into their accustomed oblivion, the religious influence did not. Opposition to abortion became a cornerstone of Reagan social policy. Early goals, such as constitutional amendments and legislative bars to abortion, were not strongly pushed and were not enacted during the presidency. Yet significant progress was made in quiet ways. So consistent was the antiabortion stance of federal judges appointed, pro-choice opponents charged, that this became a litmus test for judgeships. Support for prayer in public schools, while pursued with less zeal, was a strongly held public position. Reagan pressed for federal funding for parochial and religious schools, officially regarded as a desirable alternative to the secular humanism imputed to public schools. And a whole cluster of "family values" permeated the public rhetoric of the presidency.

The absence of public indications of church attendance or other religious practices should lead no one to conclude that Reagan's support of these positions was entirely political. There was every indication that these are values in which he deeply believes. "The starting point," says a White House spokesperson, "is that Ronald Reagan is an evangelical Christian."

Christian Programs at Loggerheads

With quite different styles, then, the two most recent presidencies have opened the doors to religious influences on public policy in unprecedented ways. But even more striking than the difference in style, between the public piety and evangelicalism of the Carters and the closely guarded privacy of the personal religion of the Reagans, has been the difference in substance. The religiously motivated programs of action espoused by the two most recent presidents have been at opposite ends of the Christian spectrum.

The final third of the twentieth century has been characterized generally by activist expressions of Christian faith. The traditional conservative truism that "religion and politics don't mix" has been out of favor even with traditionalists (though the deeply religious Gerald Ford strongly affirmed it). Throughout the twentieth century, liberal Christianity has been identified with programs of social and political action. Conservative Christianity through most of the century has focused on personal piety and salvation of souls, rejecting such activism as inappropriate. The rise of a moderate evangelicalism in the second half of the century began the breakdown of this traditional dichotomy, with movements such as Evangelicals for Social Action and Sojourners. Jimmy Carter reflected this orientation: a religiously conservative evangelical espousing the social activism of the liberal left.

Starting in the 1970s, the liberals and evangelicals were joined on the political battlefields by the fundamentalists of the far right. The William Sloane Coffins and Harvey Coxes of the mainline left began to hear from the Jerry Falwells and Pat Robertsons of the fundamentalist right. And, embarrassingly, the Christian action programs of the two wings of Protestantism have been not just different in emphasis, but on a collision course. If there were any political issue on which Coffin and Falwell found themselves on the same side of the fence, each would be mortified. The peace and justice agenda of the mainline and evangelical left has not just been different from the pro-life, school-prayer, family-value agenda of the religious right; each group has strongly opposed the positions of the other.

The peace and justice religious values of the Carter presidency and the pro-life, pro-traditional family values of the Reagan presidency have coincided, of course, with the secular values of the two political parties whose standards the two have borne. It would be easy to ascribe the differences entirely to secular forces. Many of the policy-makers and administrators of the two presidencies have held the same views as their religiously motivated colleagues, without any bow toward divine authority.

Yet the high visibility and strong influence of religion on the two most recent presidencies cannot be dismissed as accidental or meaningless. His religious conviction was part of the essence of who Jimmy Carter was, and he genuinely saw his political choices as expressions of his faith. The formative role of religion in the Reagan program reflected a close kinship with religious right constituency groups. The strength of the influence of these groups has been such as to bring them into contention in the late eighties for dominance in the Republican party itself.

Signs of the Times?

The high visibility and strong influence of religion in modern presidencies have reflected some deeply significant signs of the times. As we shall note in some detail later, the two great moral crises of the sixties and seventies, Vietnam and Watergate, which left the country with an unsettling anxiety about its moral health, prepared a unique historical opening for the conspicuously religious and palpably "moral" candidate, Jimmy Carter. And at a deeper and more enduring level, a long-gathering concern about the absence of moral values in an increasingly secular society—the "naked public square," to use the metaphor coined by Richard John Neuhaus—had created a vacuum demanding to be filled.

Christmas 1986 brought an incident symbolic of profound change in the American society whose coins still bear the motto "In God We Trust." The Salvation Army in Fresno, California, in support of its annual holiday fund-raising activities, placed signs in city busses saying, "Sharing Is Caring—God Bless You." After receiving two complaints, the city attorney ordered the signs removed because of their religious content. The near-total secularization of the public square, represented by an interpretation of the separation of church and state which does not permit a public "God bless you" at Christmastime, has been a matter of growing concern to large numbers of Americans. Far beyond the ranks of a few fundamentalists seeking to remove *The Wizard of Oz* and *The Diary of Anne Frank* from the public school reading lists of their children, mainstream moderates as well have become increasingly restive.

There is some question as to whether the moral emptiness of the public square can be filled by a religious presidency. But as Theodore Roosevelt observed, the White House is a bully pulpit. The symbolic role of the president as embodying American values makes the office a visible target. And there is substance in the perception that the presidency is the one place in the American system where the religious convictions of one person can make a real difference in public policy. The personal piety of Carter and the religious constituencies invited into policy formulation by Reagan have brought religion into public life in ways that may change the whole balance of church and state in this multifaith society.

The extent to which religious aspirations have become intertwined with the presidency was signaled by the pre-1988 candidacies of the Reverend Jesse Jackson and the Reverend Pat Robertson for the presidential nominations of their respective parties. Here, indeed, was the ultimate step beyond Carter's personal faith and Reagan's religious constituency groups: the vision of the preacher as president. Perhaps neither Robertson nor Jackson entered the contest expecting he would actually win his party's nomination. But each came armed with a religiously based program to meet America's needs, expecting to make a significant impact on his party's platform and to win greater influence within it.

How are we to understand the vigorous entry of religion into the councils of the presidency in our times? What led to the election of a born-again Jimmy Carter and to the unprecedented influence of the religious right in the Reagan presidency? Is the Carter style of conspicuously sectarian Christianity appropriate to the highest office of a religiously pluralistic country? How could two Christian evangelicals, Carter and Reagan, have come out in such radically different places? And how is the country to come to terms with the difference between the two programs of Christian action these two presidents have supported? What about an ordained minister in the White House? Even if neither Robertson nor Jackson is ever elected, what is the significance of their candidacies? Is it possible for religiously based values to fill the vacuum of the naked public square in pluralistic late twentieth-century America? Is the presidency the right vehicle for the promotion of such values? These are questions posed by the new mixture of religion and politics in the presidency in our times.

2

Religious Liberty and the Public Faith: Toward the "Gentlemen's Agreement"

ONE MIGHT ASK why the country had not previously experienced a "born-again presidency" like Carter's. Why was the "religious right," furnishing one president's social agenda and fielding a candidate such as Pat Robertson to take his place, a new phenomenon? The United States is a nation rooted in Puritanism and Christian Evangelicalism. Its motto is "In God We Trust." Its history is replete with "Great Awakenings." Nationwide evangelical Christian movements have led to the abolition of slavery and the prohibition of alcoholic beverages. Until the mid-twentieth century it continued to regard itself as a "Christian nation," and it added "under God" to its Pledge of Allegiance as recently as 1954. Why had religion in the White House so rarely become an issue, or a focus of attention, prior to the Carter presidency?

A brief look at past presidents, and the way they have dealt with America's multiple religions, can provide answers. By and large, they have kept their distance. And it is against this background that the religious dimensions of modern presidencies loom so large.

The dilemma lies in the fact that a president, who is president of all Americans and who symbolizes the national unity, can believe in only one of the many religions of the citizenry. A rich mix of denominations and faith groups has characterized the nation from its beginnings, and a unique system of religious freedom grew out of this mix. The birth of the American nation is widely credited with having brought a new pattern of democratic republicanism into Western history. Not so widely recognized is the fact that it also brought a brand-new religious configuration. Never before had there been a society in which civil and religious institutions were independent of each other. Never, indeed, had a nation been formed from such religiously diverse peoples that a single national religion was, from the beginning, out of the question.

Social scientists point out that nation-states, historically, have been held together by commonly held values and purposes. The cultural belief system has traditionally been provided by the national religion, which has been "established" and maintained in that position by the official backing and support of the government. Such was the pattern in every European nation from which the original colonists immigrated to the shores of the New World. Dissenting groups were sometimes tolerated, sometimes frowned upon, sometimes persecuted by governments convinced that support of the established church was necessary to the common welfare. But they were always "dissenters" from the "official" religion. Every immigrant to the American shores had in his or her background a society which assumed without question that an established church was essential to nationhood.

Sources of Religious Diversity

The origins of religious liberty must be traced back to the fifteenth-century Protestant Reformation, which had put an end to the religious hegemony of the Roman Catholic Church in the West. Protestantism's emphasis on the Bible alone as the source of religious authority, and on the spiritual authority of each person as his or her own priest (the priesthood of all believers) at the human level, was inherently individualistic. Wherever Protestants held sway, religious conformity could never be fully enforced.

But the authority of government kept diversity within bounds. The historic pattern, calling for a common religion undergirding a commonly held value system for nation-states, continued to prevail after the Reformation. The Latin phrase *cuius regio, eius religio* described the right of the head of state to determine the faith of his subjects, a principle which was given official standing by the Peace of Augsburg in 1555. In Protestant Europe the German and Scandinavian countries were officially Lutheran. Scotland, Switzerland, and the Netherlands were Calvinist (Reformed). England combined Calvinist theology with Catholic ecclesiology to produce its own distinctive Anglicanism. National borders became religious as well as geographic lines, and each country had its own established church.

Protestants were inherently a cantankerous bunch, and dissent was always present; with no ultimate appeal beyond the authority of the Bible, it was inevitable that different people would interpret Scripture in different ways. And perhaps, in post-Reformation Christendom, it was equally inevitable that religious freedom would in time become the universal pattern. This, indeed, has been the course of subsequent history, even in those nations (including much of Europe) where established churches continue to enjoy government support. But at the time of the original migration from Europe to the colonies of the New World, the most dissenters could hope for was toleration.

Colonial Established Churches

With the possible exception of a few such visionary misfits as Roger Williams, who were generally regarded by co-settlers as outrageous troublemakers, it never occurred to most of the original American colonists that their own pattern might be otherwise. Those who had been dissenters back home proceeded to set up establishments of their own in the new colonies.

The Pilgrims who landed at Plymouth Rock had been English Independents whose pilgrimage in search of religious freedom had led them first to Holland and then on to the shores of the New World. The neighboring Massachusetts Bay Colony was settled by English Puritans, themselves a dissenting minority party within the Church of England. They were unwilling to renounce Anglicanism, as the Pilgrims had done. They were determined instead to purify it with their strict Calvinist theology and congregational polity. But their continued allegiance to the mother church was eased considerably by the ocean that separated them, and in practice their Congregationalism was quite independent of the Church of England.

Neither Pilgrim nor Puritan (who shortly made common cause) considered the possibility of extending religious freedom to others. They demanded conformity within the "Holy Commonwealth" they had established, and dissenters like Roger Williams and Anne Hutchinson were invited to establish themselves elsewhere. Apart from Rhode Island, where Williams provided so open a climate that even a Jewish community found a peaceable reception, the Congregationalism of the Puritans quickly became the established church throughout the New England colonies.

The Virginia settlers were led by profit-seeking English gentlemen, untroubled by technicalities of religious dissent, and they automatically accepted the Church of England as the religion of the colony. Establishment was formalized by law in 1624, with clergy serving under the religious authority of the Bishop of London back home. Religion was by no means neglected. The colonial "glebe" system set aside a portion of tobacco land in each parish for the support of the clergy. Lay squires on the parish vestries exercised tight control over the choice and tenure of Anglican ministers, and they long resisted the appointment of American bishops who might dilute their power over the colonial clergy. The preeminent place of the Anglican Church in the colony's religious life, however, was unquestioned.

Other colonies to the south, ignoring the occasional presence of communities of French Huguenots or Scottish Presbyterians, similarly established the Church of England.

The Middle Colonies: Religious Freedom Creeps In

The Reformed Church was established by the Dutch in New Amsterdam. Early Swedish settlers sought to make their Lutheranism the official religion of their new colony in Delaware. But neither establishment stuck. It was in these middle colonies that a thoroughgoing pluralism first developed.

The priority of commerce over religion provided a climate of religious civility for the Dutch settlers in New York. They had arrived with no zeal to convert the natives and no spiritual mandate in their charter. Catholics, Calvinists, English Puritans, Lutherans, and Mennonite Anabaptists all made themselves comfortable among them before the middle of the seventeenth century. Governor Peter Stuyvesant, who arrived in 1647, tried to turn back the clock. He sought valiantly to reestablish the authority of the Dutch Reformed

Church and to exclude Lutherans and Jews. But the pattern was already fixed, and the Dutch West India Company (influenced, perhaps, by the fact that it had some Jewish stockholders) insisted on openness to all. A group of Jews arrived in 1654, and in 1656 the company ordered freedom of worship extended to them.

In Pennsylvania, William Penn, like Roger Williams in Rhode Island, founded a colony in which religious freedom was based on moral and religious convictions. The Quakers, dissenters in England and generally regarded there as a contentious bunch, set a pattern of genuine openness. Penn's "holy experiment" became a sanctuary for all who believed in God. Large numbers of Scottish and Scotch-Irish Presbyterians settled in New Jersey and Pennsylvania before beginning their migration southward along the valleys of the Appalachian ridge. They were joined by Lutherans and Roman Catholics, as well as Moravians, Mennonites, Amish, and various other continental pietists. Their churches flourished. By the middle of the eighteenth century there were more churches per capita in the middle colonies than in either New England or the South.

The Calverts of Maryland, well aware that a Catholic establishment would not be tolerated in an English colony, sought only freedom for their own worship. They provided a climate of considerable openness, adding to the pluralism of the region. So despite the assumption of the colonies to the north and south, each in its own region, that the European pattern of established churches would continue, overall religious diversity on the American continent made it inevitable that the developing pluralism of the middle region would prevail in any ultimate union.

Special Case: Roger Williams and Rhode Island

Yet the wide array of churches and religions was not the only factor making for freedom of religion on the new continent. The Rhode Island colony, a tiny haven of religious freedom in the corner of New England, birthplace of the Baptists of America and site of its first Jewish synagogue, has special significance. It was here that Anne Hutchinson and her followers came, exiled from Massachusetts Bay. So many oddballs and misfits gathered in the colony that for a time it was disparagingly referred to by the holy as "Rogue's Island." But here, under the somewhat idiosyncratic leadership of

Roger Williams, was exemplified in its purest form the principle that ultimately lay at the heart of the American proposition: that religious freedom must be guaranteed *for religious reasons.* Williams set up a community in which church and state were separated, not because of any concern for democracy, but to keep the hands of government totally out of church affairs.

Williams was driven to the acceptance of other religions in his colony—even those whose beliefs he abhorred—by the logic of his Calvinist faith in the sovereignty of God. He believed that God alone is the final authority: no church, no system of doctrine, no human being. And God alone, therefore, is the final judge between churches, systems of doctrine, and human beings. Freedom of conscience was for him the compelling principle—so much so that "I commend that man, whether Jew or Turk or Papist, or whoever, that steers no otherwise than his conscience dares."

The significance of Williams's position extended far beyond the boundaries of tiny Rhode Island. It was the position to which the logic of its pervasive Calvinism ultimately brought the emerging nation. Though pragmatic and rational considerations had much to do with the pattern which finally evolved—the inescapable reality of pluralism and the reason of the Enlightenment—Williams's principle was the religious foundation on which the American proposition was ultimately built. Despite all the battles and struggles for advantage between true believers, if religious America had not basically *believed* in religious freedom the system could not have survived.

Crossing Denominational Lines

As the colonies grew and flourished, sectarianism proliferated even in those with established churches. But a commonality of experience across denominational lines was also developing. Clergy shortages, in all the denominations transplanted from the Old World to the New, left many churches without ministers of their own. Colonists found it easy to switch denominations, temporarily or permanently, to take advantage of the services of whatever minister was available. An Anglican rector in South Carolina complained about it in 1711: "[People] must have one religious leader or another," he said. "Wanting a true and faithfull one [that is, an Anglican] they'd rather follow an Anabaptist, a Presbyterian, or a Quaker than be without one." The sectarianism of the developing nation was thus moderated by people who were familiar with the worship and church life of other denominations. The American custom of "shopping around" for a church was off to an early start.

The Great Awakening of the early eighteenth century contributed to both developing trends: numerous denominations on the one hand, but considerable line-crossing and mutual respect on the other. This massive wave of revivals, which swept the colonies from New England to Georgia beginning in the 1730s, brought more than spiritual fervor. Moving through all denominations, established or otherwise, it initiated what was to become the distinctive American style of Christianity. As church historian Martin Marty has suggested:

> The Great Awakening can be seen as a move toward the developing of modern religion in the West. At its heart was the notion of choice: you must choose Jesus Christ, must decide to let the Spirit of God work in your heart and—note well!—you may and must choose this version of Christianity against *that* version. Where once a single steeple towered above the town, there soon would be a steeple and a chapel, Old First Church and competitive Separatist Second Church or Third Baptist Chapel—all vying for souls.

The Great Awakening style of competing churches, based on personal choice, building on an already pluralistic pattern growing out of the religious diversity of the settlers, ensured a pluralistic nation. But at the same time, similarities were developing. The winds of revivalism and pietism that swept through all the American denominations provided a new commonality of experience. The groundwork was thus laid for the kind of transdenominational evangelical Protestantism that later gave to American culture the commonly held belief system it required.

Two Streams: Calvinism and the Enlightenment

John Calvin, of sixteenth-century Geneva, was in an indirect way one of the founding fathers of the American experiment. New England Puritanism, rigidly Calvinistic, did much to shape the systems and institutions of the emerging nation, and numerous historians, notably Perry Miller, have pointed to the importance of the Puritan influence. But it should be noted that in addition to New England Congregationalists, most of the other major denominations of the pre-Revolutionary period were as well shaped or strongly influenced by Calvinism. The Presbyterians, who made up the third largest group, were directly descended from Calvin by way of Scotland. The Baptists, offshoots of English Separatists, who began to proliferate with the Great Awakening, showed strong Calvinist influence. Both of these groups were, like the Congregationalists, outgrowths of Puritanism in the British Isles. The Dutch Reformed were Calvinists by way of the Netherlands. Even the Anglicans were closet Calvinists. The "39 Articles," which formed their doctrinal base in that period, were strongly Calvinistic. So Calvinism, though modified in significant ways by the pietistic revivalism of the Great Awakening, provided the dominant theological tradition of Revolutionary America. Sidney Ahlstrom has suggested that "Puritanism provided the moral and religious background of full seventy-five percent of the people who declared their independence in 1776."

But if John Calvin be granted honorary "founding father" status, so, also, must John Locke. For the second major religious influence in the Revolutionary period was the Deism of the Enlightenment. It lacked Puritan Calvinism's deep roots in American history. It was a significant religious movement in America for a brief period of less than half a century. But that time span (roughly the last forty years of the eighteenth century) was a crucially formative one in American history. It was the period of the Declaration of Independence, the Revolution, and the writing and adoption of the Constitution. And Deism's leading adherents, Washington, Jefferson, Franklin, and Madison, were towering figures among the founding fathers. Its influence, therefore, was massive.

Thomas Jefferson and James Madison wrote the original versions of the Declaration of Independence and the Constitution respectively. Along with Revolutionary General George Washington, these influential Deists became three of the first four presidents of the new nation. (The other was John Adams, a New England Unitarian, also strongly influenced by the Enlightenment.)

So dominant was the formative role of Washington, Jefferson, and Madison that Reinhold Niebuhr places their "Virginia Deism" alongside New England Calvinism as one of "the two great religious-moral traditions which informed our early life."

The Deist-Calvinist "Consensus"

Washington, Jefferson, and Madison were all Anglicans, the conventional affiliation of Virginia gentlemen. It is not certain that Jefferson maintained a formal affiliation at all, though he worshiped in Anglican churches. Washington was a reasonably faithful church attender and at times a vestryman of Truro Parish. None of the three, however, was an orthodox believer. They rejected the supernaturalism and the particularism of conventional Christianity. Consequently they were often denounced by fiery evangelicals as devils incarnate. Yet their conclusions were remarkably close to those of the Calvinists in three areas critical to the religious and moral undergirding of the new republic.

First, they shared with the Calvinists a conviction that a sovereign God was shaping America's destiny. Both groups believed that America had been "called out by God to create a new humanity." The new nation was God's "American Israel." It was the Creator who had endowed citizens of the new nation with "certain inalienable rights," among them "life, liberty and the pursuit of happiness." Along with the Calvinists, the Virginia Deists attributed the bounty and promise of the new nation to a divine Providence.

Second, the Virginia Deists shared with the Calvinists a conviction that human sin required a government of elaborate checks and balances. Perhaps in the case of Madison this was a reflection of the Calvinist doctrine of original sin. He had studied at the Presbyterian College of New Jersey (later Princeton) rather than William and Mary, usually attended by conventional Virginia Anglicans. There he had been strongly influenced by Presbyterian Divine John Witherspoon.

In Jefferson's case it was clearly the tyranny of the nonrepublican governments of the Old World, which he saw as absolutely evil. John Locke, the Enlightenment figure who most strongly influenced the Virginia Deists, appears himself to have been influenced by Calvinism in this regard. In any event, all the early presidents, especially Jefferson, Adams, and Madison, wrestled with the problems of virtue, depravity, and checks and balances.

Finally, the Enlightenment Deists shared with the Calvinists a conviction that the American republic could flourish only as religion flourished. They did not particularly care what religion it was. Enlightenment thought held all religious conviction to be no more than "opinion." The Deist founding fathers considered one religion as good as another. As Jefferson observed regarding the religious diversity of Pennsylvania and New York, religious pluralism could, indeed, support public order. The various sects, he said, "flourish infinitely. Religion is well supported; of various kinds, indeed, but all good enough; all sufficient to preserve peace and order."

But neither Jefferson nor any of his colleagues doubted that religion itself was necessary to preserve peace and order. The debate (carried on most definitively in Virginia) was over structure: various forms of establishment, or the kind of freedom, in which all religions could flourish. None of the Deist founding fathers entertained or supported the kind of antireligious attitudes that led the French Revolution, a scant decade later, to a totally secular state in which Sunday was abolished and the cathedral of Notre Dame turned into a "Temple of Reason."

The Deism of the founders has been troublesome to conservative American Christians over the years. Popular American Christianity has usually been coupled with an avid patriotism which has all but canonized the founding fathers. During the 1986 bicentennial year of the Virginia Statute, a sermon on religious liberty, which included a statement that Thomas Jefferson had been a Deist who did not accept the divinity of Christ, brought an angry challenge to the preacher from a parishioner at the close of the service. A recent book on God and country announced with some excitement the discovery of a book of prayers written by George Washington when he was about twenty: "some of the most beautiful prayers we have ever read." Quoting several of them, it concluded, "The man who wrote these words was no Deist, but a very devout Christian."

To try to read the Deist founding fathers as evangelicals is not only to distort the record, but to miss the point of their contribution to religious liberty. It is precisely *because* of the influence of the Enlightenment that they were able to establish a nation with the kind of free religious climate which has enriched all varieties of American Christianity.

Had it been left to the Presbyterians, the Baptists, and the traditional Anglicans of the Revolutionary period to come together and hammer out a system of religious liberty, the chances of their success would have been slight indeed. Mutual suspicion was too intense and partisan conviction too pervasive. Though all subscribed to a common core of belief, sorting it out and agreeing on it would have been too threatening to other fiercely held convictions.

But the Deists were sufficiently detached to do the job. Those scant forty years when the Enlightenment forcefully affected the American religious scene were the most critical forty years in the religious history of the nation, and the Deist founders managed them well.

John Courtney Murray, the scholar whose writings have most clearly voiced Roman Catholic affirmation of the "American proposition," has seen the American consensus as rooted not only in "recognition of the sovereignty of God, which radically distinguishes it from the 'Jacobin' tradition of continental Europe." It is also rooted in an ethical concept of political freedom which has "moral authority only to the extent that it issues from an inner sense of responsibility to a higher law." In this sense, says Murray, "democracy is more than a political experiment; it is a spiritual and moral enterprise. And its success depends on the virtue of the people who undertake it."

Two realities, then, led to a new kind of religious environment in the new country created out of the thirteen American colonies. One was an amazing kind of diversity in which no one of the many religious groups was sufficiently strong and dominant to aspire to establishment. This ensured a pluralistic system. As Murray has put it, "Pluralism was the native condition of American society." The other was a dominant Calvinist culture modified by the revivalism and pietism of the Great Awakening, which made common cause with rationalist conclusions derived from Enlightenment Deism. The combination ultimately produced a national consensus for full religious freedom rather than an alternative based on "toleration." Significantly, though, it was a freedom firmly rooted in religious assumptions rather than mere indifference.

The Virginia Debates

Virginia was the workshop in which the ultimate shape of the American system of religious freedom was hammered out by these two forces. While the pattern of pluralistic freedom was already firmly in place in the middle colonies, nine of the thirteen colonies still had established churches, in whole or in part, at the time of the Revolution. Dissenters were tolerated in all of them; the day when anyone was persecuted for religious beliefs was long since past in this haven of freedom. Yet an established church with full toleration for dissent—the pattern already well on its way to adoption in European countries—seemed the logical outcome to most. And it was in the state with the longest history of a formally established church but the strongest strain of Enlightenment rationalism—Virginia—that the new structure of religious freedom took shape, over a ten-year period, beginning in 1776. Two future presidents, Jefferson and Madison, were its architects.

Thomas Jefferson, having resigned his seat in the Continental Congress, turned his attention in 1776 to the affairs of his native state and took up a seat in the Virginia House of Delegates. In the fall of that year he introduced a series of proposals and resolutions aimed at eliminating all the old restrictions on religious freedom, many of them no longer enforced, from British and Virginia law. Jefferson was, in effect, proposing something radically new: complete freedom of religion, an end to all efforts at state control, a government in whose eyes all religions were fully equal. No action was taken at the time. The Revolution was in full swing, and Jefferson soon became Virginia's wartime governor. His famous "Statute for Establishing Religious Freedom" was formally placed before the Assembly in 1779 as part of a new code of law for the newly independent state, the product of a Committee of Revisors which Jefferson had chaired.

It was not, however, enacted. Virginia was still unready for such sweeping change. Despite the low esteem in which all things British were then held, there was strong sentiment among the ruling classes for retention of a favored status for the Anglican Church—soon to be severed from all ties with the old country and renamed the Protestant Episcopal Church.

The establishment of Episcopalianism in the new state was never a likely outcome. Dissenters outnumbered Anglicans, even if the English connection were not an obstacle. But among those opposing or despairing of Anglican establishment, another alternative seemed more promising: a tax not to support a single established church but "for the support and maintenance of several Ministers and Teachers of the Gospel who are of different Persuasions and Denominations." So convinced were Virginians—Deists as well as followers of more conventional creeds—that religion was a necessary undergirding for public life that a complete severing of formal ties with the churches seemed to many unthinkable. This proposal for a "multiple establishment," which came to be known in the Virginia debates as a General Assessment, was the major alternative to Jefferson's call for full religious freedom.

Multiple establishment had been explored by several other new states. The Maryland Constitution, adopted in 1776, had established Christianity in general. In 1778, South Carolina had adopted a constitution making the "Christian Protestant religion" the official religion of the state.

The Select Committee on Religion of the Virginia House of Delegates adopted the South Carolina provision almost intact, taking out "Protestant," proposing simply the "Christian Religion" for state establishment, and adding elaborate requirements for financial support of the Christian religion by General Assessment. This bill, like Jefferson's, was not adopted. The years immediately ahead were years of active fighting in Virginia, and after the Revolution there were years of maneuvering and debate.

Jefferson himself was not deeply involved in the struggle over religious liberty. At the time his Statute for Establishing Religious Freedom was introduced he was, as governor, no longer a member of the House of Delegates. After the war he accepted an appointment as American Ambassador in Paris and was removed from the scene.

Patrick Henry, long known as a friend of dissenters though he was himself an Anglican, became concerned in the postwar period over an apparent decline of religion, and he assumed leadership of the General Assessment forces. In 1784 he introduced a new bill replacing the elaborate provisions of the earlier South Carolina model. It simply provided for a property tax, with each taxpayer determining the denomination to which his money would be given and allowing those who did not choose a denomination to support the building of schools in their county.

It was to counter this bill that James Madison, in 1775, wrote his famous "Memorial and Remonstrance Against Religious Assessments," which along with Jefferson's statute is one of the two classic documents conveying the thinking of the founding fathers which underlay American religious freedom.

Patrick Henry was a formidable opponent, the most popular man in Virginia at the time. Madison's ultimate victory, in behalf of Jefferson's bill, was due as much to his astute political manipulations as to the merits of its contents or the tide of public opinion. But with some complex maneuvering in the House of Delegates, and with the help of the Presbyterians and Baptists—the two largest dissenting sects in the Commonwealth—Jefferson's act was passed by the legislature in January 1786.

Jefferson's Virginia Statute set the pattern for the nonestablishment clause of the First Amendment to the Constitution, written by Madison. Its simplicity and brevity, "Congress shall make no law Respecting an Establishment of Religion, or prohibiting the free exercise thereof," contrasted with the long and carefully reasoned document Jefferson had authored. But the essentials were there. By the time of the First Amendment's adoption, in 1791, the issues were no longer widely debated.

The provisions of the First Amendment applied only to the federal government. Several states continued to support established churches for some years. But the basic principles worked out in the Virginia struggle became, in time, those of the new nation. Full freedom and equal treatment for all religions, rather than favored treatment for one and toleration of others, became the American pattern.

The Other Half of the Issue: Religion and Public Virtue

From the beginning, however, the debate that led to religious freedom had another side. One concern was that of providing full freedom of conscience and equal protection for all in a society with many religions. But the other concern was how to form a national culture. All were agreed—established church advocates, Deists, and sectarians—that the moral underpinnings of a society were dependent on its religion. It had been the strength of this concern that had led so many to insist on the necessity for some kind of established religion—even a multiple establishment—when it was obvious that no single religion commanded the majority support an established church required.

This was the concern behind the recurring debates over the foundation of "virtue" in the new society. A republican government, dependent on the wisdom and judgment of "we, the people" rather than elites, made "public virtue" an absolute necessity. James Madison debated with Patrick Henry over a General Assessment, says University of Virginia historian William Lee Miller, but "Madison did not yield to Henry in his caring about this civil moral substance in the people." Benjamin Franklin, who first used the term "public religion," did so in the context of his concern for the public virtue essential to a democracy. Through his writings he assumed, says Martin Marty, that "such a faith could draw on the points of agreement or overlap in the religion of the churches, on what Franklin called 'the essentials of every religion.' " These essentials "were not to be used to save souls or make sad hearts glad, but they did assist the society in its search for some sort of moral consensus to support public order."

Separation of church and state, as the new system of religious liberty came to be called, was institutional but never cultural. It applied to "church" but not "religion"; the "state" but not "society." It was the intention of the founders, in a pluralistic nation, to separate institutional churches from the structures of the state, for the protection of both, but *not to separate religion from society.* Quite the opposite. The problem was how to *integrate* religion and the society—to undergird the republic with virtue—in the unavoidable absence of a relationship between church and state.

The Deist founders saw in "Reason," the touchstone of the Enlightenment, a force strong enough to draw out of all the competing religions of the former colonies the common beliefs and moral qualities the new nation required. In this their confidence may have been misplaced, and, indeed, Deism as a religious movement did not outlive the founders themselves. It was rather the Calvinist/Puritan heritage, transcending denominational lines and common to the vast majority of the citizenry, that provided the religious foundation on which "public virtue" rested. "The Calvinists," says Miller, "whether supporters or opponents of a state church, whether supporters or opponents of religious liberty, were purpose-filled followers of a purpose-filled God in a purpose-filled society in a purpose-filled universe." This became the spirit of the nation.

The extent and the depth of the embedding of religion in American society is often overlooked in a secular age. The religious roots of many of its basic institutions still influence the culture. American higher education is an example. The nation's first universities—

Harvard and William and Mary, later Yale and Princeton—were all established primarily to educate the clergy. The nationwide network of private colleges, nearly all originally denominational, had similar origins. American higher education, almost until the twentieth century, was largely the product of its churches. To debate separation of church and state without an accompanying awareness of the original and historic integration of religion and culture is to distort the American reality.

The Second Great Awakening

The Second Great Awakening, following the Revolutionary period, did much to cement the common religious basis for "public virtue" that enabled the new society to function.

The First Awakening, prior to the Revolution, had set the pattern. Sweeping through all the established denominations, it had given American Christianity the common experience of revivalism, with an overlay of pietism, modifying the Calvinistic belief system. It had set the American style of personal choice, the voluntarism that has characterized denominationalism ever since. The Methodists and Baptists (who fit the style most comfortably) were growing at the end of this First Awakening. But the major groups from the colonial period—the Congregationalists, the Anglicans (now Episcopalians), and the Presbyterians—were still the largest and most powerful.

Around 1800, a scant ten years after the ratification of the First Amendment completed the process by which religious liberty was legally instituted, the second wave of revivalism and religious enthusiasm began to sweep the country. The camp meetings and fiery preachers of the Second Great Awakening accompanied the westward movement of the nation. And now the Methodists and Baptists came into their own. The West was churched primarily by them, not by the Congregationalists, Presbyterians, and Episcopalians of the original colonies. Congregationalists and Presbyterians adapted as well as they could to the new style, and they moved westward (guided by an orderly "Plan of Union" that allowed their missionaries to work together in expanding into the Old Northwest). Evangelistic zeal, however, was not their forte. The Disciples of Christ, one of the first native American denominations, was formed by revivalistic ex-Presbyterians in tune with the frontier style. By mid-century the Methodists and Baptists had become the largest of the Protestant groups.

The American system of fiercely competitive but nevertheless cooperative and relatively friendly denominations, sharing a common core of basic conviction, was a product both of the pluralistic beginnings and the unifying experience of the two Great Awakenings in the formative years. While its origins were Protestant, it was able as time went on to expand its parameters to include the entire Judeo-Christian community of faiths.

It is easy to conclude that denominationalism is the religious counterpart of the private enterprise economic system. And in a sense it is. The willingness for each group, large or small, to follow its own vision, coupled with competition for converts, funds, and influence, is "free enterprise" in the realm of faith. But at a deeper level both religion and economy, as well as other aspects of American society, reflect the religiously based commitment to freedom, equal opportunity, and divinely led purposefulness of the original American dream.

Democratic Evangelicalism: the Protestant Consensus

The revivalist pietism of the Second Great Awakening, added to the Calvinistic Puritanism of the religious base, had created what religious historian Sidney Ahlstrom calls Democratic Evangelicalism. This was the Protestant consensus that became the de facto "established religion" of the nation and remained dominant until well into the twentieth century. The religious basis for a civic morality, which the founding fathers had considered so essential for republican government, was firmly established.

It was rooted not in the churches alone. A vast range of independent voluntary associations was another major outgrowth of the Second Great Awakening. Crossing denominational lines and bringing together Christians of all kinds for various religious and charitable purposes, these nineteenth-century parachurch groups, representing the whole Protestant spectrum, also cemented together the nation's Democratic Evangelicalism, both expressing and shaping the evangelical Protestant consensus.

The astute French observer Alexis de Tocqueville—the first to explore the relationship between religion and American democracy—reporting on his travels in America in the 1830s, provided a widely quoted analysis:

> Upon my arrival in the United States, the religious aspect of the country was the first thing that struck my attention; and the longer I stayed there the more did I perceive the great political consequences resulting from this state of things, to which I was unaccustomed. In France I had almost always seen the spirit of religion and the spirit of freedom pursuing courses diametrically opposed to each other; but in America I found that they were intimately united, and that they reigned in common over the same country.
>
> Religion in America takes no direct part in the government of society, but nevertheless it must be regarded as the foremost of the political institutions of that country; for if it does not impart a taste for freedom, it facilitates the use of free institutions. Indeed, it is in this same point of view that the inhabitants of the United States themselves look upon religious belief. I do not know whether all the Americans have a sincere faith in their religion, for who can search the human heart? But I am certain that they hold it to be indispensable to the maintenance of republican institutions. This opinion is not peculiar to a class of citizen or to a party, but it belongs to the whole nation, and to every rank of society.

Civil Religion

Tocqueville may be regarded as the first to identify what has in modern times come to be known as "civil religion." In his chapter on "The Main Causes Tending to Maintain a Democratic Republic," he sought to demonstrate that the "spirit of religion" and the "spirit of liberty" had worked together in the American experience.

The term "civil religion" was coined by Jean Jacques Rousseau, who used the phrase in *The Social Contract* and prescribed the content of a simple civil religion, acceptable to all, which he considered appropriate for state sponsorship. The term has entered contemporary American discourse through a famous 1967 essay by sociologist Robert N. Bellah on "Civil Religion in America." The civil religion Bellah identified is a body of religious symbol and belief, embedded in the founding documents of the nation and enunciated by the founding fathers, which has been a central force in American life. Its themes have been prominent in nearly every presidential inaugural address. Its rituals are celebrated in patriotic ceremonies, Memorial Days, Thanksgiving Days, and state funerals. It has had deep meaning in times of crisis. This civil religion, says Bellah, is clearly distinguished from, but not antithetical to, the denominational religions of America. It is selectively derived from Christianity, but by no means the same thing as Christianity. The average American has seen no conflict between the two.

Bellah's evaluation of civil religion was strongly affirmative: "I would argue that the civil religion at its best is a genuine apprehension of universal and transcendent religious reality as seen in or, one could almost say, as revealed through the experience of the American people." The phenomenon itself was the same one to which Tocqueville had pointed. Throughout the nineteenth century it was so intertwined with the evangelical Protestant consensus which dominated American society that no one noticed its existence.

The founding fathers were selectively quoted, and their Deism overlooked, as they were baptized retroactively into Protestant evangelicalism. William Lee Miller suggests that "eventually popular American attitudes did to Thomas Jefferson something like what Jefferson did to Jesus: they granted him very high honor indeed, but at the same time were highly selective in what was to be taken from his teaching, and in what he was to be interpreted as having stood for." But the lofty religious sentiments of the founders, the strong Calvinist impulse to make the nation over into the image of righteousness, and their own evangelical piety were for the nineteenth-century Protestants a seamless robe. No one spoke of a civil religion because the dominant religious consensus filled that role without any sense of incongruity.

Changes were taking place, however, which by the middle of the twentieth century were to undermine the evangelical Protestant consensus and its claim to legitimacy as formulator of the values and religious images by which the nation lived. A major force was immigration from central Europe, all through the nineteenth century, which brought in large numbers of Roman Catholics and ultimately made them the largest single religious denomination. Early on they had accepted and adapted to the Protestant ethos. By the twentieth century, however, their strength and self-confidence made this unnecessary.

The old Protestant consensus, obviously outdated, began to give way to a new formulation of the "Judeo-Christian tradition." In the fifties the three "official religions" of America, Protestantism, Roman Catholicism, and Judaism, were seen as jointly providing the religious undergirding for public life.

A prime formulator of the Judeo-Christian consensus was the Jewish philosopher Will Herberg, whose 1955 book, *Protestant-Catholic-Jew*, described what he called the "civic religion of the American Way of Life." This "American Way of Life," he said, is the common faith which provides an "overarching sense of unity" to American society. It synthesizes all that Americans, on the existential level at which life is lived rather than the conceptual level of belief systems, consider to be good, right, and true. Herberg viewed this "common religion" somewhat negatively. Its influence, he said, had secularized and devitalized the historic Jewish and Christian faiths. But he helped to popularize the concept. There was at mid-century a considerable measure of confidence that the three major American faiths could, jointly, undergird American society.

The confidence, however, was short-lived. There were growing Protestant divergences within as well as between denominations. The struggle between modernists and fundamentalists in the late nineteenth and early twentieth centuries, focusing on such issues as evolution and the social gospel, had ended Protestant unity, initiating a broad polarization which has endured in various forms to the present time. Protestantism as a cohesive religious grouping alongside Catholicism and Judaism became increasingly problematic in the second half of the twentieth century. The post-World War II period brought new waves of non-European immigration and growing numbers of non-Judeo-Christian religions. American pluralism gave the impression of such wide-ranging diversity that the provision of a single religiously based value system for the society seemed questionable. Intellectuals in the universities and bright, highly educated people who dominated the mass media, the new technological fields, and much of government—dubbed the "new class"—tended to see religion as antiscientific and irrelevant in modern society. Overall, the growing secularism of the culture made religion seem less and less important.

It was in this context that the concept of civil religion began to be examined by scholars. The social sciences had rediscovered the work of Max Weber and Emile Durkheim. A new generation of sociologists, including Peter Berger, Thomas Luckman, and Andrew Greeley, were examining civil religion as they had the role of religion in society. Peter Berger's *The Sacred Canopy* described religion as a fundamental basis of a culture. Bellah was part of this movement in sociology, and his focusing on the historic phenomenon of civil religion may have been related to the fact that American religion in general appeared by the sixties to have lost its historic role in the society.

Is There Really a Civil Religion?

Since Bellah's 1967 essay, the civil religion phenomenon has been debated vigorously. Adherents of traditional denominations have opposed, as Herberg did, its tendency to devitalize or even replace these more personal and fully formed religions. Its more repellent manifestations—an uncritical identification of the interests of God and country; idolatry of flag and patriotic symbols; misuse of religion as a means to civil ends; extreme interpretations of "manifest destiny"—are rejected by most Americans as legitimate religious expressions. Some observers have challenged its very existence, and others have labeled or defined it in different ways.

But those who take issue with Bellah have nevertheless conceded the historic reality of some common religious values in this multifaith society, whether labeled "civil religion" or "public religion," "public faith" or "the religion of the Republic."

The debate over American civil religion has often focused on the wrong issues. Perhaps because Bellah identified it as "a genuine apprehension of universal or transcendent religious reality," the question has tended to be "Is it a real religion?" If it is, conventional religionists are instantly on guard, since it constitutes a competitor, a threat. Some of the philosopher advocates of a civil religion—Rousseau, who coined the term, and John Dewey, who sought a "common faith" for early twentieth-century America—were, indeed, looking for a generally acceptable (and therefore "least common denominator") substitute for conventional religion. Citing them in analyses of civil religion has, therefore, contributed to the problem.

In its origins or its history, however, American civil religion has never functioned as a substitute for or competitor with the nation's "church religions." It omits the entire salvific element of Christianity, centered in the crucifixion and resurrection of Jesus Christ. This element is central for evangelical Christians. The public faith is, therefore, from the Christian standpoint, totally inadequate for personal salvation. But not even the founding fathers proposed it as a substitute for the faith communities in which Americans found their salvation. The public faith *has depended on* the denominational religions.

Martin Marty has pointed to the difference between an "ordering faith" and a "saving faith." The latter, provided by denominational religions, serves to "save souls, make sad hearts glad, give people wholeness, [and] provide them with the kind of identity and sense of belonging they crave. . . ." But people who find these needs met in various ways in their various churches have also been aware that civil society must be rightly ordered. In their common heritage, and out of their common experience of living together, they have found a workable common faith for this ordering of their society.

Civil religion developed only because the saving faiths were present in such astonishing vitality and diversity. It evolved as an essential bridge between the various church religions of a multifaith society and the requirements of public order in a spiritually united nation.

This, then, is the civil religion or public faith:

1. It is the unique product of a multifaith society seeking a common basis for the ordering of its national life: a bridge between that unified national life and the multiplicity of faiths.
2. It is not, and does not seek to be, a meaning-endowing, spirit-nourishing religion; it is an ordering faith rather than a saving faith.
3. Its effectiveness in its unifying role depends on the vitality of the various saving faiths that provide its moral undergirding.

The two-sided equation of the founding fathers is still at the heart of the American proposition: *institutional separation* of church and state in a multifaith society, but *cultural integration* of religion and society to produce a workable consensus undergirding "public virtue." To focus on the former and forget the latter, as we have tended to do in the second half of the twentieth century, is to misread the system and American history. The civil religion has made that integration possible.

Civil Religion and the Presidency

One historic role of presidents, performed faithfully, but perhaps not sufficiently recognized as an essential function during the period of the Protestant consensus, has been that of symbolizing the religious unity of the national faith. In a sense the presidents have created and maintained the civil religion. Apart from the founding documents, the verbal expressions of civil religion in American history, as cited by Bellah and others, come almost entirely from the public statements of presidents. As Bellah notes, inaugural addresses are particularly rich repositories.

Through most of the nation's history, as we have seen, the Protestant consensus was so general, and the verities of civil religion were so thoroughly embedded in the assumptions of the major denominations, that few people were aware of its separate existence in their own belief systems. But denominations were real, and the competition between them was fierce, and fringe sects not sharing the general Protestant consensus were all around. So in certain contexts the distinction between public and denominational religion was always maintained.

The presidency, the central symbol of American unity, was foremost among these. Bellah and others have found presidential speeches such rich sources of the content of the public faith for an obvious reason: presidents, by common consent, could only voice those commonly held convictions relating to national life that *constitute* the civil religion. A Baptist president could not, in an inaugural address, denounce infant baptism. A Mormon president could not cite the authority of the angel Moroni. A Jewish president could not quote the Talmud, nor could a Catholic president appeal to papal pronouncements. For none of them was the salvation of souls an appropriate topic.

Indeed, the gentlemen's agreement governing the presidency went further than that. It trusted the Baptist, who shared in the general Protestant consensus, to leave such matters as the mode of baptism to the realm of ecclesiastical niceties, but it unofficially barred the Mormon, the Jew, or the Catholic, who were not part of the Protestant mainstream, from holding office. An examination of the religion of the first thirty-four presidents of the United States (up to Kennedy) reveals that all were avowed Christians, and all were identified with one of the historic American Protestant denominations. Nine were Episcopalians, eight Presbyterians, five Methodists, and five Unitarians, two Reformed (from the Dutch Reformed tradition), and one each, Congregationalist, Quaker, Baptist, and Disciples of Christ.

Religious fervor was not required, as evidenced by the fact that four of the thirty-four may not have been actual members but only adherents of the denomination preferred. Fervor, indeed, may have been an obstacle. As politicians who have survived long enough to reach the top, presidents have known instinctively that religious sentiments can build consensus but can also be divisive.

Of the thirty-four, only Woodrow Wilson allowed deep personal religious commitment to become evident in presidential policy-making, and he was a special case. He presided over the nation at a time when public fervor was characteristic of the population at large. Note, for instance, the passage during his administration, on a wave of evangelical passion, of the eighteenth amendment to the Constitution, prohibiting alcoholic beverages.

The rest kept any evidence of deep religious commitment behind the curtains of private life. By any measure, Chester A. Arthur, who succeeded the assassinated James Garfield to the office, was one of the lesser lights of the presidency. But he voiced a key presidential discovery: "I have learned that Chester A. Arthur is one man, and the President of the United States is another." Nowhere was this more evident than in presidential religion. Only the commonly accepted verities of the civil religion were visible in public life.

Based on the evidence of history, it is probably fair to say that until the middle of the twentieth century there was a general assumption—a gentlemen's agreement—that the presidency would be held by a conventional Protestant Christian, with no visible moral blemishes, practicing his religion (since masculine gender was assumed) with gentlemanly moderation and enunciating the common religious verities on which all were in general agreement.

Indeed, the pattern held well into the second half of the twentieth century. The prominence of religious issues in the 1960 election campaign of John F. Kennedy, the first Roman Catholic president, showed how deeply embedded the traditional pattern had been. As we shall note later, it was Kennedy's clear and unequivocal promise to *adhere* to the traditional pattern, together with the widespread perception that he was a conventional rather than a zealous Catholic, that made his election possible. Johnson and Nixon conformed to tradition. Gerald Ford was deeply religious but a transitional figure. It was not until the 1976 election of evangelical Southern Baptist Jimmy Carter that the gentlemen's agreement was consigned to the dust heap of history.

3

Panorama of Past Presidents: Priests of the National Religion

IN 1905, President Theodore Roosevelt commissioned the American sculptor Augustus Saint-Gaudens to design a new penny, as well as ten- and twenty-dollar gold pieces. Saint-Gaudens recommended, for purely aesthetic reasons, that the words "In God We Trust" be eliminated. The president concurred, and the coins were minted and issued in November 1907. Then the storm broke. There was an avalanche of condemnation of this "godless coinage." Some of his more caustic critics suggested that what Roosevelt wanted on the coins was "In Theodore We Trust." Congress passed a bill to restore the motto after July 1, 1908, and the president signed it, presumably with considerable relief.

The two-level game of "church and state" designed by the founding fathers has not been easy to play. Church and state have not separated readily, nor have religion and society uncomplainingly worked together in undergirding the public virtue essential to government by the people. The lines have been hard to discern, and conflicts have been inevitable.

Presidents have been key players in the church-state game. We noted in the last chapter the gentlemen's agreement, which through most of American history has kept the White House occupied by middle-of-the-road Protestant Christians whose moderation on religious issues has kept sectarian problems from arising and presidential interference in church-state affairs at a minimum.

This, however, is an essentially negative understanding of the presidential role as merely one of steering clear of the church-state minefield. Presidents have also filled a far more positive role. They have been the major formulators of the civil religion which has provided the moral and spiritual basis of American unity.

Not surprisingly, the greatest formulations have come at crisis points in national life. Nearly all presidents have voiced appropriate religious sentiments on public occasions. But the central affirmations of American public faith have come from the presidents of the Revolutionary period, especially Washington, Jefferson, and Madison; from Abraham Lincoln in the Civil War period, and from Woodrow Wilson at the time of the First World War. Any collection of the major "scriptures" of the public faith would depend heavily on the words of these five presidents. We shall therefore examine their contribution to public religious life in some detail before moving on to look at modern presidents.

The Role of the Presidents: Washington, the Father of the Pattern

George Washington, the first president, had not been deeply involved in the earlier Virginia struggle for religious liberty. He had, of course, been too fully occupied at the time with fighting the Revolutionary War. But he had not originally sided with Jefferson and Madison. He would have preferred a "liberal and gentle establishment of religion," and he found Patrick Henry's proposal for a General Assessment acceptable.

As he wrote to George Mason (October 3, 1785), "Although no man's sentiments are more opposed to *any kind* of restraint upon religious principles than mine are; yet I must confess that I am not amongst the number of those who are so much alarmed at the thoughts of making people pay toward the support of that which they profess, if of the denomination of Christians; or declare themselves Jews, Mahomitans or otherwise, and thereby obtain proper relief." However, he went on to say, because the question had become agitated, he hoped the bill would die, thus becoming "productive of more quiet to the State." Clearly, Washington was a pragmatist rather than an ideologue on the matter.

With the principle of religious liberty set, however, he made a unique contribution to its implementation. As first president and as symbolic father of the country, he established the normative pattern for the presidency under the new system that Jefferson and Madison had designed, including not just the institutional separation but the equally important cultural linkage. After taking the oath of office on April 30, 1789, in Federal Hall, New York, he added, "I swear, so help me God"—words not part of the oath. And every president since has similarly invoked God's help.

It was Washington's special genius to bring together the various squabbling factions—regional, political, social, *and* religious—that formed the new nation. Whether commanding the Continental Army, presiding at the Constitutional Convention, or defining the role of president, he had the ability to stand above the fray, embracing and appealing to all groups and parties, using his authority sparingly, intervening at critical moments, "father" to all, embodying the spirit of unity.

His role in defining the civil religion for a multifaith society was played out in this way. As he wrote to the members of the New Church in Baltimore (January 27, 1793):

> We have abundant reason to rejoice that in this Land the light of truth and reason has triumphed over the power of bigotry and superstition, and that every person may here worship God according to the dictates of his own heart. In this enlightened Age and in this land of equal liberty it is our boast that a man's religious tenets will not forfeit the protection of the laws, nor deprive him of the right of attaining and holding the highest offices that are known in the United States.

When anti-Catholicism arose in the Continental Army, Washington dealt with it quickly and decisively. His correspondence with religious bodies, the clergy, and particular congregations was voluminous. He wrote letters to governing bodies and ruling authorities of Presbyterian, Protestant Episcopal, Methodist, Baptist, Quaker, and Dutch Reformed denominations; to gatherings of clergy in various cities and denominations; to Jewish congregations in Newport and Philadelphia, to a committee of Roman Catholics. Most of the letters were similar in tone. He always conveyed the highest respect for the religion of the recipients. He generally affirmed, as he did to the clergy of Philadelphia, March 3, 1797, that "Religion and Morality are the essential pillars of Civil society." He lauded religious liberty, condemned any kind of intolerance, and promised (as to the Methodist bishop of New York, May 29, 1789) "that I shall always strive to prove a faithful and impartial patron of genuine, vital religion." In none of these letters did he depart from that impartiality, revealing anything about his own religious affiliation or practice. But so warm and understanding were his communications that some of the recipients assumed he was "one of theirs."

Washington's official addresses and communications contained similar religious sentiments, and they were his own. Presidents in those days used no speechwriters. The words with which he began his first inaugural address set a pattern of appeal to the Almighty which became normative for future presidents and set the tone of the public religion:

> It would be peculiarly improper to omit in this first official Act my fervent supplications to that Almighty Being who rules over the Universe, who presides at the Councils of Nations, and whose providential aids can supply every human defect, that his benediction may consecrate to the liberties and happiness of the people of the United States, a Government instituted by themselves for these essential purposes. . . . In tendering this homage to the Great Author of every public and private good, I assure myself that it expresses your sentiments not less than my own; nor those of my fellow-citizens at large, less than either.

In 1789, Washington issued the first official Thanksgiving Day proclamation, following a joint resolution from both houses of Congress requesting that he do so. In originating some of the official ceremonies of the civil religion, in emphasizing the relationship of commonly held religious convictions to national life, in calling for full religious freedom and mutual respect among all, Washington first formulated the civil religion or national faith which was to express the common commitment of a diverse but religious people to "one nation under God."

Jefferson and Madison

The major contributions of Thomas Jefferson and James Madison to the evolving pattern were made before they assumed office. It was their leadership in establishing the original principle of separation of church and state, rather than any presidential actions, that fixed their place in the history of religion and the presidency.

Jefferson, while president, worshiped at Christ Episcopal Church in the capital. Washington had been largely immune to criticism, but Jefferson was a frequent target of evangelical critics who identified his Deist sentiments with "infidelity." Yet his encouragement of all religions served the nation well in a period when patterns of pluralism were still forming. Jefferson had proposed establishing professorships for each "sect" at the University of Virginia: "By bringing the sects together, we shall soften their asperities, liberalize and neutralize their prejudices, and make the general religion a religion of peace, reason, and morality." An interesting sidelight on his religious faith is his compilation of Jesus' sayings, *The Life and Morals of Jesus of Nazareth* (sometimes erroneously referred to as "The Jefferson Bible"). He said, regarding it:

> I have made a wee little book which I call the philosophy of Jesus. It is the paradigm of his doctrines, made by cutting the texts out of the book and arranging them on the pages of a blank book, in a certain order of time and subject.
>
> A more beautiful or precious morsel of ethics I have never seen. It is a document in proof that I am a real Christian, that is to say, a disciple of the doctrines of Jesus.

The importance Jefferson attached to religious freedom is evidenced by the epitaph he wrote for himself: "Author of the Declaration of Independence, of the Statute of Virginia for Religious Freedom, and Father of the University of Virginia." (No mention of the presidency!)

Madison's presidency, like that of Jefferson, added nothing to his pioneering work in establishing the basic system of religious freedom. There is some evidence that he was friendlier to conventional Christianity than either Washington or Jefferson. By some accounts he attended church regularly; by others, he rarely attended. He did, however, regularly conduct family worship. By the time of his presidency his great contribution to the American pattern was behind him. But the fact that his shaping of the basic system of religious liberty took place earlier does not detract from his enormous contribution to the pattern within which the presidency unfolded.

Theologian of the National Faith: Abraham Lincoln

If the original themes of the American civil religion were set by Washington, Jefferson, and Madison, the definitive statements came from Abraham Lincoln during the great national crisis brought on by the Civil War. It was a moral crisis, both in terms of the slavery issue, which was its central ethical dilemma, and in terms of national unity, which the public religion also defined in moral terms. The great themes of human freedom and equality were central for Lincoln, and the survival of the nation itself was seen as an article of religious faith.

Moral crises drive societies to search out their spiritual resources, and it was the special good fortune of the American people to have at the helm, not only a leader of unique political gifts, but one whose religious understanding of the issues before the nation was deep and profound. In the words of Martin Marty, "Lincoln stands at the spiritual center of American history and increasingly is seen as the theological thinker whose reflections are most apt and most profound." It is a special irony, then, that he is the only American president known never to have joined a church.

Lincoln's kind of unchurched Christianity was, of course, widespread at the time. Disparagers of religious influence in national history like to point to the relatively small percentage of Americans who were church members in earlier periods. By some estimates less than 10 percent had their names on church rolls in 1800. Historian Patricia U. Bonomi has, however, laid to rest in a definitive way the myth that low membership meant little influence. Her carefully researched and extensively documented study of eighteenth-century America depicts a pervasive level of religious influence, on political as well as social and cultural life, which is perhaps hard for twentieth-century secularists to imagine. It fits well, however, with Tocqueville's portrait of the early nineteenth century.

In the Kentucky of Lincoln's childhood, as in most of the frontier West, periodic camp-meeting revivals, rather than established congregations, provided the major gatherings for worship. Many ardent believers had no formal church membership. But the biblical message the churches transmitted was widely accepted, and the Protestant Christian ethos was deeply embedded in the public consciousness.

Let it be granted that lack of opportunity in the frontier West was not Lincoln's reason for nonmembership. He rented a pew in the First Presbyterian Church of Springfield, Illinois, of which Mrs. Lincoln was a member, and he developed a friendship with its pastor. He frequently attended New York Avenue Presbyterian Church in Washington. But he never joined. Henry C. Demming, a congressman from Connecticut, reported that when he was asked why, Lincoln replied, "When any church will inscribe over its altars, as its sole qualification for membership, the Savior's condensed statement for the substance of both law and gospel, 'Thou shalt love the Lord thy God with all thy heart, and with all thy soul, and with all thy mind, and thy neighbor as thyself,' that church will I join with all my heart and soul." But church member or not, Lincoln kept a Bible on his desk in the White House. He was obviously familiar with its content, and its language permeated his rhetoric.

The Civil War brought deep divisions to the American churches, many of which were not healed until well into the twentieth century. Yet despite these divisions, the third quarter of the nineteenth century was a period of considerable religious homogeneity. The Second Great Awakening had been a transdenominational wave of spiritual fervor through all the churches. A common evangelistic style, a common biblical frame of reference, a common hymnology, a common Calvinistic sense of divine mission, a common moral stance, provided a community of understanding to which Lincoln spoke eloquently.

Lincoln's leadership in defining the national faith was, of course, rejected by southern Christians at the time. He was, in their wartime context, the very symbol of evil. But so compelling were his appeals to the God worshiped by both sides, so impartial his moral judgments, so healing his expressions of religious caring, so unifying his spiritual perceptiveness, that ultimately he spoke to North and South alike and became the definitive spokesman for the American civil religion. His words provided a base on which broken unity could be rebuilt and wounds could be healed. Lincoln's role as high priest of the American faith was fully as important as his political and military roles in bringing the country through its trauma into renewed nationhood.

Lincoln saw the Declaration of Independence as the great source of moral authority for the Union. While the Constitution may have protected slavery in its guarantees of property rights, the Declaration had established the higher principle of "liberty and justice for all." His interpretation may have been different from Jefferson's original intent, as mid-nineteenth-century Protestantism was different from late-eighteenth-century Deism. But his sense of the American proposition was sure. "Our republican robe is soiled, and trailed in the dust," he said in 1858. "Let us repurify it. Let us turn and wash it white, in the spirit, if not the blood, of the revolution. . . . Let us readopt the Declaration of Independence."

Lincoln brought to the public religion a theological depth that had previously been missing. The founding fathers had understood the reality of evil and had built a system of checks and balances into the government as a means of restraining it. But they had treated evil as a deficiency of the "moral sense" rather than depravity. Their enlightenment faith in the power of human reason had mitigated the awareness of evil with a profound optimism about human nature.

Lincoln had no such illusions. He once remarked that the Bible teaches us that all men are sinners, but he reckoned that we would have found that out merely by looking about us. Sinful human nature, he said bluntly, cannot be changed. He saw the Civil War as the tragic result of the original sin of slavery. Yet he had a remarkably sophisticated awareness that sin was not limited to one side. Near the end of the war, in his second inaugural address, he said that both the North and the South read the same Bible, prayed to the same God, and invoked His aid against each other. It may seem strange, he claimed, while reviewing slavery, that any man should dare to ask a just God's assistance in wringing his bread from the sweat of other men's faces, but the North dared not in this case judge lest it be judged. Thinking of the two contenders, he added, "The prayers of both could not be answered; that of neither has been answered fully. The Almighty has His own purposes."

The divine will, the note on which he ended, was a theme to which Lincoln frequently returned and one on which he made a major contribution to American civil religion at its best. A recurring pitfall—and one of the reasons some critics reject the positive value of civil religion—is the tendency to identify the will of God with immediate national goals. Thus Lincoln's contemporary Julia Ward Howe in her famous "Battle Hymn of the Republic":

I have seen him in the watch-fires of a hundred circling camps;
They have builded him an altar in the evening dews and damps;
I have read his righteous sentence by the dim and flaring lamps;
His day is marching on.

I have read a fiery gospel, writ in burnished rows of steel,
"As ye deal with my contemners, so with you my grace shall deal";
Let the Hero, born of woman, crush the serpent with his heel,
Since God is marching on.

Lincoln made no such identification. After the battle of Bull Run, in September 1862, Lincoln said, "The will of God prevails. In great contests each party claims to act in accordance with the will of God. Both *may* be, and one *must* be wrong. God cannot be *for* and *against* the same thing at the same time." Why, he asked plaintively on another occasion, if God had wanted to reveal His will, had He not done so directly to the president, who wanted to know that will and had to lead the actions? But he had, instead, to "study the plain, physical facts of the case, ascertain what is possible and learn what appears to be wise and right."

Lincoln moved the common faith of the republic beyond its Deist origins to its classic form. While steering clear of the sectarianism and particularism of the Protestantism of his day and retaining its universal qualities, he deepened its understanding of human evil and broadened its concept of God's sovereignty. At the same time he removed it from its naive identification of American goals with God's will and introduced the element of God's judgment on all parties, all sections, all undertakings. Clearly Lincoln stands at a pivotal point in the American civil religion.

Protestant Crusader: Woodrow Wilson

Arguably the most religious of pre-contemporary American presidents, in the conventional church-related understanding of religion, was Woodrow Wilson. "Wilson's Christian faith was the driving force of his life," says historian Robert S. Alley. "No one in the history of the White House could equal his mastery of the Bible, nor could anyone surpass his knowledge of theology."

His roots were impeccably Christian—and Calvinist. His father, his grandfather, and an uncle were all Presbyterian ministers. After serving the Confederacy as a Civil War chaplain, Wilson's father had taught at Columbia Theological Seminary in South Carolina. Young Woodrow, along with the seminarians, absorbed a stern Calvinist morality. He had a conversion experience at the age of nineteen, in 1875, and he considered following the family tradition by becoming a minister. At Davidson College he combined religious and political studies. After a nervous breakdown he dropped the idea of the ministry. For the rest of his life, however, he remained the kind of man who knelt to pray each night at bedtime.

An inveterate moralist, a Christian crusader who based his calls to righteousness squarely on "the revelations of Holy Scripture," Wilson might be regarded as the one major exception to the historic pattern of "gentlemanly moderation" in presidential religion. Lincoln, the only previous president with anything like Wilson's theological sophistication, had nevertheless been a nonchurch member, accused by his enemies of infidelity—a "saving grace" that had balanced out his innate religiosity and kept him firmly within the limits of the gentlemen's agreement.

But Wilson, though no religious moderate, did fit his times. He rode into the presidency on the crest of a national wave of evangelical Protestant zeal, which though already undermined by a century of Catholic immigration and several decades of growing Protestant polarization, was in the midst of its last hurrah.

The period from the Civil War to the First World War, a time of rapid industrialization and of massive Catholic immigration from central Europe, was nevertheless the period in which Protestant dominance of popular culture reached its highest point. The major Protestant denominations were as staunchly particularistic as ever on internal matters such as the appropriate mode of baptism or communion. But they presented, as the eighteenth century moved toward its close, a united front in matters of mission and public influence.

The world mission movement, cooperatively dividing mission fields among the denominations into "spheres of influence" through "comity agreements" (which, for instance, cavalierly "gave" north China to the Southern Baptists and south China to the northern Baptists) and operating to a considerable extent through nondenominational parachurch agencies, was a unifying force. So were the nondenominational voluntary societies that were bearers of the reforming impulse in the nation itself: Bible and Tract societies, the American Sunday School Union, the Christian Endeavor Society, and the YMCA. In 1836 the Methodists had dissolved their own Bible Society in favor of support for the American Bible Society. Protestants were agreed on the Christian basis of public well-being and their own role in underwriting that well-being.

President Grant, troubled by the persistent corruption and incompetence in Indian agencies, had turned them over to the Protestant denominations to be operated as missionary work. Sidney Mead takes it as a commonplace that "toward the end of the nineteenth century Protestantism largely dominated the American culture, setting the prevailing mores and the moral standards by which personal and public, individual and group, conduct was judged. If culture is the tangible form of a religion, in the United States that religion was Protestantism."

The spirit of the times may be summed up in a quotation from Philip Schaff, writing for the American Historical Society in 1888:

> Christianity is the most powerful factor in our society and the pillar of our institutions. It regulates the family; it enjoins private and public virtue; it builds up moral character; it teaches us to love God supremely, and our neighbors as ourselves; it makes good men and useful citizens; it denounces every vice; it encourages every virtue; it promotes and serves the public welfare; it upholds peace and order. Christianity is the only possible religion for the American people, and with Christianity are bound up all our hopes for the future.

The preeminent symbol of the period was the Prohibition movement, Protestantism's great crusade, which had been gathering strength all through the post-Civil War period. The success of the movement was largely due to the coalition of Protestants of all varieties, clergy as well as laity, that backed it. Liberals and conservatives transcended their differences. The "mainline" denominations of America's historic mainstream were the core: Methodists, Baptists, Presbyterians, and Congregationalists.

The eighteenth amendment was passed by Congress in 1917. From the present perspective, which sees Prohibition as an utter failure, it is hard to comprehend the overwhelming consensus that supported it at the time. The process of ratification by the required thirty-six states was accomplished in just over a year. In the end forty-six of the states ratified the amendment, with only Connecticut and Rhode Island—both heavily Catholic—refusing. Eighty percent of the legislators in the entire forty-six states supported it. In six states it was unanimous. Little wonder, then, that the sense of a united Protestant America was extremely strong. For the self-confident Protestant majority, civil religion and evangelical faith were one and the same. The victory was seen as a striking advance for "Christian civilization."

Though its day was almost over, it was this tide of Protestant hegemony that swept Wilson into the presidency. The crusading spirit of American Protestantism had long been one of its prominent features. It was a spirit that transferred easily to war when "Christian civilization" was threatened, as happened in 1898, and again, on a much larger scale, in 1917–18. Lyman Abbott's book *Twentieth Century Crusade* expressed on its title page the crusading spirit of the Great War period:

> A crusade to make this world a home in which God's children can live in peace and safety is more Christian than a crusade to recover from the pagans the tomb in which the body of Christ was buried.

Wilson, then, in taking "Christian America" out of its former isolation into the mainstream of world affairs, with a sacred mission to share the blessings of freedom and democracy with less-favored peoples abroad, followed not only the Calvinist mission of his religious heritage but the spirit of the times. He saw affairs of state in biblically based moralistic terms. "I will not cry peace so long as there is sin and wrong in the world," he declared in 1911. And this was the way the America of his times saw it. God was clearly guiding the nation's destinies. At the close of the war Wilson put it in unmistakable terms:

> God has in his good pleasure given us peace. It has not come as a mere cessation of arms, a mere relief from the strain and tragedy of war. It has come as a great triumph of right. Complete victory has brought us, not peace alone, but the confident promise of a new day as well in which justice shall replace force and jealous intrigue among the nations. Our gallant armies have participated in a triumph which is not marred or stained by any purpose of selfish aggression. In a

righteous cause they have won immortal glory and have nobly served their nation in serving mankind. God has indeed been gracious.

And in the peroration of his July 1919 speech to the Senate:

> The stage is set, the destiny is disclosed. It has come about by no plan of our conceiving, but by the hand of God who led us into this way. We cannot turn back. We can only go forward, with lifted eyes and freshened spirit, to follow the vision. It was this that we dreamed at our birth. America shall in truth show the way. The light streams on the path ahead, and nowhere else.

Here was the moral purpose, the sense of divine mission which America had long applied to its own interests in its own hemisphere, gone forth to conquer the world.

Wilson had little doubt that his cause was the Lord's. In 1923, after he had left office, he said in an Armistice Day message, "I am not one of those who has the least anxiety about the triumph of the principles I have stood for. I have seen fools resist Providence before and I have seen their destruction, as will come upon these again—utter destruction and contempt. That we shall prevail is as sure as that God reigns."

The End of the Protestant Hegemony

But in terms of immediate goals, he was wrong. The dynamism of the Christian crusade did not long outlast the war. Wilson, facing enormous postwar difficulties, once quoted a Confederate soldier who had said, after a long, hard march, "I love my country, and I'm fightin' for my country, but if this war ever ends, I'll be dad-burned if I ever love another country."

The rest of the world refused to go along with Wilson's idealism abroad, the Senate blocked him at home, and his own failing health ended his presidency in weakness and disrepute. But the times had changed. The surge of crusading Protestant idealism had run its course. The shifting mood of the postwar period brought a "spiritual recession." The Student Volunteer Movement, which had fueled the missionary spirit, went into decline. Missionary giving, after reaching a peak in 1921, decreased significantly. A whole range of falling indices heralded the end of evangelical Protestant hegemony in American life.

The 1928 presidential campaign of Al Smith, Catholic and anti-Prohibition, even though it ended in defeat, marked the close of the Protestant era in American life. The Hoover victory in that campaign, says Robert Handy, was the last gasp of "dry Protestant civilization." Handy calls this period the "Second Disestablishment"—the first having been that of Jefferson and Madison. Woodrow Wilson's presidency, however, had come at the high point of the Protestant establishment, just before its collapse, and in the context of the times his break with the traditional pattern of "gentlemanly moderation" in things religious had hardly been noticed.

Post-World War I Presidents: the New Context

Wilson's successors returned to the traditional practice of keeping presidential religion in the realm of private life. In inaugural addresses and on ceremonial occasions they voiced the appropriate religious sentiments, but they led no Christian crusades. And while earlier presidents had low-keyed personal religion to avoid the pitfalls of denominationalism in an overwhelmingly Protestant culture, there was now a growing awareness of the larger pluralism that had come to characterize American society.

Although the Catholicism of Al Smith is generally believed to have played a significant role in his defeat, his candidacy in itself made it clear that the day of Protestant hegemony in American culture was over. It had been a long time in coming. Cardinal James Gibbons of Baltimore, the preeminent American Catholic prelate through most of the last quarter of the nineteenth century and the first quarter of the twentieth, had been instrumental in moving Catholics beyond their immigrant status and ethnic enclave mentality into full participation in American society. After 1908 the United States had no longer been considered by Rome as a mission field, and the American church had come of age. Cardinal Gibbons's strong leadership and his vision of a united American Catholic Church had looked for ways of transcending ethnic parishes and traditions. He had insisted, in dealing with Rome, that there be no ethnic distinctions in the government of the church. The Americanization of the church was largely his achievement.

At a Catholic congress, held in conjunction with the World's Columbian Exposition in Chicago in 1893, the words of the papal legate to the United States, Archbishop Francisco Satolli, made headlines: "Go forward, in one hand bearing the book of Christian truth and in the other the Constitution of the United States. Christian truth and American liberty will make you free, happy, and prosperous." It was Gibbons, however, who had made the pronouncement possible.

By the time of the Second World War, full participation of Catholics in what John Courtney Murray had called "the American proposition" was a given. It was another cardinal, Francis Spellman of New York, preeminent spokesman for American Catholicism throughout the war years and into the sixties, who personified Americanism as a prime Catholic virtue. So much did this become the conventional wisdom that during the postwar Cold War period Catholics were preferred candidates, regarded as least likely to be subject to subversive influences, by recruiters for such organizations as the FBI and CIA.

Increasingly, then, it had become customary to think of America as a multifaith society, and during World War II this mode of thought was institutionalized. In the movie cliché of the day, the infantry squad or the plane or boat crew always featured an obligatory Irish or Polish Catholic and a New York Jew, along with a token WASP, to symbolize the religious and ethnic partnership that was winning the war.

The military chaplaincy, which became a major institution of public religious life during the Second World War, had much to do with establishing the three-faith Catholic-Protestant-Jew pattern as the government's way of looking at American religion. Historically the Army and Navy had accepted ministers of all denominations, including a few Catholics and Jews. But like the nation itself, the chaplaincies had been overwhelmingly Protestant. In World War II the three-faith system was formally recognized and made official. Cooperation and equal treatment became the accepted standard, as Protestant, Catholic, and Jewish chaplains worked together to bring the religions of America to troops all over the world.

Presidents Roosevelt, an Episcopalian, and Truman, a Baptist, regarded the emerging three-faith pattern as normative. Roosevelt saw religion as essentially ethical and highly personal, and in his public role he emphasized the commonality of religious experience. As he wrote to Pope Pius XII in 1939 regarding the faith of common people everywhere:

> They know that unless there is belief in some guiding principle and some trust in a divine plan, nations are without light and people perish. They know that the civilization handed down to us by our fathers was built by men and women who knew in their hearts that all were brothers because they were children of God. They believe that by His will enmities can be healed; that in his mercy the weak can find deliverance, and the strong can find grace in helping the weak.

Truman frequently employed religious symbols, spoke often to religious groups, and sometimes defined policy as a religious crusade. To a group of Anglican bishops, and later to a Lutheran gathering, he asserted that the Sermon on the Mount governed "American policy in its leadership role over the moral forces of the world."

The Eisenhower Model

But it was Eisenhower, in the postwar period, who epitomized the American faith of the Judeo-Christian tradition. He moved the civil religion decisively from its old Wilsonian Protestant formulation to a new and broader Catholic-Protestant-Jew basis. He embraced the reality of a more broadly defined pluralism and enunciated clearly and forcefully its continuing relevance as the moral basis of American society. He began his first inaugural address with a three-paragraph prayer addressed to "Almighty God." And curiously, Eisenhower, like Lincoln, the earlier formulator of the public faith, spent most of his life without a formal church affiliation.

Eisenhower came from midwestern evangelical Protestant roots, with Jehovah's Witnesses in his background and a mother who was a member of a small sect called River Brethren. But his adult military experience—a lifetime of attending nondenominational Army chapels and dealing with chaplains of all three major faiths—formed his beliefs, preparing him admirably for the broader pluralism he symbolized as president. In 1948 he had announced, "I am the most intensely religious man I know," after which he had hastened to add that this did not mean he belonged to any sect. "I believe in democracy," he said.

Much has been made of Eisenhower's famous remark "America makes no sense without a deeply held faith in God—and I don't care what it is." Conventional religionists—who generally do care deeply what their own faith is—have often ridiculed it as expressing a contentless "faith in faith." And the American religious consensus of the Eisenhower years is, indeed, open to this charge. Historian William Lee Miller, in a book about the religion of the Eisenhower years called *Piety Along the Potomac*, has treated it somewhat caustically. Yet the "I don't care what it is" remark bore serious testimony to an authentic public faith. Eisenhower, says John F. Wilson, "simply assumed that the realm of common life is grounded in a public religion."

It is important to note, however, that Eisenhower did not commend religion-in-general as the answer to all religious needs. He was aware of both dimensions of the American religious system and he affirmed them both. After becoming president he was baptized into the Presbyterian church, and thereafter he remained a faithful member of that denomination. On occasion, returning from a trip on Sunday morning, he would leave his helicopter, change clothes, and head straight for services at National Presbyterian Church. After retirement he was a faithful member of the Gettysburg Presbyterian Church until his death.

If Washington, Jefferson, and Madison were the formulators of America's civil religion, then, and Lincoln was its major theologian, Eisenhower was its prime exemplar in modern times. "Not since Woodrow Wilson had there been a president who felt so much at home with public piety as he," says Martin Marty. Billboards in California during Ike's campaign for reelection carried the message "Faith in God and Country; that's Eisenhower—how about you?" The ultimate judgment of history may be that the "religious revival" of the fifties was superficial. Its emphasis on religion in general remains suspect for many whose personal commitment through church or synagogue is deeply felt. Yet the transition from an outmoded Protestant hegemony to a broader consensus was crucial. Eisenhower's place in the history of the relationship of religious faith to public life is an important one.

The American system of religious pluralism is based on genuine loyalty to institutional denominations and their faith commitments. Yet there has from the beginning been an underlying religious unity among Americans sufficiently strong to form a national culture. Eisenhower's act of joining and adhering faithfully to a denominational church confirmed the pluralism. But his articulation of the underlying unity reaffirmed the validity of the American proposition in a period when the old Protestant hegemony was clearly a thing of the past. He was the major modern spokesperson for the public religion which coexists with and is undergirded by the pluralistic faiths of America.

John F. Kennedy: the First Catholic President

The new paradigm, which recognized Protestantism, Catholicism, and Judaism as the religions of America and sought a religious basis for national life in the Judeo-Christian tradition, was authenticated by the election of John F. Kennedy. No longer was the presidency barred to non-Protestants.

Yet Kennedy's significance, as the first Catholic president, lay not so much in the fact that he broke the tradition that had governed the presidency since the nation's beginning as that he reaffirmed it. No president in history has adhered more rigorously to the classic pattern of "moderation" and to the gentlemen's agreement to keep personal faith separate from public life than he.

Kennedy's mother was inordinately pious, and the son, as president, was careful to observe all the Catholic proprieties of the family tradition: attendance at Mass, faithfully Catholic baptisms, weddings, and funerals. Yet Ted Sorensen, one of his closest associates and the family-authorized biographer, has said, "Not once in eleven years—despite all our discussions of church-state affairs, did he ever disclose his personal views on man's relationship to God." Political observer Tom Wicker found "no reason to doubt that religious belief and discipline had no effect whatever upon his Presidential conduct and judgment."

This, of course, was the promise that had paved the way for his election. From the beginning he had considered it essential that he convince the electorate that his Catholicism would not sway his presidency. He resolved to handle it directly and forthrightly, and he showed remarkable patience in doing so again and again. "I am not the Catholic candidate for President," he told a group of newspaper editors in April 1960. "I do not speak for the Catholic Church on issues of public policy, and no one in that church speaks for me." Earlier, in *Look* magazine in March of 1959, he had written: "Whatever one's religion in his private life may be, for the office-holder nothing takes precedence over his oath to uphold the Constitution and all of its parts—including the First Amendment and the strict separation of church and state." Here he was placing himself in the classic position expected of presidents, that of a clear separation between personal religion, kept in the private sphere, and public responsibility. While there might have been some question as to how "strict" the separation between church and state had been historically, certainly for the first Catholic president great strictness would be required, and he was clearly aware of it. Says William Lee Miller, "The joke was that he turned out, in effect, to be our first Southern Baptist President—one, that is, who defended a thoroughgoing separation more characteristic of that group than of his own church."

The matter of Kennedy's Catholicism was probably laid to rest as a campaign issue in his September 1960 speech to Texas Baptists in Houston. At that time, repeating once again his oft-given promises about the sharp line between private religion and public policy, he said:

> Because I am a Catholic, and no Catholic has been elected President, it is apparently necessary for me to state once again . . . not what kind of church I believe in, for that should be important only to me, but what kind of America I believe in. I believe in an America where separation of church and state is absolute, where no Catholic Prelate would tell the President (should he be Catholic) how to act, and no Protestant minister would tell his parishioners for whom to vote.

On this occasion Kennedy went so far as to pledge that he would resign should any conflict between his religious conscience and his oath to uphold the constitution arise. Whether or not the Texas Baptists were convinced, the nation at large was.

A collateral issue affecting American Catholics and the Kennedy presidency had to do with changes in the Catholic Church itself during the pontificate of Pope John XXIII. A period of unprecedented ferment and experimentation in the church culminated in the Second Vatican Council, from 1963 to 1965, which ratified and institutionalized a number of striking changes already in the wind. These included sweeping modernization of the church's worship and devotional practices, symbolized by the translation of the Mass into English (for Americans). A large number of ritual requirements (such as fish on Friday) were eliminated, thus bringing American Catholicism closer to the pattern of other denominations.

Another important change was the recognition and respect accorded other religions. In practice this significantly modified the Catholic claim, long a red flag to other Christian denominations, to be the "only true church." Barriers to marriage, child-raising, and even church attendance across Protestant-Catholic lines, all of which had earlier been negatively perceived by Protestants, were sharply reduced. In another major change lay people were given a far more prominent role in the church—also a move that brought Catholicism closer to the pattern familiar to Protestants.

While the formalization of these changes, in the decrees from Vatican II, came after Kennedy's death, the spirit of change was very much in the air during his presidency. Most important of all, perhaps, was a major alteration in the way Catholic people perceived their relationship to the church. Unquestioned obedience to ecclesiastical authority, the hallmark of an earlier Catholicism, no longer governed the religious lives of many—perhaps most—American Catholics. They adopted the right of private judgment, accepting or rejecting pronouncements of the church on particular issues, on the basis of individual conscience. This standard of private judgment and interpretation, long inherent in the biblical rather than ecclesiastical authority of Protestantism, was later apparent in the wholesale rejection by ordinary Catholics of the church's teaching on birth control.

John XXIII, who presided over Vatican II, was widely recognized as a new kind of pontiff, and Kennedy was linked in the popular mind with this new chapter in an ancient church. He was the prototypical "new Catholic" and was widely perceived as such. As Robert Alley puts it, "The vast majority of American Protestants, even those who voted against him for religious reasons, knew John Kennedy was really 'one of them.' "

Kennedy filled the traditional role of "high priest of the public religion" with consummate grace. He quoted the Bible frequently. His religious references in public speeches were apt and appropriate. And he adhered strictly, in public life, to those common aspects of religious faith shared by the entire Judeo-Christian tradition. Not once, in his public religious leadership, did Protestants or Jews find anything offensive in his Catholicism.

Kennedy confirmed and strengthened the model set by Eisenhower, which came to be regarded in modern times as normative for the American presidency. It offered a religious interpretation of America's place in history under the sovereignty of God, based no longer on the Protestant America of the nineteenth century but on the broader Judeo-Christian and biblical tradition. It provided a public morality drawn from these biblical and Judeo-Christian sources. The presidency demonstrated a private commitment to a personal, denominational religion, kept separate and distinct from the public faith with which it was fully compatible.

And the Other Thirty

Washington, Jefferson, and Madison have been highlighted in this chapter because they established the pattern: separation of church and state but close interaction between religion and society. They also established the president's role in such a society. Lincoln was the "theologian" of the civil religion, the most thoughtful and sophisticated articulator of the public faith. Wilson's importance lay in his uniqueness—as the most overtly religious of the pre-modern presidents and the one whose personal religion had the most effect on his approach to public policy. His violation of the traditional pattern was, however, a reflection of the spirit of his times. Eisenhower reformulated the public faith, in terms of the Judeo-Christian tradition of the post-Protestant period, and was its most articulate modern spokesperson. Kennedy confirmed the Eisenhower model, demonstrating that a Catholic could fill the same role and symbolizing vividly, as the first Catholic president, the end of the old Protestant hegemony.

What about the other thirty presidents in American history up to the seventies? They varied denominationally from Millard Fillmore, the Unitarian, to Herbert Hoover, the Quaker. In terms of public evidence of the fruits of their personal faith, they varied from the rectitude of John Adams, who near the end of his life wrote to Dr. Benjamin Rush, "I have been a church-going animal for 76 years," to the scandals surrounding Warren Harding and the resignation of Richard Nixon under an ethical cloud.

They provide a plethora of footnotes on the relationship of religion to the presidency. John Quincy Adams, while president, served as a trustee of New York Avenue Presbyterian Church in Washington, and on several occasions loaned the church substantial sums of money to pay current bills.

Andrew Jackson recorded in his diary that he read three to five chapters from the Bible each day.

James Buchanan, after retirement from the presidency, was refused membership in a New York Presbyterian church because of his earlier limited endorsement of slavery and was held in limbo for four years before being finally admitted to the church rolls.

Andrew Johnson toyed with the idea of becoming a Catholic but out of respect for his Methodist wife and the political power of the Know Nothings, did nothing about it.

Rutherford Hayes, whose ardently prohibitionist Methodist wife was known as "Lemonade Lucy," was probably not a formal church member but knelt and prayed following family devotions each morning at the White House breakfast table.

James Garfield, before entering politics, was a lay preacher of the Disciples of Christ church.

Benjamin Harrison, a Presbyterian deacon, elder, and Sunday School teacher, was labeled by Theodore Roosevelt "a cold-blooded, narrow-minded, prejudiced, obstinate, timid old Psalm-singing Indianapolis politician."

Grover Cleveland pronounced his training as a minister's son "more valuable to me as a strengthening influence than any other incident in my life."

William McKinley, a former Methodist Sunday School superintendent, liked to gather friends (including members of Congress) for Sunday-night hymn sings at the White House.

Dutch Reformed Church member Theodore Roosevelt was such a vigorous hymn singer that a popular story of the day had him reorganizing the Heavenly Choir after death, calling for 10,000 sopranos, 10,000 altos, 10,000 tenors, and concluding, "I'll sing bass."

Lyndon Johnson, who wanted to please everybody, probably attended more Washington churches, Catholic and Protestant, than any other president.

More important than this presidential religious trivia, however, is the fact that all the other thirty followed the expected pattern with regard to religion in the White House. The public image presented by each of them was that of conventionally religious rectitude accompanied by personal allegiance to (if not always membership in) one of America's religious denominations. Their personal religious convictions and their participation in denominational religion were kept in the private sphere. Nearly all attended church. But they kept their distance. Separation of church and state meant for them separation of public policy and private religion.

As we have noted before, however, separation of church and state is only half of the religious freedom issue as confronted and resolved by the founding fathers and as worked out in the years since. The other half is the interrelationship of religion and culture. Throughout American history, as we have seen, this close relationship between religion and society has prevailed alongside the institutional separation of church and state. Here presidents have had a positive role, as symbolic high priests of the public religion that has undergirded American life. With varying degrees of enthusiasm and success, all have played their roles. They have made appropriate references to God and to the religious dimensions of national life on ceremonial occasions, officiated at national rituals, and served as spokespersons for the national faith. Their personal religion—whatever its nature—has generally not been allowed to intrude into public life.

Seymour Fersh, in 1961, made a study of the 170 annual state-of-the-union messages of presidents up to that year, including their religious dimensions. Characteristically, these messages have included religious references—usually of a generalized nature—at the beginning and the end. The annual Thanksgiving proclamations since the time of Grant (prior to which Thanksgivings were proclaimed sporadically but not annually) have followed a formalized pattern reflecting a basic belief that God has created and sustained the common life and that the nation continues to be dependent on God's providence.

In earlier years presidents occasionally proclaimed national days of humiliation, as John Adams did on May 9, 1787, to "satisfy divine displeasure." Three such days of humiliation were proclaimed during the War of 1812, after which there were no more until the three proclaimed by Lincoln during the Civil War. The last of these was a "day of public humiliation, prayer and fasting" set by Wilson for May 30, 1918. The demise of this custom is no doubt related to the fact that humiliation has gone out of fashion in American denominational religion as well as in national life. Twentieth-century Americans do not take well to humiliation, even implied humiliation, as Carter discovered with his announcement of a national "malaise" in 1978.

Presidential deaths, however, have called forth "days of fasting and prayer" (after the death of Harrison); or "a special period for again humbling ourselves before Almighty God, in order that the bereavement should be sanctified to the nation" (Lincoln); or "sorrowful submission to the will of Almighty God" (Garfield). State funerals, memorial days—all these have called forth presidential leadership in the rituals of the civil religion.

The overall pattern has been a consistent one. Presidents from Washington through Kennedy—whatever their personal religious convictions—have faithfully filled their symbolic role as head of the civil religion. Indeed, they have been the major articulators of the public faith, and their leadership has sustained it in its unifying function. Historically, the presidency has always been the symbolic focal point for the public religion.

4

Spinning Off into the Sixties: the Demise of the Moral Consensus

WHAT HAPPENED to change the historic pattern? The contemporary presidency, and particularly the new way in which religious and moral issues have become prominent in presidential politics and policies today, can only be understood against the background of the social upheaval of the 1960s.

For many years to come the sixties will probably be seen as a watershed period for American society. Suddenly nothing was the same, and everything went screeching off in new directions. A full generation later the images of the decade are still vivid: civil rights protest marches and sit-ins at lunch counters; the "youth revolution" and the "generation gap"; *Hair* and the sexual revolution; drugs and "hippies"; huge marches in Washington protesting the Vietnamese War; young men running off to Canada or Scandinavia to avoid the draft; a president forced to give up his quest for reelection. It was a time of massive social change, still not fully sorted out and understood. And not least among the old verities tossed out in the turmoil of that upsetting decade was the long-established religious equilibrium, for the sixties also brought massive changes in the American churches.

It is, of course, an oversimplification to ascribe to a single decade a wave of social turmoil which obviously had earlier roots, which at its height spilled over into the first half of the next decade, and which has had persistent consequences since. Indeed, if the decade of greatest change were precisely fixed, it would probably be 1965 to 1975. But perception is sometimes more important than precise dating. "The sixties" will probably long be the symbolic designation for an era in which American society seemed to have turned itself upside down.

New Directions on the Religious Scene: the Proliferation of Faiths, Cults, and Value Systems

On the religious scene the Catholic-Protestant-Jew paradigm of the Eisenhower years had been a continuation of the basic pattern of the past. The America of the 1950s was no longer a Protestant nation, true, but a genuine community of interests between various religious groups had continued to exist.

The entry of Catholics into the civil religion had, in fact, brought substantial gains. John Courtney Murray, in the fifties and sixties, offered some of the most thoughtful analyses of the American proposition yet produced. Catholicism's natural law tradition was an uneasy bedfellow with Protestant dependence on biblical revelation. But it provided nevertheless a way of looking at interfaith commonalities which accorded well with the words of the founders. Catholics and Jews had joined with Protestants in a substantial religious consensus undergirding public life.

But not for long. New permutations of pluralism were on the way, and they appeared to herald a new configuration. Changing immigration patterns brought to the American shores numbers of non-Europeans who turned out to be non-Judeo-Christian. Hindus and Moslems began to show up in appreciable numbers and to form self-conscious communities, building mosques and temples here and there. The "boat people," who were welcomed in the aftermath of Vietnam, were Buddhists—or even Montagnard Animists.

Changes within traditional American society further broadened the bounds of pluralism. The civil rights revolution produced the Black Muslims, a radical protest against white Christian culture, and the beginning of a religious movement that ultimately wandered at least partway into orthodox Islam. Experimentation with Eastern religions became popular with young counterculturists, who professed to find a connection between "Zen and the Art of Motorcycle Maintenance." Sects and cults began to proliferate, some of them extreme expressions of traditional religions, but others taking unfamiliar directions: Hare Krishna, the Divine Light Mission of Guru Maharaj Ji, the Unification Church of Sun Myung Moon, Scientology. The numbers of people involved were never large, but the media spotlight was intense, and the impression given was that of limitless proliferation.

Other developments, too, undercut the old consensus. The "Secular City," hailed enthusiastically by Harvey Cox and others in the sixties, turned out to be something less than the total revolution in religious consciousness it had then appeared to be. It did, however, point to a general secularization of culture which has had far-reaching consequences. The "new Class" of opinion-makers, heralded by Milovan Djilas in his 1957 book by that name, and later analyzed by a number of American writers, was dominated by secular-scientific modes of thought which allowed little room for transcendence.

cFuturologists Herman Kahn and Anthony Wiener, in a 1967 look at the remainder of the twentieth century, assumed an increasingly "sensate" culture, which they described as "empirical, this-worldly, secular, humanistic, pragmatic, utilitarian, contractual, epicurean or hedonistic. . . ." The new class dominated the major universities, the media, and the nation's cultural life in such a way as to give an image of thoroughgoing secularism. The sixties, says historian John F. Wilson, "marked a stark repudiation of that spiritual ethos which had persisted throughout the life of the nation."

The striking decision by Federal Judge W. Brevard Hand in Alabama early in 1987 that "Secular Humanism" was, in effect, a religion that was being unconstitutionally supported by textbooks in public schools, and requiring the removal of some forty such texts from use in the state's schools, was highly controversial. Though reversed on appeal, it raised an intriguing issue. Most people had regarded secular humanism not as a religion but as the absence of religion. Judge Hand's designation reflected the reality, though, that for numbers of people (including many who dominated the intellectual life of the nation) a secular-scientific world view had replaced religious modes of thought. Another dimension was thus added to the society's religious pluralism.

The "sensateness" of a humanistic culture was further strengthened in the sixties by a fresh wave of hedonism, signaled by such code phrases as "the new narcissism," "the me generation," and "doing your own thing." Undergirded by the "humanistic" or "third force" psychology of Abraham Maslow, Carl Rogers, Erich Fromm, and others, in which self-actualization had become the highest value, a new and stridently self-centered value system replaced for many people the older religious values of self-sacrifice. The much-heralded sexual revolution, ushered in in the sixties with great fanfare (and out, in the eighties, with less fanfare, under the threat of AIDS), was, perhaps, the ultimate expression of the "self-fulfillment ethic." The new values were vividly described by public opinion pollster and analyst Daniel Yankelovich in his 1981 book, *New Rules: Searching for Self-Fulfillment in a World Turned Upside Down*.

A further analysis of the continuing effect of the "therapeutic" ethic of self-fulfillment was offered a few years later by sociologist Robert Bellah and others in the widely read book *Habits of the Heart: Individualism and Commitment in American Life*. Although the self-fulfillment movement may by then have been past its prime, its effects were still to be seen not only in the continuing hedonism of a persistently sensate culture but in popular cults such as est and Lifespring and in New Age religious movements of the late eighties.

The Changing Shape of Pluralism

In all these ways, then, the very meaning of "pluralism" appeared to have changed. When the American system of religious liberty was designed by the founding fathers, it was essentially a pluralism of Protestant denominations, with different backgrounds, traditions, and fiercely competitive attitudes but with a common Calvinist heritage and a common style of pietistic evangelism. It made room for a few Catholics, Jews, and even an occasional "Mahomitan," to whom, having properly declared himself, Washington was willing to extend toleration. But it was basically a Protestant pluralism, and so it continued through most of the nineteenth century.

As Catholics gradually increased in numbers and worked their way into the mainstream, it became a broader Christian pluralism. By the mid-twentieth century it had become a Judeo-Christian pluralism. Still, however, its areas of agreement undergirded the public faith, first formulated by the founding fathers, proclaimed definitively by Lincoln, reaffirmed on ceremonial occasions by president after president, and accepted by the citizenry as central to the national experience throughout the nation's history.

Beginning in the sixties, however—as the term "pluralism" became a popular buzzword—its meaning took on quite different implications. The change was in some ways more apparent than real. Statistical data continued to show an underlying religious and ethical consensus which remained remarkably stable. But media attention to non-Judeo-Christian religions and proliferating sects and cults, a secularized society in which traditional religions no longer seemed to have a significant role, and a new, nonreligiously based value system focused on gratification of the self all combined to produce an apparent change of context. Pluralism came to be understood as the absence of any kind of commonality in religion, as a system in which no meeting of minds was possible, and in which religion had to be relegated entirely to the realm of private idiosyncrasy. It was regarded by many as little more than another way of "doing your own thing" if you were so inclined.

Moral Crises of the Sixties Era: Vietnam and Watergate

Perhaps equally as significant as the context of social change were the moral crises of the sixties era: Vietnam and Watergate. Neither was limited temporally to the one decade. American participation in the Vietnamese War, which had begun almost unnoticed with the introduction of military advisers to assist South Vietnamese "defenders of democracy" in the early sixties, and had gradually escalated until the Tonkin Gulf incident brought open intervention in 1964, did not end until 1973. The Watergate affair, perhaps in some ways the child of the Vietnamese War, did not even begin until 1972 and was not brought to its sorry conclusion until 1974. Yet both crises belonged in a special way to the sixties—a decade which did not end, in spirit, until 1975.

Moral revulsion toward the Vietnamese War ultimately engulfed most Americans and finally forced the war's end in a precipitous withdrawal without semblance of victory. It is a story yet to be fully understood. Novelists, playwrights, and filmmakers, rather than historians and ethicists, have been its major analysts in the early post-Vietnam years.

Certainly the intervention began as a moral undertaking—even a moral crusade—in the Kennedy spirit of "bearing any burden" to protect the free world from the Communist threats. That interpretation long persisted in many circles. The present Roman Catholic archbishop of New York, Cardinal John J. O'Connor, then a Navy chaplain who had recently served with Marine Corps troops in Vietnam, wrote a 1968 book defending the American involvement on classic, just war grounds and praising its "civic action" program aimed at "winning the hearts and minds of the Vietnamese people" as a morally admirable venture. He has since distanced himself from that position, as have many others, but at the time it was widely shared.

The forces behind the transformation of the Vietnam intervention, in the public eye, into a morally repugnant undertaking were complex. Certainly some of the repugnance grew out of the unwillingness of a privileged and self-indulgent generation of young men—in the context of the sixties—to give up "their own thing" for the misery of combat and an all-too-possible death. Yet the absence of clear moral purpose on the part of the nation that sought to send them into that misery and danger was a major factor contributing to that unwillingness. As Eisenhower had said, "Belief in an underlying cause is fully as important to success in war as any local spirit or discipline induced or produced by whatever kind of command or leadership action." The moral purpose symbolized by Eisenhower's designation of World War II as a "Crusade in Europe," in the title of his famous book, was missing for the Vietnam generation.

The fact that the Vietnamese War was the first in history to be fought in plain view of the public on television screens also had much to do with convincing Americans that it was immoral. War has always been a brutal and sordid business. But never before had the brutality been so visible. Widespread drug use among American troops was reported in exhaustive detail, as were the burning of Vietcong villages, the harsh treatment of civilians believed to be Vietcong, and the "fragging" of officers by their own troops.

Particularly abhorrent incidents, such as the My Lai massacre, came to symbolize a kind of moral depravity which the public simply refused to accept as characteristic of America. Similar incidents may have taken place in earlier wars, but they had been hidden from view. This time the My Lai report was preceded by too many evening newscasts showing American troops torching the grass huts in too many native villages.

Watergate was the climax. We shall examine later the role of President Richard Nixon—a conventionally religious man who had church services conducted weekly in the East Room of the White House but who became the symbol of moral bankruptcy. The story of this traumatic chapter in the history of the presidency is too well known to require repeating. But as Vietnam had come to represent the absence of morality in national policy, so Watergate came to represent the absence of morality in the presidency itself.

A high level of polarization marked American politics throughout the Vietnam and Watergate period. Supporters and opponents of the Vietnamese War were in sharp and sometimes violent confrontation right up to the bitter end. Indeed, it was the sharpness of the confrontation and the utter absence of communication on Vietnam that gave to the period known as the sixties part of its watershed quality. Similarly, defenders and detractors of Nixon were angrily polarized throughout the Watergate affair; hardly anyone felt lukewarm about him. It is, therefore, all the more remarkable that the collective moral judgment of the nation finally reached such a high level of consensus. Few, in the end, would have claimed that either Vietnam or Watergate was morally defensible.

The era of the sixties was a complex period. The civil rights revolution, ending a long and shameful period of general, socially sanctioned, and legally supported discrimination against black Americans, was a monumental achievement. Though the task is unfinished, the basic step toward equality for all Americans was irreversible. The role of the churches in bringing about the change was a proud chapter in American religious history, and the Reverend Martin Luther King, Jr., was one of the few authentic heroes of the period.

The elimination of many barriers to the full participation of women in all aspects of American life was also a major achievement, accompanying the sexual revolution of the times. The growing numbers of women in elective and appointive government offices, in the managerial levels of business and industry, and in all parts of the work force, have enriched the whole society.

It was, however, clearly a period of moral crisis: the overturning of traditional values, the ethic of self-fulfillment, the apparent absence of consensus in an increasingly pluralistic society, together with the twin traumas of Vietnam and Watergate, all had moral dimensions. And it has been the moral crisis—with its underlying religious implications—that has so strongly affected the presidency in our times. All this goes a long way toward explaining the election in 1976 of the deeply religious and transparently "moral" Southern Baptist, Jimmy Carter, who promised to restore "a government as good as the American people." This phenomenon will be examined in greater detail in later chapters.

Meanwhile, Back at the Churches: Religious Responses to Cultural Change and Moral Crisis

Religious influences on the presidency, however, have also been shaped by some striking events in the churches, as American religion has dealt with cultural turmoil and moral crisis. An additional piece of the context, then, is an examination of what has happened on the religious scene in the post-sixties period.

In the spring of 1987, religious news, long relegated to the back pages or a special weekly feature page in the papers, suddenly became the stuff of headlines. Religious figures were hot properties for TV news-maker interviews. Attention was focused on the television evangelists. First Oral Roberts raised national eyebrows with a threat that unless his supporters contributed $8 million quickly, the Lord would "call him home." Then the PTL (for Praise the Lord or People That Love) empire of Jim and Tammy Faye Bakker collapsed. Bakker resigned, confessing marital infidelity.

A series of highly public battles ensued, first with his finger-pointing fellow evangelist Jimmy Swaggart, whom Bakker accused of attempting a "hostile takeover." Later he turned on fellow evangelist Jerry Falwell, whom he had initially asked to take over his ministry but then attacked publicly as he sought to get it back. Revelations of million-dollar salaries, unlimited and unaudited expense accounts, and a tastelessly lavish life-style on the part of the Bakkers followed as the PTL organization went into bankruptcy. The Internal Revenue Service and Justice Department, as well as state and local officials, began lengthy investigations. Months later, Bakker's self-righteous accuser, Jimmy Swaggart, was himself brought down amid revelations that he had been involved in similar sexual knavery.

But the headlines and the tawdry tales of apparent greed and corruption focused on only a few religious TV entrepreneurs. Behind the public hoopla lay a pattern of massive change in American religious life. The TV ministries were only one part (and not the most important, though the most visible part) of a rapidly growing evangelical movement in American Protestantism. Accompanying the rise of evangelicalism had been a sharp decline, both in numbers and influence, on the part of the traditional "mainline" churches. And along with these two changes had come a realignment of political attitudes on the American religious scene.

Decline of the Mainline

The term "mainline" has been applied to the historic Protestant denominations that both led and reflected mainstream American life through most of the nation's history. These are the denominations that provided the Protestant consensus in the nineteenth and early twentieth centuries: Episcopal, Methodist, Presbyterian, Congregationalist (now the United Church of Christ, after joining with other denominations), Disciples of Christ, Reformed, Lutheran (earlier ethnic enclaves, but by this time mostly mainstream), and Baptist (except for the Southern Baptists, whose post-Civil War isolation had kept them out of the mainstream). Most of them are mainstays of the National Council of Churches, which has served as their cooperative voice.

Through the post-World War II period and the Eisenhower years they had grown steadily in membership and influence. They were viewed as generally liberal, both in religion and politics (in which they were actively involved). They constituted the publicly perceived "Protestantism" of the "Protestant-Catholic-Jew" paradigm of the fifties. The large black Protestant churches, and the small conservative white churches, were there, but they were largely ignored as the mainline got the attention.

The turning point can be dated precisely in terms of statistics. Every one of these large, historic denominations reached its high point and began its decline in membership at the height of the sixties turmoil, in either 1967 or 1968. In the twenty years following, the Disciples of Christ declined by 29 percent. The Presbyterians (two denominations in the sixties, but united into one by the eighties) jointly lost 26 percent of their membership. The Episcopal Church decreased by 18 percent; the United Church of Christ by 16 percent; the United Methodists by 15 percent; the Lutheran Church in America by 11 percent; the Reformed Church in America by 11 percent, and the American Lutheran Church by 9 percent. The American Baptists had arrested their decline in the early eighties and shown modest growth near the end of the twenty-year period, but overall had also declined significantly.

The numerical decline was accompanied by polarization within the mainline denominations. The managerial revolution had given liberal mainline leadership the tool it needed to capture control of the central bureaucracies. Even the foreign mission agencies, which had long been the stronghold of mainline conservatives, came under their sway. With the organizational restructurings that swept through all mainline churches in the late sixties and early seventies, their dominance was institutionalized. Church machinery was controlled by activist liberals, with an agenda of social and economic change. Meanwhile, the public at large—including many mainline church members—had become increasingly conservative. The result was a deep internal cleavage between liberal, activist leadership and more conservative laity. Racked by internal dissension, the historic mainline churches lost influence as well as members.

Rise of the Evangelicals

But the fall of the mainline is only half of the story. Equally as significant has been the rise of the conservative wing of Protestantism. The TV ministries—all evangelical—have received major attention. But conventional church membership has also shifted. The more conservative churches within Protestantism and the once-ignored "fringe" denominations have been growing at a rapid pace. While the Methodists—once the largest Protestant denomination—have declined by 15 percent, the Southern Baptists—now the largest—have grown by 26 percent. Some of the smaller conservative and pentecostal denominations have grown even more precipitously. A dramatic case in point is the Assemblies of God, the denomination of Jim Bakker and Jimmy Swaggart. The Assemblies have increased by a massive 242 percent in the last twenty years. This pentecostal denomination is now larger than several of the major mainline denominations that far exceeded the Assemblies in size at the end of the sixties, including the Disciples of Christ and the United Church of Christ. The Church of the Nazarene has grown by 41 percent, and the Seventh-day Adventists by 61 percent; the smaller Christian and Missionary Alliance by 61 percent, and the Church of God (Cleveland, Tennessee) by 107 percent. This dramatic reconfiguration of American Protestantism lies behind Jerry Falwell's often quoted remark that the mainline has become the sideline.

The rise of evangelicalism has been accompanied by other kinds of change. It has brought new institutional arrangements, with independent evangelical parachurch groups taking over much responsibility for mission and ministry from formerly powerful denominational agencies. It has brought a shift in the center of gravity of church life, from the denominational hierarchies to the local congregations, where lay people are able to exercise control. Protestantism, which despite its denominational diversity was a relatively constant and fairly predictable factor in national life for the first century and a half of American history, has, since the 1960s, taken on a radically different shape.

What Is an Evangelical?

The term "evangelical" has a long history in Protestant Christianity. It is generally applied to the kind of biblically based Christianity, with an emphasis on personal faith in Jesus Christ as savior from sin and a desire to share that faith with others (evangelism), that was characteristic of American Protestantism through the eighteenth and nineteenth centuries. In countries other than the United States, non-Roman Catholic Christians are frequently known as "evangelicals" rather than "Protestants."

Because contemporary American use of this and other terms tends to be confusing, it is perhaps well to take a brief look at terminology. In modern times the term "evangelical" has come to be used as a means of distinguishing conservative Protestants from the more liberal, less biblically focused, and more social activist form of Protestantism represented by the leadership of the historic mainline denominations. So understood, it encompasses an extremely broad and inclusive movement, which most observers consider to be dominant in contemporary American Protestantism. In includes very large numbers, and probably a majority, of the grass-roots members of the old mainline denominations, who are alienated from denominational leadership, as well as the growing conservative denominations. Within this overall movement, however, are several subcategories:

Fundamentalists are the most conservative theologically, insisting on a test of orthodoxy (the five "fundamentals") and literal interpretation of the Bible.

Charismatics, also known as *pentecostals* (the terms tend to be used interchangeably although there is a technical distinction), are less concerned about theological niceties than fundamentalists and are more feeling oriented. They emphasize "the baptism of the Holy Spirit," an intensely felt experience which brings "spiritual gifts," often including "speaking in tongues" and spiritual healing.

Evangelicals comprise a less precise category, since the term "evangelical" is used in two ways. It sometimes means the whole conservative movement, including fundamentalists and charismatics. But it is also used to designate the more moderate group (probably the majority) within the broader evangelical movement, who are in the classic biblically based, personal-salvation-through-faith-in-Christ tradition of Protestantism. Evangelicals in this sense wish to distinguish themselves from theological liberals, but are less rigid and ultraconservative than the fundamentalists and less focused on specific spiritual gifts and experiences than the charismatics.

Evangelicalism: Background

The modern evangelical movement must be understood against the background of the historic division in American Protestantism between two factions generally designated liberal and conservative, though numerous other terms have also been used. Its antecedents go all the way back to the origins of American history, when ultraliberal Enlightenment Deists, like Thomas Jefferson and James Madison, were castigated as "infidels" by the more conservative Calvinists and Revivalists. As we have seen, however, Deism as a major movement was short-lived, and through most of the nineteenth century a Protestant evangelical consensus was so widespread as to be perceived as almost universal.

In the last two decades of that century, however, the rise of the Social Gospel movement, led by Walter Rauschenbusch and others who were deeply stirred by evils related to industrialization and urbanization, provided a focal point for a new liberalism. Already in place was a native strain of liberalism represented by New England Unitarianism and by such figures in America's past as Ralph Waldo Emerson. The emergence of Darwinian biology and the secular-scientific world view imported into major American universities (Johns Hopkins, Harvard, and the University of Chicago being the leaders) from German universities were already shaping American intellectual life. All these forces fed into a growing religious movement that came to be known as "modernism." It sought to make religion compatible with the science, the technology, and the intellectual mind-set of the modern world.

It was countered, however, by increasingly vociferous defenses of traditional Christianity from the conservative side. The term "fundamentalism," which came to designate the most determined opponents of modernism, was popularized by a series of twelve small books, written by distinguished conservative theologians from Great Britain, Canada, and the United States, called *The Fundamentals: A Testimony of the Truth.* Financed by two wealthy Los Angeles laymen, Lyman and Milton Steward, the volumes were published from 1910 to 1912, and within that period a total of three million of the books were distributed. The "five fundamentals" of belief, which came to characterize the movement, were the inerrancy of Scripture in every detail, the virgin birth of Christ, the "substitutionary" theory of atonement (Jesus' crucifixion as payment for the sins of all humanity), the physical resurrection, and the physical second coming of Christ. Around these fundamentals rallied the opponents of modernism.

The symbolic climax of the battle came with the famous "Scopes Monkey Trial" in Dayton, Tennessee, in 1925, which pitted fundamentalist champion William Jennings Bryan against Clarence Darrow, the liberal defender of evolution. While skirmishes lingered on for decades, the modernist victory in that trial signaled the growing dominance of the liberal faction in the ruling circles of the historic Protestant denominations that then dominated American society.

After losing their bid for control of the mainline denominations, the fundamentalists went into decline. Their remnants controlled only the small conservative denominations and the independent Bible colleges outside mainline Protestantism. By and large they moved into a separatist stance, isolating themselves from the mainstream.

Contemporary Evangelical Renascence

The election of Southern Baptist evangelical Jimmy Carter to the presidency in 1976 was the event that brought the resurgence of evangelicalism to public attention. The year 1976 was labeled "the Year of the Evangelical" by newsmagazines; both *Time* and *Newsweek* ran cover stories on the evangelicals, and suddenly they were a hot item.

The evangelicals represented by Jimmy Carter were not, however, the same as the old fundamentalists. A more moderate strain of evangelicalism had begun to develop among the "outs" on the fringes of Protestantism in the forties and fifties. Reflecting the social environment of a scientifically oriented culture, it had become increasingly uncomfortable with the antiscientism of the extremists. It had sought intellectual respectability. The liberalism of the dominant mainline churches was rejected, but so was the rigidity of fundamentalism. Wheaton College in Illinois, Fuller Theological Seminary in California, and Gordon-Conwell in the East, and the journal *Christianity Today*—all independent and nondenominational—were the major axes around which the new evangelicalism developed.

Much of the numerical strength of the evangelical movement, however, has come from the mainline churches. Large numbers of grass-roots conservatives had stayed in the major denominations after the modernist-fundamentalist controversies of the twenties and thirties, and through the forties and fifties they had been content to remain there. The neo-orthodox consensus which dominated the mainline churches in that period had been a middle-of-the-road position, sufficiently orthodox in spirit for most conservatives, at least as preached and understood at the level of the local congregation. But as the neo-orthodox middle-of-the-road consensus gave way to the radical theologies of the sixties and seventies—the "death of God," the "secular Christianity" of the avant-garde theologians of that period, and the various liberation theologies that followed—mainline conservatives became restive. Capture of the mainline bureaucracies by social activists committed to sweeping, worldwide social and economic change—sometimes perceived by conservatives as taking Marxist directions—left the conservative laity uncomfortable about denominational mission undertakings.

The evangelical renewal reached a "critical mass" when the leadership from outside the mainstream and the restive conservative laity within the old mainline denominations began to coalesce into a new and major force.

Fundamentalist Resurgence

Meanwhile, in the same period, the old fundamentalism was undergoing something of a renascence of its own. Television was the major instrument of its revitalization.

Not all TV evangelists are fundamentalists. Billy Graham, the first major Christian leader to make extensive use of mass-media evangelism, had been one of the central figures in the development of the new and more moderate evangelicalism. Others who later started major television ministries, such as Robert Schuller of California's Crystal Cathedral, might also be classified as moderate evangelicals.

Jerry Falwell, however, probably the current TV evangelist best known to the general public (though not the most widely watched), proudly labels himself a fundamentalist. He has been the central symbol of the current resurgence of the fundamentalist movement. Falwell's base is the Thomas Road Baptist Church in Lynchburg, Virginia, an independent Baptist congregation which he began in 1956. To the original church has been added a much larger institutional establishment which now includes Liberty University and Liberty Baptist Seminary for the training of fundamentalist clergy. The heart of Falwell's TV ministry is his *Old Time Gospel Hour*, which originates at the Thomas Road Church. For part of 1987 he also became chairman of the board of the PTL ministry, taking over when Jim Bakker, its founder, ran afoul of moral and legal problems. His fundamentalism presented some problems, however, for the looser, charismatic PTL organization, and he bowed out after a few months. Pentecostal Jimmy Swaggart, who before his 1988 fall was one of the most widely watched TV evangelists, would also have been described as a fundamentalist.

Pat Robertson became widely known as a TV evangelist through the *700 Club* and the Christian Broadcasting Network, based at Virginia Beach, Virginia. Though he severed his relationship with them and reached out to a broader constituency in pursuit of the 1988 Republican presidential nomination, he remains a major figure in TV evangelicalism. Robertson avoids the fundamentalist label. Like PTL's Bakker (who got his start on Robertson's *700 Club*), he is a charismatic, and in the past there has been a fairly sharp cleavage between the fundamentalists and the charismatics among the TV evangelists. Falwell, along with other traditional fundamentalists, rejects the charismatic emphasis on miraculous healing and other gifts of the Holy Spirit, and he refused to endorse Robertson's pre-1988 presidential candidacy. Apart from the charismatic emphasis, however, Robertson's theology is reasonably close to that of the fundamentalists.

Fundamentalism in contemporary Protestantism is essentially a nonecclesiastical movement. The denominations that label themselves with this term are few and small (and some, like the Independent Fundamental Churches of America, would probably resist being called denominations). There are many independent congregations that wear the label, and large numbers of individuals who consider themselves fundamentalists are members of more inclusive churches and denominations. The importance of fundamentalism as an organized force in contemporary America, however, lies mainly in the mass-media ministries. It is also, as we shall note in more detail later, closely identified with the conservative political movement known as the religious right.

The scandals and struggles among the television evangelists were media blockbusters, since the principals were TV celebrities. The moral failures, the excesses of conspicuous consumption, and the apparent financial irregularities among top leaders, however, have not significantly dampened the ardor of the rank and file. Neither TV religion nor fundamentalism should be written off as finished.

Struggles within Protestant evangelicalism are commonplace. They are normally settled by "free enterprise" initiatives, the formation of new denominations or parachurch groups. But they are part of the vitality—not the weakness—of the rise of evangelicalism and the massive changes in contemporary American Christianity.

However difficult it may be to distinguish between evangelicalism, fundamentalism, and pentecostalism, the importance of the overall evangelical movement in contemporary America becomes crucial in understanding the effect of religion on the presidency in our times. For it is out of this new cutting edge of American Christianity—the moderate evangelicalism of Jimmy Carter and the fundmentalism of the new religious right, which has had the ear of Ronald Reagan—that religion has made a major impact on the White House.

The extent to which the resurgence of religious conservatism in the seventies and eighties has been a response to the developments mentioned earlier—the secularization of American culture, the self-fulfillment ethic, the moral crises of Vietnam and Watergate—would be difficult to demonstrate conclusively. Many factors have been at work. Not least, from the standpoint of those involved in the evangelical renewal, has been the transcendent factor: the action of the Holy Spirit in renewing the church. But clearly much of the focus has been on moral issues, on the recovery of a moral and spiritual quality that once undergirded the common life. However else it may be explained, the evangelical renewal in American Christianity cannot be divorced from the widely perceived cultural changes that have been its background.

Evangelical Political Activism

The biggest change of all, perhaps, is the way evangelicals of all kinds have entered politics. The term "new religious right" has political rather than theological implications. So does the term "the evangelical left," applied to such groups as Evangelicals for Social Action or the Washington-based Sojourners. Even the charismatic wing of evangelicalism, in the person of Pat Robertson, has become politically involved. His quest for the 1988 Republican presidential nomination brought a downplaying of his role as preacher. Prior to his formal declaration of candidacy, he resigned from the Baptist ministry. For most of his adult life, however, he was that rarity, a charismatic Southern Baptist minister.

All this has been a radical break with the customary pattern of most of the twentieth century. For years it was commonplace to characterize American Christianity in terms of liberal social activism and conservative pietism, liberal involvement and conservative separatism, liberal this-worldliness and conservative other-worldliness. Martin Marty analyzed a century of historic trends in terms of two continuing parties, the "Public Protestants" and the "Private Protestants," and most observers saw this as an accurate delineation. Reams of research found sociopolitical involvement to be the surest litmus test for categorizing liberal and conservative Christians. The stereotypical conservative statement was "Religion and politics don't mix."

In the seventies this neatly ordered typology collapsed. The private Protestants went public. The first tremors came with the new evangelicals of the seventies, who felt compelled by their Bible-centered gospel to press actively for applications of that gospel in public affairs. It was with this movement that President Jimmy Carter was identified. Their political concerns, however, tended to be the traditional concerns of the liberal mainline: peace, world hunger, economic justice, justice for women and minorities. Mainliners were suspicious of their pietistic style, and sometimes of their motives, but by and large welcomed them to the activist fold.

The Rise of the Christian Right

At the end of the seventies, the Christian right, symbolized by Jerry Falwell and the Moral Majority, burst onto the political scene with a totally different agenda. Suddenly there were two "Christian programs" on the field. And, embarrassingly, they were on a collision course. They took opposite sides on most major social issues. Peace causes, as defined by mainline liberal church agencies in terms of disarmament, a nuclear freeze, opposition to any kind of draft, and, in extreme cases, "resistance" through civil disbedience or withholding of taxes were confronted by the peace-through-strength advocates of the religious right. Old left anti-nukers faced new right pro-nukers. Abortion rights, defended by the old religious left (and especially Christian feminists), were challenged by vociferous pro-lifers of the new religious right. Old left calls for "radical change of oppressive economic systems" (which often decoded as replacement of private enterprise—particularly multinational corporations operating in the Third World—by state-run economies) were countered by calls for "economic freedom" from such neoconservative groups as the Washington-based Institute on Religion and Democracy. And Christian morality, for the new religious right, had to do not primarily with the liberal sins of racism and sexism but with a whole new (or more accurately, old) set of "family values."

The Christian right was not suddenly converted to a "social change agenda." It was reacting to a perceived threat. In the post-sixties period the basic values to which it was committed, understood as religious values, were apparently being swept away under a determined onslaught from the left. And the agent, often, was the court system, which operated under less restraint in bringing about social change than the executive and legislative arms of government.

"Something had to be done," said Jerry Falwell in describing the situation that led fundamentalists to become politically involved. "The government was encroaching upon the sovereignty of both the church and the family. The Supreme Court had legalized abortion on demand. The Equal Rights Amendment, with its vague language, threatened to do further damage to the traditional family, as did the rising sentiment toward so-called homosexual rights." Fundamentalism, then, insofar as it is represented by the Christian right in politics, is consciously reacting to the success of the secular and Christian left.

More moderate evangelicals have divided on political issues. Some—probably the majority—have supported the conservative political program of the fundamentalists. Falwell, most famous spokesman for the new religious right, has been careful to avoid identifying his political arm, earlier known as the Moral Majority and more recently as the Liberty Federation, with fundamentalism, or even with Protestant Christianity. It has sought to embrace a wider range of evangelicals. It has made common cause with Catholics on the issue of abortion and with Jews on support for Israel. Many nonfundamentalist evangelicals have embraced this conservative program.

But some evangelicals have adopted more liberal public policy positions. Jimmy Carter was not alone in drawing from conservative Christianity a justice-based political agenda.

Most politically involved charismatics, too, have favored the program of the religious right. Although Jerry Falwell has refused to support his presidential candidacy, Pat Robertson's political program has differed scarely at all from that of the Moral Majority. But some charismatics, like some moderate evangelicals, are drawn to the peace and justice agenda of the evangelical left. Evangelicals have become a potent political force, but certainly not a united force, as recent presidents have learned.

Why Has It Happened?

We began this chapter with a look at "the sixties," that watershed period of massive social and cultural change: the new kinds of pluralism that many perceived as making any national consensus impossible; the self-fulfillment revolution that rejected old Christian values of self-sacrifice in favor of a "new narcissism"; the dominance of the "new class" and secularization of culture, which was certainly not new to the sixties but which took special forms in that period, and the moral crises of Vietnam and Watergate.

With all these changes, however, America remained an extraordinarily religious society. The early-nineteenth-century observations of Alexis de Tocqueville, noted in an earlier chapter, about the remarkably pervasive "religious aspect of the country," are often thought of as describing a period and a culture long gone. Yet foreign observers in modern times, too, have come to similar conclusions. Said Dietrich Bonhoeffer shortly before mid-century, after a sojourn in the United States:

> Nowhere has the principle of separation of Church and state become a matter of such general, almost dogmatic significance as in American Christianity, and nowhere, on the other hand, is the participation of the Churches in the political, social, economic and cultural events of public life so active and so influential as in this country where there is no state church.

Here, still current, are the two dimensions of the original American experiment: institutional separation of church and state, but cultural integration of religion and society.

Public opinion polls show amazingly little change in the religious beliefs, attitudes, and practices of the majority of the American people since the 1950s. Still today, from 94 to 98 percent (depending on the poll) believe in God; 90 percent are convinced that heaven exists; 80 percent believe Jesus is God and see Him as their personal Savior. And about half the population is made up of more or less regular church attenders. The Ten Commandments are regarded as applying fully today by from 96 percent ("Thou shalt not kill") to 68 percent (the less popular "keep the Sabbath holy").

A contemporary Italian observer, Furio Colombo, contributing editor of the leading Italian daily newspaper *La Stampa* and professor at Columbia University's School of International Affairs, writing in the eighties, made observations highly reminiscent of Tocqueville in the 1830s and Bonhoeffer in the 1940s. Noting that the 1980 presidential campaign had pitted "born-again Jimmy Carter against Moral Majority champion Ronald Reagan, with evangelical preacher John Anderson as the third competitor," he said, in the preface of his book *God in America: Religion and Politics in the United States*:

> My assumption in *God in America* is that religion is to American culture, politics and life what ideology is to French, Italian, Spanish, and other European cultures, politics and life—a key, a matrix, a way of explaining and organizing otherwise confusing events.

The contrast between the basic religious continuity and the massive cultural changes associated with the sixties helps in understanding what is going on in American religion. The changing shape of American Christianity is, at least in part, the response of an incorrigibly religious people to the crisis of the sixties. It may be regarded as a turning away from the accommodation to the secular world, which has been the consistent characteristic of religious modernity. It represents a return of religion to its classic function, that of providing a meaning system, a "sacred canopy," under which life unfolds. It brings a recovery of transcendent authority in religion, of traditional belief systems and religiously based values.

Other interpretations of the dizzying changes in religious life may be offered. But however interpreted, the change is real. American Protestantism can no longer be thought of in terms of the historic mainline denominations, with all others dismissed as "the fringes." Evangelicals, fundamentalists, and charismatics are now at the center of American religious—and political—action.

The Turning Point: Nixon to Ford

THE NIXON PRESIDENCY began with a flurry of religiosity. A committee on religious observance had been established far in advance of the first inaugural. Churches and synagogues across the country were asked to pray for the new president. A collection of quotations, Bible readings, and prayers was distributed widely on inaugural day, as were ten thousand copies of a card depicting "Praying Hands," with the words "Thanksgiving, Blessing, Dedication, Guidance." Billy Graham opened the inaugural ceremony with prayer, and "spiritual heritage" was the key phrase in Nixon's address.

Richard Nixon was a Quaker by birth and childhood training but not a Quaker in the commonly understood sense. The East Whittier Friends Church, to which his mother belonged and in which he was brought up, is affiliated with the Southwest Yearly Meeting, which is quite similar to other evangelical Protestant denominations. Services there, in Nixon's childhood, would have been scarcely distinguishable from those in other evangelical churches, with hymns, public prayers, Scripture, and sermon—in sharp distinction to the unstructured silence and the peace emphasis of eastern Quakers. Nixon did, when it seemed advantageous, identify himself with the Quaker peace tradition, and undoubtedly his commitment to peace was real but it was not the classic Quaker pacifism.

Richard Nixon and Watergate

From one perspective President Nixon may be regarded as as much victim as perpetrator in the Watergate affair, with which he is indelibly identified. His dedication to the public good was evidenced by many presidential achievements, notably in relationships with the Soviet Union and in a bold new opening to China. The effectiveness of his pragmatic statesmanship has long been recognized and his books are widely read. Fifteen years after Watergate he has been grudgingly conceded "elder statesman" status. But Watergate remains his major monument.

A conventionally religious man, whose ardent prayers at critical moments became part of the public record, he was a loving husband and father. Nixon was best known religiously for his close friendship with Billy Graham. After Watergate, Graham felt that he had been taken in by Nixon. At the time, however, the friendship was real, said Pat Buchanan, a former Nixon speechwriter in a 1987 interview. Buchanan, himself a Catholic, recalls an occasion when the White House staff went en masse to a Graham crusade: "We went up to Billy Graham's thing . . . in Pittsburg. He hauled us all in there to the stadium one day—even I was there. All I remember, there were these organized advance guys saying Billy Graham's advance guys were the only ones in the business who could compete with them!"

"Was that the president's idea, that you all go to the Billy Graham crusade?" he was asked.

"It was his idea. There was a lot of politics in that—no small amount."

Buchanan regarded Nixon, however, as a privately pious person, a "believing Christian." The president, he said, had great respect for traditional Catholicism, having been deeply impressed by the devout faith of his secretary, Rosemary Woods, whom he held in high regard.

Nixon is also remembered in religious circles for his East Room church services. Attended by three or four hundred invited guests, these services were led by prominent clergy invited from all over the United States. Guest preachers were carefully in structed in the proper protocol by Bud Wilkinson, former Oklahoma University football coach, who warned that the sermon must be limited to fifteen minutes, since "the President doesn't like long messages."

Regarded by some as a symbol of the "imperial presidency" and viewed with suspicion by many religious leaders as "captive Christianity," the services were controversial. No doubt the Nixons' desire to worship was sincere. But the services were also politically useful as a convenient and easy way to reward the faithful, since invitations to attend were regarded as a "hot ticket."

Nixon's closest approach to a church relationship during his presidency was with the Key Biscayne Presbyterian Church, near the Florida home to which he frequently repaired (for the suntan his TV image required as well as for rest). Nixon's friend Bebe Rebozo, a Key Biscayne resident, attended the church regularly. The Reverend John Huffman, its pastor, met the president walking on the beach one day, accompanied by Rebozo and Pat Buchanan. Rebozo introduced them and Huffman invited Nixon to his church.

"If I can talk Bebe into coming, maybe I'll visit you," the president said.

Huffman replied, "He's in church every Sunday, Mr. President, except when you're in town."

"I can't believe it!" Nixon said teasingly.

After that he became a fairly regular attender when at Key Biscayne. At the end of the Vietnamese War, a special service was scheduled at the church at the request of the president, who "wanted to be in prayer" at 7:00 P.M. on Saturday night when hostilities officially ceased. Arrangements were made for a network pool to cover the service for a worldwide telecast, whereupon Ron Ziegler, the White House press secretary, gave Huffman a sermon to use, prepared by a White House speechwriter (the son of a rabbi). When Huffman indignantly rejected it, Ziegler backpedaled. No other attempt was ever made to influence Huffman's preaching.

Huffman had a number of conversations with Nixon after services, was invited several times to the White House, and came to regard the president as an authentic Christian concerned about the moral dimension of the presidency. He was deeply shocked when the full story of Watergate became known, having earlier understood from personal discussions with Nixon that he was innocent and having defended him publicly on that basis.

Nixon was probably no more or less "moral" than many other practical politicians who have reached the highest office through the rough and tumble of the American electoral system. Perhaps the disillusionment of Vietnam had already established the climate in which his own debacle played out. But his resignation to avoid impeachment for malfeasance was, and will probably remain, a symbol of moral bankruptcy at the highest level. The cumulative impact of the affair was devastating: the smallness, the vindictiveness, the deviousness that pervaded the atmosphere in the Oval Office; the sleaziness of behavior and gutter-level language revealed in the secretly recorded tapes; the contrast between carefully crafted image and underlying reality; the parade of White House aides at the highest level, marching off to prison, one after another, as convicted felons; the president himself, an unindicted co-conspirator in the obstruction of justice, gratefully accepting a pardon.

The undermining of traditional morality by all the forces collectively known as "the sixties" had already prepared the way. But no one factor loomed larger than Watergate in ushering in the era of religious presidencies. Nixon marked a turning point. Religion is still regarded by most Americans as the wellspring of morality, and the need for morality in public life was deeply felt after Watergate. History has demonstrated that at least symbolically, and perhaps substantively, public morality and its undergirding religious faith tend to be defined for the nation by its presidents. In the years ahead religion would be an important factor in the presidency.

What Is Public Morality?

The question of what constitutes public morality is not an easy one. Indeed, the meaning of morality itself is hotly debated among ethicists today. And differences between Christian ethicists of various orientations are quite as great as those between Christians and their secular counterparts. But these fairly esoteric debates over the nature of morality are beyond our present purposes. What matters, from the standpoint of religion and the presidency, is what the average American means by public morality.

At the risk of oversimplification, it is clear that there are at least two competing definitions of public morality in the field today. Both have biblical roots, and both thus are illustrations of the dependence of American society on its religious base for the values by which it lives.

"Be Good" Morality: The most common, simple, and widespread understanding of public morality is a direct application of the stan-

dards of *personal* morality to public life. At this most basic level, morality simply means being good and avoiding evil. The biblical understanding of the requirements of love of neighbor—respect, kindness, compassion, and help—provides the positive "goods" to be sought. The Ten Commandments provide a foundation of "thou shalt nots"—evils to be avoided.

Clearly the application of this kind of personal morality to public life was what Jimmy Carter meant when he called for "a government as good as the American people." Such a basic-level public morality condemns dishonesty, deception, greed, sexual misconduct, and other personal moral lapses on the part of public officials, and calls for honesty, integrity, and devotion to the public welfare. It was here that Nixon was found wanting. And it was this widespread demand for personal morality in public life of which Gary Hart ran afoul early in the campaign leading up to the 1988 election.

The social program of the contemporary religious right is a variation of this form of "Be Good" morality. It is private morality, publicly applied. Opposition to abortion and homosexuality, support for family values, and prayer in public schools are applications of these principles of biblically derived personal morality, not just to the behavior of public officials, but to society at large. Opponents take issue, not with their voluntary adoption as standards of personal morality, but with their mandatory application to all through law or constitutional amendment.

"Do Good" Morality: There is a second kind of public morality that focuses not on personal behavior but on the goals and intentions of public policy itself: doing good for society rather than just being good personally. The call for social justice—also with biblical roots, particularly in the Old Testament prophets—is in this category. Social justice (for ethnic minorities, women, or the disadvantaged, for instance) cannot be achieved on an individual level by moral persons and then applied in public life—even by large numbers of individual persons. Nor can freedom, or peace. These goals can be achieved only through collective actions of public structures. And the personal morality of the officials involved may be irrelevant to whether or not such collective actions are initiated or achieved. Thus Richard Nixon's initiative in opening up relations between the United States and the People's Republic of China may have been a moral public policy, in terms of the goal of world peace, regardless

of whether he lied, deceived the public, or was otherwise guilty of personal moral failures as a public official.

Religious Polarization and Public Morality

But what it means to "do good" for society is not nearly so evident as what it means to "be good" in public life. Definitions vary with religious orientation. For the religious left it has generally meant social justice. The left has seemed far more interested in "doing good" (justice) than in "being good"; liberal Christianity has been perceived as having little interest in "old-fashioned" personal morality. To the extent that the religious left is heir to the spirit of the sixties, there is some merit in the perception. The turmoil of the sixties tended to undermine the first kind of morality as a basis for public life. The questioning of all authority (including religious authority), the rejection of traditional values (essentially religious values), the perception of a kind of fragmented pluralism that precluded any religiously based consensus—all these tended to devalue "thou shalt nots" and "thou shalts." Further, the self-fulfillment ethic growing out of humanistic psychology and related sources was an explicit rejection of the self-sacrificial other-centeredness of traditional morality ("love thy neighbor" as the highest social value) in favor of a self-centered standard ("do your own thing," "whatever turns you on"). While the religious left did not buy into the whole counterculture package of the sixties, it was far more strongly influenced by it than was the religious right, which rejected it. The left has generally shown more interest in justice as a moral goal for public policy than in the application of personal morality at the public level.

Resurgent conservatism, on the other hand, has championed the "Be Good" kind of public morality. The code phrase "family values," which has to do with the effect on society of the deterioration of traditional sexual morality and of related family structures, points to a central issue. But a wider concern has covered a whole range of traditional (biblically derived) personal moral standards as applied to public life.

Extremists on both sides have tended at times to emphasize one kind of public morality so strongly that the other kind has appeared to be negated. Thus the sixties radicals who proclaimed that "the real pornography is Vietnam" seemed to be implying that the old kind of pornography—sexual exploitation and pandering—no longer mattered. At the other extreme, ideologues of the religious right have at times appeared to be so wrapped up in the pro-life movement that they have not seemed concerned about justice issues.

We shall look repeatedly in future chapters at the competing programs of the old religious left (nuclear disarmament, economic justice, and justice for women and minorities) and the new religious right (opposition to abortion, family values, and prayer in public schools). They are focused on two different kinds of public morality, sometimes with the implication that the two are mutually exclusive.

But the two kinds of public morality can, of course, coexist. Indeed, they are related and interdependent. As Reinhold Niebuhr, perhaps the greatest and most original American theologian of the twentieth century, suggested, justice [at the public level] is the equivalent, in a sinful world, of love [at the personal level]. Both kinds of morality are necessary in public life.

There is, moreover, more overlap than is sometimes perceived. The religious right does have a "Do Good" morality—a moral public policy goal—of its own, comparable to justice, in its emphasis on freedom as a biblically based moral value. The neoconservative movement in religious circles has made freedom, along with democracy, a central public policy emphasis. Justice and freedom are certainly not mutually exclusive, although the polarization of contemporary religion would sometimes make it appear so.

World peace, as a moral goal, crosses religiopolitical lines. Liberals tend to associate it with justice and conservatives with freedom. Liberals tend to seek it through nuclear disarmament, conservatives in "peace through strength." No moral endeavor has deeper biblical roots than peace.

Increasingly, also, religious people from across the ideological spectrum are interested in a restoration of personal morality to public life. No longer—if it ever was—is this a concern of the right alone.

The Naked Public Square

Out of the moral uncertainty of the turmoil of the sixties, and out of Vietnam and Watergate, has come a broad and general call for a renewal of the moral foundations of public life. Essentially, this call is simply a resumption of an historic American quest, what mainline Protestant leader Martin Marty calls "the search for some sort of moral consensus to support public order."

From the time of the founding fathers the other half of the freedom-of-religion issue has been the concern that "public virtue" be undergirded by a religious consensus. This, for many decades, was a major emphasis of the "Public Protestants," who saw an active role for Christians in advocating those policies and supporting those programs that made for the common weal and the public good. Indeed, the sense of identification with the mainstream of American life and concern for its well-being was the original meaning of the term "mainline" as applied to the major historic denominations.

One of the more fateful changes growing out of the turmoil of the sixties was the transformation of this mutually supportive relationship between the Protestant mainline and the well-being of the American mainstream into an angrily adversarial one—at least insofar as the bureaucratic leadership of the mainline denominations is concerned. The roots of the transformation may have been nurtured in the identification of the then-young avant-garde Christian leadership with the rebellious young adult generation in its 1960s challenge to "the establishment." Certainly the Vietnamese War was a major factor.

As members of that generation moved into leadership in the mainline denominations, almost without exception they identified with war-opposers and draft resisters, who saw the Washington establishment in the Johnson and Nixon years as "the enemy." They were nurtured on the radical theologies of the sixties and seventies—the "death of God," the "secular city," and "religionless Christianity"—all of them antireligious establishment and antitradition in character. More recently the liberation theologies from South America and the Third World, which if not actually sympathetic with Marxism have at least tended to use Marxist analysis as a theological tool, have been influential on liberal leadership.

The rejuvenated anti-Communists of the Reagan era have tended to view them with suspicion, and liberals have reciprocated by viewing nearly every administration initiative—along with resurgent conservative groups, religious and secular, that have supported these initiatives—with similar hostility. Their opposition to government policy has been generalized into a kind of automatic antagonism to the role assumed by America in world affairs. Says liberal spokesman

James Wall, editor of the mainline flagship publication *The Christian Century*, "The mainline church social activists have had many participants who never met a revolution they didn't like. Riverside Drive [New York headquarters of the National Council of Churches and several mainline denominations] has its supply of those now-graying folk who harbor resentment against U.S. capitalism and allow this resentment to lead them to embrace uncritically left-wing movements in the Third World."

One effect of all this has been to largely remove the mainline denominations (at least insofar as their leadership is concerned) from their traditional value-formation and consensus-creation roles as bearers of mainstream religious and moral concerns. But the vacuum has been filled by others. The decay of public virtue, with the perceived eclipse of the Judeo-Christian tradition in the face of proliferating pluralism and the apparent absence of religiously based values in public life, has been a major focus of the rising evangelical tide in American Christianity.

From the mainline perspective the very name "Moral Majority" (appropriating for its own use the term "moral") has tarred the moral search with the brush of the religious right. In a predictable reaction the secular and religious left have dissociated themselves from "moral majoritarian" causes.

Yet the concern for recovery of a moral base is far broader than that encompassed by the specific issues of the religious right. Sociologically it is a recognition that the society cannot long survive without a commonly held basis and purpose. Historically it is a growing awareness that the bicentennial celebrations of the Declaration of Independence and the Constitution have pointed us back to something underlying America at a more basic level than laws and political institutions. In the popular mind it is a growing conviction that crime and drug abuse, and perhaps corporate greed and official malfeasance as well, are out of hand in a way that cannot be addressed by more laws and "programs."

The wider call is not associated solely with the application of "Be Good" morality in the public realm. It is interested in "Do Good" public morality as well: a religiously based collective commitment to the pursuit of peace, freedom, and social justice. It is basically concerned for the underpinnings of American life, not the moral applications alone.

The 1984 publication of *The Naked Public Square*, by Lutheran theologian Richard John Neuhaus, a former radical anti-Vietnam War activist who is now a leading neoconservative, provided this rising tide of concern with its definitive metaphor for the absence of a commonly agreed-on morality in public life.

In 1985 the Brookings Institution, long regarded as a bastion of liberal ideology in the nation's capital, published a major study on *Religion in American Public Life* by Senior Fellow A. James Reichley. Its focus on what Neuhaus had called the naked public square, and its emphasis on the role of America's churches in remedying the situation, surprised many. Said Reichley, "From the standpoint of the public good, the most important service churches offer to secular life in a free society is to nurture moral values that help humanize capitalism and give direction to democracy."

The sense of something missing at the moral core of public life, and of the necessity for a religiously based answer, is extraordinarily widespread in America today. The late eighties saw a rapidly growing concern about the vapidity of school textbooks from which all references to religion had been removed, with liberal organizations such as People for the American Way joining more conservative groups in seeking remedies. Political philosopher Allan Bloom's best-selling 1987 book, *The Closing of the American Mind*, written from the perspective of higher education, excoriated the relativism which has removed all moral absolutes. The sense of an urgent need to recover a moral base for American society has been wide and deep and rapidly growing.

On this area of concern, evangelical Protestants of all stripes tend to come together, along with many mainstream Catholics and Jews. Liberal mainliners as well—notably church historian Martin Marty—have been deeply troubled by the erosion of the national moral consensus. Liberal editor James Wall sees the issue as far broader than the kind of concern raised by fundamentalists. "Christians from across the spectrum are exercised over the loss of moral fiber," he said in an interview. "I share that concern. The absence of morality, in public life and private life, is the basic issue today." Although Wall disagrees with Richard John Neuhaus on many issues, notably on what he perceives as an unwarranted attack on mainline Protestantism, he shares Neuhaus's alarm over "the naked public square."

The Stage Set for a Religious Presidency

The stage was set, then, by the mid-seventies for a striking change in expectations of the presidency. It was not a consciously planned strategy. No political party or influential politician said "What we need is a religious president." Most people were not even aware of the shape and strength of the developing pattern. But the social forces were all in place: the sixties revolution against traditional values; the apparent development of a kind of fragmented pluralism that precluded moral consensus; the growing moral judgment about Vietnam and the moral revulsion at Watergate; the growing awareness of moves to secularize government and the emptiness of the public square.

The religious counterforces had been gaining strength at the same time: the rise of evangelical and fundamentalist movements, pursuing different and sometimes opposite political goals but united in their conviction that morality must be restored to national life and determined to make a political impact. And it all came together in the form of unprecedented attention on the religious dimensions of the presidency.

The disarray of American religious life in the post-sixties period has made the task of presidents in symbolizing a religious base for public life extraordinarily difficult. But the striking prominence of religion in post-Nixon presidencies has been no accident. As foreign observers over a century and a half have reported—Tocqueville, Bonhoeffer, Colombo—religion still occupies a central place in American life, despite the general secularization of culture and the influence of the "new class." And though not always consciously recognized as such, a critically important task of all presidencies since Nixon has been the effort to find a religious base for filling the emptiness of the public square.

Gerald Ford

From this perspective Gerald Ford was in many ways the right person in the right place at the right time. The facts that there were no obvious or discoverable moral blemishes on a long political career, and that he was widely regarded as a good and upright person, were significant elements in his selection as appointive vice president, following the murky departure of Spiro Agnew from that office. His background investigation by the FBI, prior to his confirmation by Congress, was probably the most exhaustive ever undertaken in connection with a public figure. Mr. Ford, in a 1987 interview, agreed with that assessment:

"There were other options that Mr. Nixon had at the time he nominated me. But I think the consensus is that because of my clean political record it would be far easier for me to be confirmed than some of the other possibilities."

But Ford was more than "Mr. Clean." His life had demonstrated a religious basis for political morality that inspired confidence. He was a lifelong, faithful Episcopalian, a regular churchgoer, whose family life as well as his political career had been shaped by his religion. Asked about his religious background, the former president recalled a churchgoing childhood in Grand Rapids, Michigan:

"I was born Leslie King," he said. "My mother divorced my father when I was very young. She subsequently [married] Gerald R. Ford, Sr. I have no recollection of any religious upbringing with my real father. I was much too young. So my religious background really relates to my stepfather, and, of course, my mother. Both . . . were Episcopalians. They belonged either to St. Mark's Episcopal Church or Grace Episcopal. During my youth we attended both Grace and St. Mark's.

"Both my mother and father were very devout churchgoing members. My father—stepfather—served in the Vestry, and Mother was associated with various women's groups. . . ."

The churchgoing pattern that marked Ford's youth continued into adulthood. He was married in Grace Episcopal Church in Grand Rapids, and the young lawyer soon took his wife, Betty, to Washington as a newly elected congressman.

"During our married life when we were in Washington," said the former president, "we attended with our children Emmanuel Church on the Hill, which was connected with the [Virginia] Theological Seminary, in Alexandria. My wife taught Sunday School there. I periodically spoke, at the request of the minister, to the congregation. I was not a vestryman, but I participated in various men's functions, dinners, etc., at Emmanuel. All of our children were born in Washington, and were baptized . . . at Emmanuel."

Ford recounts in his presidential memoirs, *A Time to Heal*, that while his children were growing up he tried hard to reserve Sunday as "family day," returning for the day if he was traveling. Sunday always began with the family attending church together. One of the Ford sons, Michael, entered the Christian ministry, attending Gordon Conwell Theological Seminary and later serving as associate pastor of a Presbyterian Church in Bellfield, Pennsylvania.

Throughout his life, Ford said, "I would say that there was little or no deviation from our connection with the Episcopal Church. . . . We have continued that relationship out in California, in the Rancho Mirage area, with the local St. Margaret's Episcopal Church," he added.

While serving in Congress, Ford was a member of a weekly prayer group. "That started about 1962," he said in response to a question about it. "It was the inspiration of Congressman Al Quie, of Minnesota. Congressman Mel Laird of Wisconsin, Congressman Charles Goodell of New York, and Congressman John Rhodes of Arizona—the five of us used to meet once a week in the Capitol, for a very short but very serious time of prayer and meditation."

As vice president, Ford continued to meet regularly with the group at the Capitol. Asked if they met while he was president, he replied, "Periodically they would come to the White House, for a very off-the-record gathering—and, of course, our prayer meetings in the Capitol were all off the record. They were not publicized; it was simply a get-together of us, on our own free will."

Prayer has been a regular and significant part of Ford's life. The night he learned that President Nixon would resign, and that he would become president, Jerry and Betty Ford prayed together. Said Ford:

> I concluded with a prayer from the 5th and 6th verses of Chapter 3 of the Book of Proverbs: "Trust in the Lord with all thine heart, and lean not unto thine own understanding. In all thy ways acknowledge Him, and He shall direct thy paths."
>
> Fifty years before, I had learned that prayer as a child in Sunday School. I can remember saying it the night I discovered that my stepfather was not my real father. I had repeated it often at sea during World War II. It was something I said whenever a crisis arose.

The Nixon Pardon

The most fateful decision of the Ford presidency, the decision to pardon Richard Nixon, was also accompanied by prayer. The president publicly asked the prayers of others, for guidance. On the morning he announced his decision, he later recalled, "I wanted to go to church and pray for guidance and understanding before making the announcement. So at eight o'clock Sunday morning, I attended services at St. John's Episcopal Church on Lafayette Square. I sat alone in the Presidential pew, took Holy Communion, and then returned to the Oval Office."

Commenting on the religious dimensions of the decision, the former president referred to a sermon, preserved in the Ford Presidential Library at the University of Michigan, which was preached by the Reverend Dr. Duncan E. Littlefair in Grand Rapids shortly after the pardon. The sermon dwelt at some length on prudential dimensions of the pardon, with a reminder to the congregation of the widely shared knowledge in President Ford's own hometown of his integrity, decency, honesty, and honor. Theologically, Dr. Littlefair treated the pardon in terms of the biblical doctrine of forgiveness. He referred to the fact that we wonder and marvel at Jesus, on the cross, who was able to forgive his enemies who were killing him.

> Is this only words? Do we mean it? Then will we struggle a little in our religion to rise to it sometime, somewhere? Could we not then muster a little forgiveness for Richard Nixon, for one who has wronged us but one who has served us as well for many, many years and, according to millions of us, served us well whatever his faults of character and whatever his later misdeeds? If we claim the glory of an innocent man forgiving those who kill him, it doesn't seem so much that we rise to that level. What a mockery of our religion if we cannot.

Mr. Ford indicated in the interview that while there were pragmatic reasons for the pardon, which were quite distinct from his religious beliefs, the sermon reflected his own religious convictions about it.

Gerald Ford's closest religious relationship during his presidency appears to have been with the Reverend Billy Zeoli, president of Gospel Films, in Muskegon, Michigan. Zeoli had developed a close relationship and served as "personal chaplain" to a number of sports personalities and other celebrities.

"Over the years, while I was a congressman," said Ford in the 1987 interview, "I got to know Billy Zeoli. He was a very active religious leader in the Grand Rapids area—attractive, dedicated, a very fine religious leader. He was especially close to my family, my wife and my children. And so when I became vice president and president, we continued that relationship."

On the day Ford was selected to be vice president, Zeoli was in Washington, as his guest, to deliver an invocation at a session of the House of Representatives. From then on Zeoli sent Ford weekly inspirational messages, usually a verse or passage of Scripture and a brief prayer, throughout the period he served as vice president and president. Mr. Ford found them extremely helpful, and later, when Zeoli published them in book form, he wrote an introductory "Appreciation" describing what they had meant to him. Zeoli also traveled to Washington "almost every month" for a personal visit, a time of "talking, reading the Word of God, and praying together" with the president. He went to Washington when Mrs. Ford had cancer surgery and prayed at her bedside.

In view of this, the former president was asked in the interview if Zeoli had, in effect, been his "pastor" while he was president.

"I wouldn't say my pastor," Ford replied. "He was a very dear friend who was devoted to our family. . . . We had a very close relationship, but I would not categorize our relationship as he being my pastor."

Like the Capitol Hill prayer group, it was a personal relationship, separate from church life. Mr. Zeoli is not an Episcopalian, and Mr. Ford did not know his denominational affiliation.

While in the White House, Mr. Ford continued his regular churchgoing, attending St. John's, across Lafayette Square from the executive mansion.

"When I became president we terminated the Sunday church services in the White House which Mr. Nixon had instituted," he said. "I did not feel that that was a proper thing to do, although when the Nixons had such services, when we were invited we attended. But we felt that those services were not quite appropriate in the White House itself." Ford indicated that he was able to attend church at St. John's about half the time. This, given the demands of office, probably constituted quite faithful attendance.

In light of the fact that both Nixon and Reagan cited security precautions as the reason for not attending public church services, and that Ford himself had been the object of two assassination attempts, he was asked if security was an issue for him in connection with church attendance:

"Oh, no," he replied, quickly dismissing it. "That was never a problem."

Classic Pattern: "Religion and Politics Don't Mix"

Mr. Ford draws a sharp distinction between his religion, which he regards as a private matter, and his public responsibilities. He has been a faithful believer and churchgoer all his life, and there are many evidences of the depth and authenticity of his faith. Little is said about religion, however, in his memoirs, *A Time to Heal*. This is in sharp contrast to the memoirs and autobiographical writings of President Carter, who writes of his religion frequently and freely.

President Ford, indeed, comments in his book on the difference between the two: "Throughout the [1976] campaign, Carter talked about his religious convictions in a way that I found discomfiting. I have always felt a closeness to God and have looked to a higher being for guidance and support, but I didn't think it was appropriate to advertise my religious beliefs."

Zeoli, in the introduction to his book, speaks of the intense privacy of Ford's religion: "Christianity, for him, is an internal personal matter, never something to call attention to. He could have done many things to get political mileage from his Christian life, but he stoutly refused to do so."

"I feel very strongly that one's religious convictions and dedication are personal," the former president said in a 1987 interview. "I never, during my twenty-eight and a half years in public office, sought to promote or exploit my religious background. I believe in prayer. I believe strongly in the Bible. I think I am a reasonably conscientious person as far as the church is concerned. But I never tried to mix my religion with politics."

Conceding that the public has a right to know the religious background of a presidential candidate as voters make their personal judgments, he felt nevertheless that the two spheres are sharply separate. "My feeling about politics and religion went back well before I was in the White House," he continued. "I just never mixed my religious beliefs with my political activity. And I feel very strongly that organized religion should not get involved in organized government. They should be totally and completely separated."

Mr. Ford's views and practices have followed a classic pattern of American Christian piety. He understands religion in terms of personal belief, resulting in a moral life characterized by prayer and faithful churchgoing rather than in terms of social or political activism. He adhered to the traditional pattern for the presidency, keeping his religion in the private realm, sharply separate from the public realm. And his classic conservative view that "organized religion should not get involved in organized government"—which he repeated several times and with deep feeling in the course of the interview—is unchanged by recent developments. He discreetly refused to comment directly on the entry of religious conservatives into politics via the Moral Majority and similar groups. But even though they are not churches, he considers them "organized religious groups," which he believes should not be involved in politics.

Mr. Ford, then, belongs to the post-Vietnam, post-Watergate generation of presidents in which high standards of personal and public morality are demanded for this office, with its great influence as well as symbolic significance. His clean record had much to do with his selection and confirmation. His is a religiously based morality, according well with the still-general perception that personal moral qualities are associated with religious faith.

Yet he was intensely private about his faith. And ironically this unelected president, who at the height of the Watergate debacle came into the job at least in part because of his reputation for honesty, integrity, and moral character, three years later was narrowly defeated after a campaign in which the Watergate scandal, and Mr. Carter's honesty, integrity, and perhaps especially his religion, were significant elements.

Asked whether, given the fact that Americans consider moral values to be related to religion, a wider public awareness of his own deep religious faith might have made a difference in the context of that election, the former president refused to speculate. Agreeing that his clean political record had been an important element in his choice for the job, he went on to say:

"Mr. Carter, I think the record clearly shows, had an open [to the public] conviction, from a religious point of view. And if he didn't, many of his friends, throughout certain areas of the country, used that politically. I would under no circumstances ever do that myself."

The social forces in the nation that were beginning to point toward a greater religious influence on the presidency were in the Ford years still in their infancy and as yet unfocused. Vietnam and Watergate loomed large, but the social effects of the sixties revolution were not yet clear. Evangelicalism was rapidly gaining strength, but it still lacked the symbol of a Jimmy Carter to fix the public eye on it.

Finally, and perhaps most important, Ford was too closely associated with Nixon to escape guilt by association. The combination of having been Nixon's handpicked and appointed successor, as well as the one who pardoned him, meant that inevitably some of the negatives rubbed off. His was a religious presidency, largely unrecognized as such, and he gave way to the more overt religiosity of Jimmy Carter.

Enter "The Deacon"

"THE DEACON" was the code name for President Jimmy Carter used by the Secret Service in plain-language communications.

Questioned in a 1987 interview about the importance of his Christian faith and his reputation for Christian morality in his 1976 election to the presidency, Carter said, "The country at that time was searching for someone who would publicly profess a commitment to truth and integrity, and the adherence to moral values—concerning peace, human rights, the alleviation of suffering—and I put forward these concepts which are very deeply ingrained in my own character and political motivations, and it just happened at that particular time that what I had to offer was what the American people wanted. I promised that I would never lie to the American people, that I would have a government as good as the Americans were, that my foreign policy would be based on moral values and standards, and this appealed to the American people."

In the annals of the American presidency, Carter was one of a kind. He displayed a combination of straightforwardness, an aura of moral rectitude that exemplified all the traditional personal and family values, and a transparently authentic religious faith that struck the right note for the time. What other politician in history would have run for the presidency with a campaign biography from Broadman Press, the publishing arm of the Southern Baptist Convention? And what other candidate would have begun that biography with a quotation from theologian Reinhold Niebuhr?

Whether by design or by serendipity, the signals were exactly right: the campaign themes of simple goodness; the highly public churchgoing and Sunday School teaching; the unembarrassed discussions of his faith; and his "witnessing." These spoke strongly to a nation reeling from the turmoil of the sixties, with its rejection of past verities, the value vacuum of the new secularism, the moral quagmire of Vietnam, and the ethical nightmare of Watergate.

What made Jimmy Carter what he was? Some observers, identifying his "simple religiosity" with the "hell fire and damnation" stereotype of southern fundamentalism, found in him contradictions, or even hypocrisy. The reality was far more complex. Four background factors played a part in making him the prototypical "new evangelical" and in shaping the religious and moral dimensions of his presidency.

The Southern Baptist Church

Clearly the Southern Baptist Church, in which he was brought up, played a major part in forming his religious beliefs and attitudes. An appreciation of this denomination—unique within Protestantism and yet quintessentially Protestant—is the starting point in understanding Carter.

At the heart of the denominational shift which has changed the face of American Protestantism, as we noted in an earlier chapter, has been the enormous growth of the Southern Baptist churches. The number of persons *added to their rolls* since 1968 exceeds the total membership of each of the predominantly white mainline denominations except the three largest. They have half again as many members as the next largest Protestant denomination, the United Methodist Church, which until the sixties was the largest American Protestant group.

Mainline Protestants have never known what to think about the Southern Baptists. They have been far too numerous not to be considered "mainstream." But they have been relatively uninvolved in the trends and issues that have dominated mainline Protestantism in the twentieth century. They took little part in the fundamentalist-modernist wars of the 1920s and 1930s, remaining staunchly conservative. With no liberal tradition, they were little affected by the neo-orthodox reaction to liberalism in mid-century.

Their roots, as the name indicates, are southern. They divided from the northern Baptists (who became the American Baptist Convention) at the time of the Civil War, and there has been no serious movement toward reuniting in the century following.

Both before and after the fundamentalist-modernist controversy of the twenties and thirties, the Deep South had remained the "Bible Belt," largely untouched by modernism. Southern branches of other mainline denominations were also biblically oriented and conservative in theology and social outlook. But by mid-twentieth century they had, at least in leadership circles, rejoined the mainstream. Traditional conservativism was left more and more to the Southern Baptists and smaller fundamentalist or pentecostal denominations. And as these groups spread nationwide they attracted like-minded conservatives in other regions. The curious outcome has been churches labeled "Southern Baptist" in such northern outposts as Alaska or North Dakota.

The Southern Baptists present in microcosm (or perhaps macrocosm, since the denomination is too large to be "micro" in any way) most of the major trends in Protestantism today. As evangelicals they have grown rapidly, while the mainline denominations have steadily declined. They have been lay-centered and highly responsive to the grass roots, while mainline clerical leadership has left its constituency far behind. They have focused on the traditional concerns of religion—the provision of worship and a meaning system, biblically based religious education, and outreach in evangelism and compassion—while the declining mainline has focused on social and political change. They have held firmly to biblical authority, while mainliners have accommodated to the relativism of the "new class." Along with the smaller conservative and pentecostal denominations (similarly lay-oriented, similarly focused, and similarly growing) they have shown a remarkable spiritual vitality.

For all their southern conservatism, however, these churches have not totally escaped the intellectual currents of modernity. A continuing battle between conservatives and "moderates"—with the two parties corresponding roughly to the fundamentalists and evangelicals on the larger Protestant scene (there are few if any real liberals)—has gone on within the denomination. There is, however, no significant charismatic party; the Southern Baptists have held the line staunchly against the charismatic movement.

The denomination is known as the Southern Baptist *Convention*, and technically it does not regard itself as a denomination at all. Each local congregation is completely independent. It maintains a "Cooperative Program," operating through large boards, but its basic national identity is the annual convention, attended by "messengers" from each local congregation wishing to send them. The contest for the presidency of the convention in the mid- and late eighties reached such levels of political interest that the numbers of messengers exceeded all previous records, and officials were hard put to find convention centers large enough to hold them. The prize was the president's power to appoint board members for Southern Baptist seminaries and denominational agencies, and each year the fundamentalists have won it. By the late eighties, as their control of agencies and seminaries tightened, moderates began to talk of a possible split in the denomination. Their 1987 gains in the state conventions, however, made such a split unlikely.

The struggle for dominance in the Southern Baptist Convention has taken place since the Carter presidency. But it demonstrates the longtime presence of a moderate faction, of which Carter was one of the more liberal representatives.

The Southern Baptist Culture of Carter's Youth

In the twenties, thirties, and early forties, when Carter was growing up, such divisions were not apparent. Southern Baptist culture in the rural South, in the pre-World War II period, provided an environment which in many ways was as truly an ethnic enclave as any Little Italy or Chinatown.

Church occupied such a central place in the life of Southern Baptists of the period—socially, educationally, and culturally as well as religiously—that its formative influence would be hard to overestimate. Carter's press secretary and fellow Southern Baptist, Jody Powell, alluded to it in a 1987 interview:

"He, like I, grew up where as a child most of the public speaking you heard was preaching, and so without even thinking about it, that becomes part of your way of speaking."

Carter's mother, "Miss Lillian," spoke in a similar vein of the place of the church in his childhood environment. Plains, Georgia, didn't even have a beer joint, she said. A church and a school—that's all there was.

From earliest childhood Carter attended Sunday School at Plains Baptist Church. He was a member of the Royal Ambassadors—"R.A.s"—a missionary education group for young boys, with six tiers of ranks from "page" to "ambassador plenipotentiary." He professed his faith in Jesus Christ as his personal savior and was baptized into church membership at age eleven, in 1935. He got his first training in public speaking by "taking parts" in the Sunday evening BYPU (Baptist Young People's Union). He was ordained a deacon (the ruling office in Baptist churches) in 1958. He ushered, took offerings, preached lay sermons, led in public prayer, and pronounced benedictions. No activity was more central in his life than church.

The relative isolation from other churches or religions (Southern Baptists were staunchly antiecumenical) created a somewhat ingrown world view. Carter later commented, for instance, on the way his perception of China was shaped by Southern Baptist missionary fervor and his assumption that others saw it the same way:

> Sometimes my visitors were amused at the way my Deep South Baptist ideas crept into discussions. Once when we were discussing the Far East, I remarked that the people of our country had a deep and natural affection for the people of China. When most of the group laughed, I was perplexed and a little embarrassed. It took me a few moments to realize that not everyone had looked upon Christian missionaries in China as the ultimate heroes and had not, as youngsters, contributed a penny or a nickel each week, year after year, toward schools and hospitals for the little Chinese children.

To understand the Southern Baptists it is necessary to understand the importance of Sunday School in Baptist life. A Baptist may speak of "going to Sunday School" when a Protestant of another denomination would speak of "going to church" or a Catholic would speak of "going to Mass." Even today what one member of the denomination calls "the Southern Baptist cradle-to-grave Brownie-point record system" canvasses each Sunday School class to ask "How many read their Bibles daily this week? How many brought an offering? How many studied the lesson? How many are staying for church?" The point is that "staying for church," while encouraged, is optional; going to Sunday School is the basic Sunday-morning routine. The emphasis on Sunday School has been a key to the steady growth of the Southern Baptist churches; the lines of Sunday

School busses on almost any Baptist parking lot are a common southern sight.

Thus Carter's identification as a Sunday School teacher has more meaning in the Southern Baptist context than it would for other Protestants. His role as a Sunday School teacher in Plains Baptist Church, and his insistence while president on teaching Sunday School whenever possible at Washington's First Baptist Church, are to be seen in this light.

Christian Century editor and former Carter political operative James Wall, himself a native Georgian, relates that on one occasion during the period when Carter was being labeled a symbol of evangelicalism, he said to him, "I've decided that you strike me more as a Southern Baptist Sunday School teacher than as an evangelical preacher." He was alluding to the difference in style between the teacher and the evangelist, the latter image being often evoked by the label "evangelical." And he reports that Carter, who was amused by the distinction, took it as a compliment.

Sunday School is a lay activity, and Southern Baptist churches are strongly lay-centered, perhaps the most lay-centered of all the major denominations. The system is one in which the local congregation is "the church," with final ecclesiastical authority. It is a system, therefore, in which a lay leader, a deacon and Sunday School teacher, has a strong sense of his or her own religious authority. Such a layman would not be as accustomed to depending on others for religious guidance as would a layman of a more authoritative denomination.

Commenting in a 1987 interview on the role of his father in his religious formation, Carter saw him as the role model for Baptist leadership: "Daddy was actually the Baptist in the family. Mother was a Methodist, but when they were married Mother joined the Baptist Church. Daddy was a leader in the so-called Junior Department of Sunday School. He was a teacher and a deacon in the church, in the years that I remember from childhood. When I came home from the Navy, I became a teacher, and then a leader in the Junior Department, and a deacon. So I followed my father's footsteps in the Baptist Church." The pattern was a familiar one, central to the lay-dominated Baptist system, and one of considerable religious authority.

Despite the absence of a powerful central headquarters to enforce conformity in this congregation-centered denomination, however, Southern Baptist culture has been surprisingly homogenous. The pattern was quite consistent throughout the Deep South during Carter's formative years. Baptists were conservative, Bible-centered (tending toward a literal interpretation of Scripture), and strongly missionary-oriented. The central Sunday School Board, and Home and Foreign Mission Boards, having no authority of their own, were highly responsive to the spirit and needs of grass-roots Christians. Their programs and emphases were voluntarily accepted by local congregations with surprising unanimity. A certain amount of internal dissension was inevitable, and congregations had a tendency to split and resplit over a variety of issues. Yet the culture, the thought forms, the language, and the folkways of these Sunday School- and missionary-centered congregations were nearly identical from church to church.

Jimmy Carter, like most people, is, of course, the product of many cultural influences, secular as well as religious. Jody Powell, on guard lest this interviewer ascribe too much significance to the religious dimension of the Baptist background, hedged on its importance: "I think it can say more about you culturally than it does in terms of religion. That was such an interwoven part of our culture in the South, and had been for so long, that quite often the rankest sort of hypocrites were the ones who used the [religious] language most readily. I always thought he [Carter] reacted against that."

But the dominant place of the church, socially and educationally as well as religiously, in the rural southern life of his youth, meant that the Southern Baptist culture in which he was brought up left a deep and ineradicable imprint on his life and character. And Powell regarded him as "probably more devoutly religious than any modern president."

An Atypical Southern Baptist

Jimmy Carter was, nevertheless, an atypical Southern Baptist in some respects. And his "differentness" was as important an element in who he was as his conventional Southern Baptist acculturation.

Most Southern Baptists, until relatively recent times, have been "Private Protestants," staunchly resisting any "mixing of religion and politics." Historically the denomination has been a consistent champion of separation of church and state. Even today this impulse remains strong. The leadership roster of Moral Majority, for instance, is filled with Independent Baptists (like Jerry Falwell himself) but lists few Southern Baptists.

Traditionally, however, there has been a minority within the Southern Baptist community with a strong commitment to social justice. In the mid-century South the consuming justice issue was racial discrimination, and a few Baptists bucked the southern tide in this watershed struggle.

One of the most radical expressions of this minority strain within the Southern Baptist fellowship was the Koinonia Community, an interracial farm at Americus, Georgia, not far from the Carter family home. Its founder, Baptist minister Clarence Jordan from nearby Talbot County, was the uncle of longtime Carter associate Hamilton Jordan. Koinonia Community was the object of violence, threats of violence, and legal and economic reprisals throughout the period of the civil rights struggle in the South. The farm had been established in 1942, the year young Jimmy Carter spent at Georgia Tech in preparation for entry into the Naval Academy. By the time he returned from the Navy, in 1953, resentment and harassment of the interracial community were in full swing, and Carter was well aware of these nearby events, fully reported in the local newspaper, the *Americus Times Recorder*.

An earlier and more direct influence, however, was the social conscience of his mother, Miss Lillian, whom he described in an interview as the most significant factor in the shaping of his religious convictions. A strong person in her own right, Miss Lillian filled the traditional role of wife and mother but was also a registered nurse who provided medical care for blacks as well as whites in her strictly segregated community. Compassionate care for blacks might have been ascribed to the southern "Lady Bountiful" tradition, classically demonstrated by Scarlett O'Hara's mother in *Gone with the Wind*. But Miss Lillian went far beyond that, challenging the deep-rooted traditions of the segregated South.

Carter, in his campaign biography, *Why Not the Best?*, gives a vivid description of the racial folkways of the pre-World War II South. The most powerful and cosmopolitan figure in the small rural community of Archery, in which Carter lived as a child, was a black bishop of the African Methodist Episcopal (AME) Church, with responsibility for the churches of five or six states. When he had business with Jimmy's father, he would drive up in his car and send a messenger to the back door, whereupon Mr. Earl would go out into the yard and meet him.

But the bishop's son, home from college in Boston and calling on Miss Lillian to discuss his education, would knock on the front door. He would be invited into the parlor to be served tea and cookies, with Jimmy present. His father would leave, pretending it was not happening, and such visits were marked by a general "nervousness around the house," Carter remembered.

"He didn't like it," Miss Lillian said, referring to her husband's attitude, "—didn't like it at all—and he didn't understand it, either. . . . But he wouldn't talk about it with me, and he never once told me not to do it again. I guess he knew it wouldn't have made any difference. It wouldn't have done any good for him to have told me to stop seeing the colored boy in our parlor. I liked that colored boy and respected him because he was smart and because he was out there trying to get an education and trying to make something of himself. I wanted Jimmy to get to know him and hear him talk about his adventures and his schooling and all. I enjoyed it, too, of course, but really I wanted Jimmy to be exposed to something and somebody he was not normally going to be exposed to."

Describing to this interviewer her formative influence on the development of his Christian commitment to social justice, the former president said, "Mother was one of the enlightened and progressive Southerners, even when I was a child, during the Depression years. And then later, as the civil rights questions became prominent in the country, Mother was known in the community as the only supporter of the civil rights movement on a public basis among the adults. And it's obvious she had a great influence on me."

The strength of that influence became evident later, in Carter's forthright and outspoken leadership in the desegregation process: in his business (which was boycotted when he refused to join the local White Citizens' Council); on the Plains School Board; as state senator and governor. His national recognition began when public attention (including a *Time* cover story) was focused on his enlightened racial attitudes as governor of Georgia.

Christian Tradition of Service to Others

Beyond the commitment to social justice and racial equality, radical by Southern Baptist standards of the day, Carter's religious background also included a strong emphasis on service to others. The call to serve, and even to sacrifice for others, is a central New Testament theme, common to all Christian churches. In traditional Southern Baptist circles, this call to service has often been translated into missionary work and personal evangelism, as well as compassionate alleviation of suffering. Many Christians of all denominations, however, content themselves with contributing money for church programs in these areas.

Carter grew up in an environment in which the service/sacrifice theme was much more personal. Miss Lillian's nursing service to the community was well known. Her husband, Earl, once compared her to Eleanor Roosevelt: "Damned if she [Mrs. Roosevelt] wasn't a lot like Lillian—always poking around in the black houses, seeing if everything was all right, checking on the babies, taking medicine and food." Once he jokingly called his wife "Eleanor."

But though Mr. Earl himself was a traditional southerner of the period, following the custom of strict segregation in race relations, he was a closet philanthropist. He was generous in his support (financial and personal) and encouragement of blacks. Every year at high school commencement, graduating girls wore white dresses. For those who couldn't afford them, Mr. Earl paid the bill. He secretly provided college money for promising high school graduates. In the months before his death he canceled notes for money owed to him by black tenants, and at the time of his death his accounts receivable amounted to nearly $100,000. Jimmy and even his mother were surprised at the extent of his generosity. "I knew about the dresses," Miss Lillian said, "but most of the rest of it he just kept to himself."

The most striking symbol of the family's tradition of service, perhaps, was Miss Lillian's decision in 1966, at the age of sixty-eight, to join the Peace Corps, and her two years of service in India. "We were not particularly surprised," said her son in retrospect. It was a striking example of this strong woman's commitment to helping others.

What Carter has at times referred to as his "second born-again

experience," following his initial defeat fo
ship, was a noteworthy element in his relig
tered around a question asked in a sermon th
"If you were arrested for being a Christian, w
evidence to convict you?" He found that he had
in terms of being a deacon and a Sunday Schoo
a kind of actively involved Christianity which
service to others as life's central purpose. It was f
perience that he first joined one of his church's short
spending a week visiting from door-to-door among un
ilies in another state. He later described it as a week o
to God "with no strings attached," and he followed
such missions annually. The service theme, commo
tians, was for him a tradition and a personal pattern of
as words.

Theological Depth

A fourth background factor that helped to define Jimmy
a Christian was the level of his understanding of theolog
ethical issues, rare for a lay person. Protestants ordinarily le
study of complex theological issues to the clergy. Books on th
and ethics are rarely read except in seminaries and pastors'
Lay church leaders—particularly among literalistic Baptists-
erally focus their attention on the Bible itself, with the help
haps, of study guides and Bible commentaries. Even Sunday Sc
teachers and church officers venture only rarely into the eso
realm of theology.

A Southern Baptist politician who quotes Reinhold Niebuhr, the
is a startling exception. Certainly Carter was the most theologicall
literate president since Woodrow Wilson. In an interview he was
quick to disavow theological sophistication: "I don't claim to be any
expert on theology—not at all," he said. Yet his familiarity with
complex theological issues, as revealed in conversation as well as
his writings, is impressive.

Robert L. Maddox, a Christian minister who was perhaps closer to the Carter presidency than any other theologically trained observer, confirmed this judgment in a 1987 interview. As minister of the First Baptist Church of Calhoun, Georgia, to which Jack

lest son) and his family belonged, Maddox
ip to the Carter family antedating the White
; some informal, voluntary speechwriting for
invited to join the White House staff as a
he later assumed responsibility for Protestant

thoroughly familiar with contemporary theology
ments, Maddox later became executive director
ed for Separation of Church and State and man-
journal, *Church and State*. As a White House
nt was especially respected by Mrs. Carter, who
d him with a kind of informal and unofficial access
t not enjoyed by other staffers at his level.
idered Carter quite knowledgeable theologically. "Not
said, "because he did not ever pretend to be a scholar.
nore than the average layman. He knew as much Nie-
llich and Kierkegaard as a whole lot of people who have
minary. . . . They were formative people in his life. . . .
ad them, and digested them, over a long period of time.
s from a layman's point of view, not a seminary professor's
view."

nced by his mother's reading habits, Carter became a vo-
reader in adult life, and his political interest as well as his
anity led him to explore the relationship of religion to public
Though he has quoted Paul Tillich, Søren Kierkegaard, and
, he was most deeply affected by the "Christian realism" of
hr, probably the preeminent American theologian of the twen-
century.

ne first book that I ever read thoroughly by Reinhold Niebuhr,"
aid to this interviewer, "was *Reinhold Niebuhr on Politics*, which
as given to me by a friend who later became a judge—Judge Bill
Gunter. But after I read that book I expanded my library. I have
several books by Reinhold Niebuhr, and a little by his brother [H.
Richard Niebuhr], and of course, others that I read, just to compare
their theology or philosophy with Niebuhr. I'm strictly amateurish
in this approach. But when I teach Sunday School—which is every
Sunday that I'm home—I often go to Niebuhr, or some of his works,
to clarify a complicated or difficult concept. So I live with Niebuhr's
work, on a continuing basis." In a letter to Mrs. Niebuhr, following

a visit she made to the Oval Office after her husband's death, Carter spoke eloquently of her husband's work and how it had affected his thinking.

Carter's reading and quoting of Niebuhr, Tillich, and others followed a minority tradition within Southern Baptist circles but an important one. Journalist James Wooten has suggested that faithfulness to the Southern Baptist Church on the part of a "well-traveled, well-read, well-educated man with an engineer's precise mind," who "had read a great deal of the work of modern theologians whose emphases were on the social and ethical aspects of the gospel" was a kind of hypocrisy. Such a judgment reflects a failure to understand either the Southern Baptists, or modern evangelicalism, or Jimmy Carter.

Carter was deeply influenced by the Southern Baptist Church in which he was raised and of which he has remained a faithful member, not only during his presidency, but since. Yet he was and remains a Southern Baptist of a special kind. His leaving of Plains Baptist Church—of which he had been a lifelong member—and his membership in the group which formed the new Maranatha Baptist Church in the community, was over the issue of racial inclusiveness. He could not in conscience remain a member of a church that excluded people on the basis of race.

Jimmy Carter is an orthodox but not a fundamentalist Christian. On a TV talk show, along with his wife, in June of 1987, a questioner identified him as "the first fundamentalist president." Mrs. Carter intervened before he could answer, asking the former president, "Would you consider yourself a fundamentalist?"

Carter answered, "By measurement of the average Christian, I think Southern Baptists would be considered fundamentalists," and he did not explicitly disavow the term. But he went on to draw a clear distinction between his own positions and those usually identified with the politically active fundamentalists of the Christian right today. Carter believes strongly in the authority of Scripture, but without legalistic literalism of interpretation.

Summing Up

Four aspects of Carter's religious background, then, help in understanding the president he later became. First, the Southern

Baptist Church, of which he has been a lifelong loyal member. His continuing active involvement and the unpretentiousness of it are caught up in a remark by Mrs. Carter in a telephone conversation reported by Robert Maddox. Talking about Maranatha Baptist Church, she had told Maddox that the minister was the only paid person on the staff.

"We don't even pay a janitor," she added. "All the members take turns cleaning up the building. Jimmy and I were down there last Saturday night, taking our turn going through the building preparing it for Sunday."

But second, devoted Southern Baptist though he was and is, he was an atypical one, particularly in race relations and civil rights in the fifties and sixties. He came out of the minority tradition that was actively involved in seeking racial equality for black Americans. He had, and has, a strong commitment to social justice, derived at least in part from the influence of his mother and tested by his own experience during the civil rights revolution in the South.

Third, his commitment to the Christian tradition of service to others took the form of active personal involvement in justice issues. Like his mother, who joined the Peace Corps, he learned to express his commitment in deeds.

Finally, his theological understanding, particularly as revealed in his appreciation of Reinhold Niebuhr, was remarkable for a Southern Baptist layman. University of Virginia professor William Lee Miller, himself a student of the religious dimension of American history, writes that he was initially suspicious of Carter's quoting of Niebuhr and Tillich, thinking that his source, as with many public speakers seeking apt quotations, was probably a theological equivalent of Bartlett's *Familiar Quotations*. But after a lengthy investigation, he came to the conclusion that "the affinity between Carter and Niebuhr is authentic and important." Carter's career as well as his statements reflected Niebuhr's themes: "Christianity related to politics; love as the motive for social justice; realistic political skill in the service of justice."

Miller quoted Carter: ". . . There's an almost perfect concept expressed in the Christian ethic, that there's an ultimate pattern for government, but the struggle to reach it is always unsuccessful. The perfect standard is one that human beings don't quite reach, but we try to."

That, said Miller, is "not too bad a layman's softened version of Niebuhr." Carter had, and has, a fairly sophisticated understanding of ethical and theological issues related to public life, derived from his study of Niebuhr and others.

During the 1976 campaign the evangelical movement in Protestantism, which had long been gathering strength, reached the level of public awareness, thanks in considerable measure to Carter. It was a renascence of conservative Christianity, adhering to classic Bible-centered Protestantism but seeking to differentiate itself from the rigid extremes of fundamentalism. It renounced the separatism of earlier conservatives, involving itself in the world and working for social justice. Both *Time* and *Newsweek*, in cover stories that year, identified Carter as the prototype "new evangelical." It was as accurate as such labels ever are. Both religiously and politically, the Carter presidency exemplified the "signs of the times."

7

Born-Again White House

In a 1987 interview former President Carter was asked to what extent he had seen his presidency as a way of putting his Christian faith into action. Reference was made to an incident reported in his book *Why Not the Best?* in which, in a conversation with a preacher, he had compared public service with Christian ministry.

Said Carter, recalling the incident, "The minister was preaching a revival in our church, and was staying with my mother, and I was contemplating running for the State Senate. It was my first political office. He was deploring the fact that I, as an active church member—deacon, Sunday School teacher—would consider getting into the 'sordid' world of politics. I argued with him a little while, and I finally asked . . . 'How would you like to be minister of a church with 80,000 members?' I saw my State Senate position, which encompassed a district of 80,000 people, as a way to minister to their needs, not in an evangelistic or theological way, but in a practical way—their human needs. It was just a spur of the moment comment, without much prior thought, but I've always seen public service as a way to carry out part of the Christian responsibilities that I claim."

Carter was expressing the classic Protestant understanding of "Christian vocation," which does not limit the concept to preachers and priests, but affirms the call to everyone—Christian shoemaker or Christian president—to serve God in his or her vocation. Such an understanding is ingrained in the Protestant consciousness. As a deeply committed Christian, Carter probably felt more keenly than those presidents whose religion has been a conventional affiliation the imperative of a sense of Christian vocation.

Robert Maddox, commenting to this interviewer on that sense of calling, made it clear that Carter did not feel that "God had told him to run for the presidency"—the motivation claimed by Pat Robertson.

"Carter never did say that," Maddox reported. "He was not on a holy crusade. I think he was a very ambitious man, a very strong man, and simply wanted to be president. . . . But he also had a strong sense of serving and living before God. [He] realized that his sense of the judgment and affirmation of God, on his life and on his presidency, was ultimately what was important. He was a man who wanted to be president, and in the providence of God he became president, and he tried to do the very best he could as a Christian, as a man before God, in the process."

His was a "Christian vocation," then, in the classic Protestant sense. But how does one carry out a "Christian vocation" as president of all the people in a multifaith society? The tension inherent in that question is one of the basic issues relating to the Carter presidency. "I profess, as a Baptist, to separation of church and state," said Carter. His commitment to that principle was deeply felt and often reiterated.

Jody Powell was also careful in an interview to point out that Carter had adhered strictly to the separation principle: "I suspect if you looked back over his speeches and public utterances, you would find that he was less apt to be quoting Scripture all the time [than any modern president]—in fact sometimes I would put what I thought was an apt reference in a speech, and it got taken out. I don't really know what that was; my suspicion always was that he felt uneasy about flaunting religion, and certainly about giving the appearance that he was using his religion in an avowedly political way. That last was very consistent with what has been the historical Baptist attitude toward church and state. . . .

"What I'm saying is that to the extent his religion affected his behavior in office, it all operated internally. He certainly was not the sort of fellow that would ever have said, 'I think we ought to do this or that or the other, because my deep religious convictions compel me toward that decision.' But, having said that, I think almost everything he did was in a major way affected by his religious faith, because I think it is such an integral part of who he is and his view of life, from his concern for human rights, and his concern about the less fortunate in society, and the obligation of those who are more fortunate. . . . I also felt that his . . . very striking—at least to me—inner strength, being at peace with himself, and being able to take the good and the bad without being overcome by either, was an outgrowth of his faith."

Powell's admonition is an important one. The very act of examining the effect of a president's religion on his conduct of the office is likely to distort the picture. Every action, every decision, is the product of so many components and so many influences that to look at any one of them in isolation is to skew reality.

The fact that the religious influences operated entirely internally further complicates such a process. Carter consciously and intentionally refused to set up a "religious" White House. To the chagrin of some of his evangelical supporters who saw his election as a way of turning government over to "godly people," he selected his staff and his Cabinet without regard to religious affiliation or absence thereof. Andrew Young, his Ambassador to the United Nations, was an ordained minister, but as a former congressman, prominent black politician, and symbol to the nations of the Third World of Carter's human rights emphasis, his credentials were political rather than religious. Apart from Religious Liaison officials, no one on the staff appears to have been appointed primarily for religious reasons. Qualifications, ability—and closeness to Carter—were the governing factors.

"If the president had appointed a visible evangelical to the Cabinet, it could have made a difference [politically]," said Robert Maddox, who had occupied the Protestant Religious Liaison position, in a 1987 interview. "It may have been," he added, "that no clearly visible evangelical emerged, who could also lead a department.

"Pat Robertson claims," he went on to relate, "that he sent a list of names—highly qualified people—on a special airplane to Plains, and it was delivered to the president, and that was the last he ever heard. He didn't even get a 'thank you' for sending the names down."

"Did Robertson tell you that?" Maddox was asked, and the answer was "Yes."

Recommendations from religious sources were received and considered on the same basis as any others. The advisory commission on appointments during the transition period before Carter took office included religious figures (for instance, Father Theodore Hesburgh, of Notre Dame), but being "religious" earned no extra points.

In the Oval Office, Carter was all business. He was an engineer by training, a hard-nosed businessman and practical politician by experience. He was a master of detail, and he demanded such mastery from others. He had little time for small talk, and little patience with failure to do one's homework. If a subordinate had brought him a proposal and when asked for justification had replied, "God told me to do it this way," he or she would have received short shrift.

A policy issue such as the Panama Canal treaties, which will be discussed in this chapter, would not have been surrounded by God-talk. A staff member or Cabinet officer, intimately involved in the matter, might have gone through the entire eighteen months in which Panama was continually on the presidential agenda without once hearing Carter say anything that sounded "religious." This was what Powell meant by saying "He was not a Bible-banger or a Scripture-quoter, either in private or in public." It was part of what Carter himself meant by "separation of church and state."

He was who he was, and the public was well aware of the Christian dimension of who he was. That was part of the reason he had been elected. But it was that Christian person—not any religious organization, not the Southern Baptist Church, not the Bible, not the Holy Spirit—who sat in the Oval Office.

A revealing incident is related by Maddox. A congressman contacted the White House, somewhat apologetically, to say that an influential minister in his district had had a vision detailing the release of the Iranian hostages. He would not tell anyone except the president the method God had revealed to him by which the hostages would be released. Maddox telephoned the minister and talked to him at length. He was cordial and pleasant, but would talk only to the president. Maddox brought in Gary Sick, Iranian expert from the National Security Council staff, who also talked with him. Both of them felt that the minister was sincere, but would not, of course, allow him to see the president. And there the matter rested. "The Lord has told me to talk only with the President. If you do not let me, fine. But the whole mess will be on your head, not mine."

Carter did not govern by revelation. He did not govern by seeking out appropriate passages in the Bible to cite as proof texts. He did not govern on the basis of authoritative rulings by the church—Southern Baptist or any other church. And in this he disappointed many religionists.

But his was, nevertheless, a profoundly religious presidency in the sense indicated by Powell's concluding observation: ". . . having said that, almost everything he did was in a major way affected by his religious faith, because . . . it was such an integral part of who he was and his view of life."

Carter's Biblical Frame of Reference

One clue to understanding the religious influence on the person who was president is in terms of the biblical frame of reference, which for Carter was normative. In remarks to the National Association of Religious Broadcasters in 1980, on a more personal level than is sometimes customary on such occasions, President Carter said, "Rosalynn and I read the Bible together every night, not as some sort of mystical guidebook, as some might think, to give us quick and simple answers to every problem of a nation or personal life, but because we find new insights and new inspirations *in this present job* in passages we have read and known and loved ever since childhood." (emphasis added)

No one who reads several chapters of the Bible each day throughout a lifetime, who teaches the Bible to others weekly in Sunday School, all because of a deep conviction that its religious and moral authority is absolute, can fail to be deeply affected by it.

The thinking of such a person obviously has many nonbiblical dimensions. Problems or conversation having to do with science, with management, with practical politics, with history, with personalities, with any one of a multitude of ordinary or presidential concerns, have their own frame of reference. Hours or days consumed by such issues may go without any biblical connotation, even in the inner recesses of the mind. But when there are moral, or ethical, or ultimate concerns—as there are in many dimensions of ordinary human relationships as well as affairs of state—for such a person the biblical frame of reference is as natural as breathing.

With reference to a speech he had made earlier on the moral basis of foreign policy, Carter was asked by this interviewer, "Is the Bible the source of the moral basis [of American society]?"

"Well, it is for me," he answered. "The Bible and associated writings, by commentators and theologians and others—the entire gamut of religious thought. We're dealing with me personally. I don't claim that the Bible is the basis for all proper government service, or moral values, because there are other religions that have moral values, that don't look upon the Bible as the Holy Word. But for me personally it has been the guiding standard."

The Bible provided such a natural and normal frame of reference for Carter that it slipped almost unnoticed into his way of looking at things. Thus in an early interview about morality in foreign policy, John Hart of NBC News asked, "Can we talk about dictatorships, the morality of liaisons with dictatorships?"

Carter: "Well, I think the moral standards should be encompassed in 'do unto others as you would have them do unto you' [paraphrase of Matthew 7:12]. As we have relationships with other governments, I think one of the guiding principles, among others, should be, 'What's best for those people who live in the country with which we are dealing?' whether it be Angola or Russia or whether it be the People's Republic of China or whether it be our good friends in Great Britain or China."

Hart: "If dictatorship be wrong and democracy is right, should the experimental democracies such as ours have relationships with dictatorships that are wrong? Is that the kind of moral judgment you bring to foreign policy?"

Carter: "God says, 'Judge not that ye be not judged' [Matthew 7:1]. Just because I believe in democracy it doesn't mean I think that people who live in countries that might have a different form of government—socialism, communism, fascism, dictatorship as you expressed it—are wrong. I don't think our country has a prerogative or responsibility to determine the form of government for other people." The biblical quotations simply reflected his normal way of thinking.

"On occasion I saw nothing wrong with quoting Scripture to illustrate a point," said Carter to this interviewer, looking back on his presidency. "I remember, when I made the report to Congress, for instance, the day after we concluded the Camp David accords, I quoted from the Sermon on the Mount in honoring Prime Minister Begin and President Sadat. I said, 'Blessed are the peacemakers, for they shall be called the children of God.' And I thought that was appropriate."

The point is not that Carter quoted Scripture. All presidents have done so, and Powell may be right that Carter did less of it in his public addresses than some of his predecessors. The point is that he was steeped in the biblical frame of reference, and that such quotations came naturally to his mind in connection with questions like moral judgments or making peace. The biblical thought forms were there, even when Scripture was not explicitly quoted.

James Wall tells of a time during the 1976 Democratic primary campaign, in the week before the Illinois primary, when he and Carter were riding together to a political appearance. The week before Carter had come in a miserable fourth in Massachusetts, slowing his momentum for the nomination.

"How did you feel about losing in Massachusetts?" Wall asked the president.

"Rosalynn and I have discussed it," Carter replied, "and we feel it was for the best."

Here, Wall said, was biblical language in a political context. "As political language, it would have been misunderstood. I was glad he didn't say that publicly. But I understood him completely. 'For the best' is a familiar southern evangelical term. He was using it in the Christian context of 'All things work together for good to them that love the Lord.' "

Carter recognized that his personal imprint on policy was in considerable measure a product of his personal Christianity: "I think that for every person, by the time they reach adulthood, or reach positions of responsibility, whether as a military officer, or a college professor, or a business leader, or a medical doctor, or attorney, or whatever, their standards of morality, their priorities in life, are shaped by a multiplicity of factors: the influence of their parents, their neighborhood, their schooling, and in most cases by their religious beliefs. And my own character—that is, the positive elements of it—was shaped by my religious beliefs. And obviously I took those beliefs into the White House, into the governor's office and into the campaign arena, and expressed my goals and my standards very clearly to the American people. I'm sure that was a factor in their choice of me as president, and certainly a factor that shaped my own decisions in the White House. My religious beliefs were an integral part of my character."

Clearly the Carter presidency reflected a vast number of factors in the country and the administration of which the president's personal impact was only one. And equally clearly, that personal impact was the product of a number of factors of which his religion was only one. He himself has been careful to make that clear, as have those around him. But all that being assumed, the effect of his faith, both on the way he saw the country and its responsibilities, and on who he was as a person, was perhaps the most distinctive mark of this particular presidency.

The Nation's Commitment to "the Principles of God"

Beyond the effect of his Christianity on who he was as a person, a second factor contributed to the religious dimension of the Carter presidency. He was convinced that the principles on which the American nation was based were religious principles. Thus he saw a national commitment to justice, to freedom, to peace, to human rights, not as something he was seeking to impose on his fellow citizens out of his personal Christian frame of reference, but as God-given principles long ingrained in the national character by its religious origins. He assumed not just that he was personally doing God's will in emphasizing these goals as president but that this nation "under God" was already guided in such directions by that will.

Questioned about the effects of his own beliefs, he slipped easily into a discussion of the national character: "the adherence to moral values—concerning peace, human rights, the alleviation of suffering." Because it was a nation based on religious principles, he was able to say "I have never found an incompatibility between my duties as a Christian and my duties as a governor or a president." (He did, however, later on the same occasion, modify this slightly in terms of the incompatibility of his personal views on abortion with the laws he was required to—and did—enforce.)

In a 1986 address on religion and American foreign policy, before a distinctively Christian audience at Messiah College in Pennsylvania, the former president cloaked his discussion in the Christian terminology familiar to his listeners. At one point in the address he said, "[A] characteristic of *foreign policy based on religion* is the alleviation of suffering." (emphasis added) He was not intentionally suggesting that American foreign policy in his administration had been based on religion as such. Rather, he had pointed his audience to justice as the equivalent of Christian love in public life and suggested that justice is the basic guideline. In a later interview he was questioned about the phrase "foreign policy based on religion."

"In that speech I was trying to delineate the factors that make a great nation, which has a known commitment to the principles of God," said Carter. "And obviously peace, the promotion of freedom, human rights, nuclear arms control, are elements of the nation's character that are admirable—and the alleviation of human suffering is another: . . . the offering of starving people adequate food, refugees a place to stay. I always looked upon these as parts of my duties as a president . . . and I still look upon that as part of the moral obligations of a great nation like ours." Carter saw these obligations as derived from the nation's commitment to "the principles of God."

The impact on public policy of President Carter's personal religious faith, together with his conviction that the nation was based on "the principles of God," might be examined from a number of perspectives. As Press Secretary Powell intimated, it affected in a major way everything he did.

In the museum of the Carter Presidential Center in Atlanta there are six central displays, presumably reflecting the former president's own judgments as to the major achievements of his presidency. These depict "New Relations with Panama" (the Canal treaties); "Peace in the Middle East" (the Camp David accords); "Confronting the Nuclear Threat" (SALT II); "Protecting the Future" (Energy); "Commitment to Human Rights," and one display is divided between two themes, "Hostage Crisis in Iran" and "Strengthening Ties with China." Evidences might be found of religious influences in the president's personal impact in all of these areas. We shall, indeed, be looking in some degree at nearly all of them. For illustrative purposes, however, we shall examine in detail the religious dimension of the first two of these initiatives, the Panama Canal treaties and the quest for peace in the Middle East.

The Panama Canal Treaties

The building of the Panama Canal was one of the great engineering achievements of human history. The "remarkable revolution" which separated Panama from Colombia in 1903, however, and the creation within this conveniently established new nation of the Canal Zone under U.S. sovereignty did not constitute one of the proudest moral achievements in American history. The United States instigated the revolution, quickly recognized the new Republic of Panama, and ensured its survival by immediately landing sailors and Marines from gunboats which had been standing off Colón and Panama City. Dealing with a French businessman named Philippe Bunau-Varilla, who had not even visited Panama in eighteen years and whose credentials as its representative were at best questionable, the United States hastily signed in Washington on the night of November 18, 1903, a treaty (which no Panamanian had ever seen) highly favorable to American interests, bypassing an official Panamanian delegation which had already arrived in New York.

"I took Panama because Bunau-Varilla brought it to me on a silver platter," President Theodore Roosevelt is reported to have remarked privately. Publicly some years later, in an address at the University of California, he said, "Fortunately the crisis came at a period when I could act unhampered. Accordingly, I took the Isthmus, started the canal and then left Congress not to debate the canal, but to debate me."

In fairness to Roosevelt and his chief agent, Secretary of State John Hay, it should be remembered that this was a period in which the "manifest destiny" of the United States to extend its power and "bring the benefits of Christian civilization" to less fortunate peoples was widely supported. The United States had a mandate from civilization to build the Canal, the president told Congress on January 4, 1904. Even so, the public reaction at the time was sharply divided.

The Canal Zone, a ten-mile-wide strip of land across the isthmus from the Atlantic to the Pacific (cutting the Republic of Panama in two) in which the United States was granted all rights of sovereignty, made it possible for Americans to build and operate the Canal. It came, however, to be bitterly resented by the Panamanians.

Beginning early in the post-World War II period, Panamanian opposition to the treaty became a foreign policy issue. By the 1960s rioting and bloodshed in Panama reached crisis proportions. After Panama broke diplomatic relations with the United States in 1964, President Lyndon Johnson began negotiations which led to agreement on three new treaties. Opposition in Congress was so intense, however, that they were not submitted for ratification.

President Nixon began negotiations again in 1970, and once again agreement was reached in principle, but the terms were unacceptable to Congress. President Ford also sought a solution and continued the negotiation process, but was strongly opposed on the issue by then-Governor Ronald Reagan during the 1976 presidential primaries.

For President Carter, as for his five predecessors (as far back as Eisenhower), the Panama Canal was a no-win issue. Increasingly a symbol throughout the Third World, and especially in Latin America, of "might makes right," the problem went beyond the troubles in Panama itself or military concern with the security of the Canal. A solution was urgently needed.

But public opinion was strongly opposed to concessions. At the beginning of the Carter administration, polls showed that 78 percent of the American people did not "want to give up" the Canal. In the fall of 1975 a Senate resolution opposing any new treaty and the termination of American sovereignty over the Canal was sponsored by thirty-eight senators, four more than the one-third needed to defeat ratification.

For Carter as well as for the presidents preceding him who had wrestled with the issue, there was no shortage of political, military, economic, and geopolitical considerations. For Carter, however, there was also a religious dimension: the justice which in public life takes the place of love as the Christian mode of action.

He was aware of all the obstacles. "Nevertheless," he said, "I believed that a new treaty was absolutely necessary. I was convinced that we needed to correct an injustice." Before his inauguration he made a decision to press ahead and selected his representative for the negotiation team. His first presidential review memorandum (PRM 1) addressed the issue.

The fight for ratification of the treaties, which came in 1978, was a bitterly bruising battle, and one in which the still-new president used up much of his political capital. It was one of the issues over which the fundamentalist wing of the Christian evangelical movement began to desert him. Carter did get some help from one former political adversary, however. He later revealed that President Ford had given him valuable assistance through lobbying undecided Republican senators. The struggle was "one of the most onerous political ordeals of my life," said Carter. "Many times during the year when we were so discouraged, I had wondered if the results would justify the terrible political costs and the effort we had to exert. Each time, I decided that we simply could not afford to fail."

Beyond the centrality of justice in Carter's perception of the Christian imperative for public life, another dimension of his religious faith which permeated his thinking and undoubtedly affected his determination to settle the Panama Canal issue was his sense of humility, both personal and national. In remarks at the National Prayer Breakfast in January 1977, soon after his inauguration and at the time he was initiating the Canal treaty revision, Carter talked about both kinds of humility:

"If we know we can have God's forgiveness as a person, I think, it makes it much easier for us to say, as a nation, 'God have mercy on me, a sinner,' knowing that the only compensation for sin is condemnation. Then we just can admit an error or a weakness or hatred, or forego pride." Carter's treatment of the Panama Canal treaties in his presidential memoirs, *Keeping Faith*, makes it clear that the morally questionable circumstances under which the United States acquired the Canal Zone had much to do with his determination to right the wrong. He began his chapter with the words "Twenty-one years before I was born, an event took place at the home of then Secretary of State John Hay that was later to confront me with the most difficult battle I had ever faced. . . ." The event, which he then went on to describe, was the hasty signing of the infamous treaty with Bunau-Varilla. For Carter it was at least in part the admission of a national error, the forgoing of pride—the equivalent in public life of repentance for sin.

Peace in the Middle East

The commitment to peace was, in itself, a religiously rooted value for President Carter, but peace in the Middle East had special biblical dimensions for him. The title of his post-presidency (1985) book on the Middle East, *The Blood of Abraham*, reveals the strongly religious context in which he viewed the intractable problems of peace in that troubled region. Asked about the religious imagery, both in this title and that of Carter's earlier book, *Keeping Faith*, Jody Powell was equivocal: "As I recall there was considerable debate about the title of that first book, about whether it would be misinterpreted. And obviously it does have a subtle double resonance. *The Blood of Abraham* is about the Middle East, and it's almost impossible to talk about the Middle East without [a religious reference]."

Carter himself, in response to the same question, was unequivocal. The religious connotations of both titles were not accidental, he said.

"I did a lot of biblical study when I was writing *The Blood of Abraham*, in particular, because part of the book is a history of the Middle East, the region of Palestine or the Holy Land, and I went back to the time of Abraham and came forward. It was interesting to me also to read, from Paul's writings, the explanation that the early Christians were also . . . children of Abraham. This was one of the deep concerns that new Christians, particularly Jewish Christians, had in the early days of the church, because people didn't want to give up their covenanted inheritance from God in becoming Christian. . . . Paul made a very strong distinction that Abraham was rewarded not for his race, but for his faith. . . . And this is the explanation that Paul gave, that we Christians who share Abraham's faith, regardless of our race, are also children of Abraham. So this has always been reassuring to me, and I thought it was interesting to tie together the fact that Christians, who are about 15 percent of the Palestinians, and the Arabs, who are Moslems—about 85 percent of the Palestinians—and the Jews, all share the inheritance of Abraham."

Carter was quite explicit as to the religious dimension of his commitment to Israel, which was for him "the land of the Bible": "For me there is no way to approach or enter Israel without thinking first about the Bible and the history of the land and its people. The names and images have long been an integral part of my life as a Christian, but many of them took on a new and entirely different significance when I became president of the United States and joined in life-or-death negotiations to resolve some of the twentieth century's problems. It is rare indeed to find the distant past so intertwined with the immediate present, not just for historians and theologians in their classrooms and studies but for statesmen in the halls of government and military commanders in the field of battle."

So deeply was his view of Israel embedded in religious concepts that Carter regarded the existence of modern Israel as ordained by

God. "In my affinity for Israel I shared the sentiment of most other Southern Baptists that the holy places we revered should be preserved and made available for visits by Christians. . . . The Judeo-Christian ethic and study of the Bible were bonds between Jews and Christians which had always been part of my life. I also believed very deeply that the Jews who had survived the Holocaust deserved their own nation, and that they had a right to live in peace among their neighbors. I considered this homeland for the Jews to be compatible with the teachings of the Bible, hence ordained by God. These moral and religious beliefs made my commitment to the security of Israel unshakable." Though religious modes of thought were natural to Carter, on few issues did he make the religious sources of a public policy commitment so explicit as on this principle, which he regarded as "ordained by God."

Carter considered Middle Eastern quarrels essentially religious. He noted the profound effect of Judaism and Islam on governments and public policy both in Israel and in the Arab countries. To a remarkable degree, he said, "the will of God is the basis for both esoteric debates and the most vicious terrorist attacks among Jews, Moslems, and Christians."

The Camp David Accords

No achievement stands higher in Carter's estimate of the accomplishments of his presidency than the Camp David accords—the end of hostilities and mutual recognition between Israel and Egypt that accompanied them, and the basis for wider Mideast settlement (though not subsequently realized) that they provided.

As *The Blood of Abraham* makes clear, Carter considered the common sources of Islam, Judaism, and Christianity, together with the deeply religious view of life which both Prime Minister Begin of Israel and President Sadat of Egypt shared with him, to be essential elements in the equation. "During my long meetings with Prime Minister Begin, and even more with President Sadat," he said, "we discussed the three monotheistic religions and their influence on the ancient and current relationships among people in the Middle East, and also on us as individuals—a Jew, a Moslem, and a Christian—searching for peace."

Jody Powell recalled the religious dimension as having been an important part of the context of Camp David, but was reluctant to gauge the extent of its effect. "One of the first things that happened up there," he said, "was that they issued a joint statement [a reference to the joint call for prayer, issued by the three]. . . . There was that fact [their religious faith] that clearly meant something to them, because all three of them talked about it. On the one hand, it was an expedient thing to talk about—that was one thing you could say that was positive, for all three of them. I suspect it did go well beyond that . . . but I doubt if that's quantifiable."

The Bible was part of the equipment Carter took with him to the negotiations: "I went to Camp David with all my maps, briefing books, notes, summaries of past negotiations, and my annotated Bible, which I predicted—accurately as it turned out—would be needed in my discussions with Prime Minister Begin." In a later interview Carter suggested that while the religious dimension at Camp David was a relatively minor factor in the massive mix of history, conflicting national interests and regional rivalries, in one sense it made the difference between success and failure.

"Even if the religious factor was a minimal element," he said to this interviewer, "the Camp David agreement hung by such a narrow thread that I think any particular factor could have caused failure, so because of that explanation, I don't think there's any chance, in retrospect, that we could have been successful without a common faith in a monotheistic God, whom we all recognized to be the same, among me and Begin and Sadat. This may have been a greater factor with me and Sadat than it was with Begin, because I noticed that whenever President Sadat brought this up, as he often did, that Prime Minister Begin was somewhat discomfited. But I responded with alacrity, to say, 'This is a common thing on which we can build mutual peace in the future.' So to summarize . . . I would say that any substantial factor could have caused failure, and religion—a common faith—was a substantial factor."

Religious Commitment to Peace, Justice, and Human Rights

Both the Panama Canal treaties and the Camp David accords were part of a wider religiously based commitment to peace and justice. It was evidenced, of course, in other aspects of the presidency: the unratified but long-observed SALT II with the Soviet Union, limiting the strategic nuclear weapons of the superpowers; the emphasis on racial justice, symbolized by the appointment of unprecedented numbers of highly qualified blacks to federal positions.

Reinhold Niebuhr regarded justice in the political context as the equivalent of love in a sinful world. In a highly Niebuhrian analysis, Carter explained the centrality of justice in his own political agenda: "The highest calling of a Christian is to exhibit, in one's life, love. . . . As you know, in Greek there are four definitions of love. What Christ was talking about was 'agape' love, sacrificial love, love without getting anything in return. . . . So that sacrificial love, to oversimplify its meaning, is the highest possible calling for a human being. A nation is not able to exhibit that kind of a calling. A nation cannot demonstrate sacrificial love. When I was president of the United States . . . I did not have the right to sacrifice the interests of American citizens for others. So you can see, there is an inherent difference between what a human being can do, as the highest possible Christian standard, and what a nation can do. The highest possible standard of a nation is justice."

Part of the liberal left in American politics, sympathetic to if not influenced by Marxist economic analysis, has tended to interpret justice in economic terms. For them justice means some form of redistribution of wealth. Some religious liberals have also leaned toward an economic definition, defending socialist economies, denouncing multinational corporations as exploiters of Third World nations, and calling for sweeping change in "repressive" (by which they mean capitalist) economic systems. Carter's biblically based understanding of justice was not essentially an economic one, and this sharply differentiated his program from that of the radical Christian left.

Neither the commitment to peace nor to justice was uniquely a "Christian policy"; each was developed, administered, and supported within the administration by secularists and members of non-Christian religions. But Carter's personal sense of priority and personal perspective on each of them was an outgrowth of his sense of Christian responsibility.

Especially was this the case with regard to human rights. At the entrance to the human rights display at the Carter Presidential Center are the words "No issue was closer to Jimmy Carter than human rights. His religious faith and faith in liberty led him to champion this cause at home and abroad."

Robert Maddox, asked in an interview to comment on ways in which Carter's religion had affected his presidency, mentioned human rights first:

"His religion shaped his human rights policies," Maddox said. "It was clear to me that this was a passion of the president. . . . [It] grew out of his own faith, his regard for human beings, out of his years of involvement in the civil rights struggle in Georgia."

Following a prisoner exchange with the Soviets in April of 1979, involving the release of some Jewish dissidents and Russian Baptist Georgi Vins in exchange for two convicted Soviet spies, Carter saw a biblical connection: "I was to teach Sunday School the next morning, and our pastor, Reverend Charles Trentham, invited Vins to worship with us. The lesson was about the persecution of Naboth (I Kings 21), and I drew some parallels between the Bible story and religious persecution in our time." Even more basic, however, was the moral dimension. With regard to his human rights policy, the bottom line for Carter was simply "It was the right thing to do."

Respect for Other Religions

Because Jimmy Carter was a Southern Baptist, a member of a denomination that places itself outside of "mainline" American Protestantism, and because he identified strongly with the Southern Baptists, his image, with some, was "sectarian." Because his faith was strongly and distinctively Christian, not a vague "religion in general," and because it was an evangelical Christianity committed to making converts, not a liberal ecumenism that finds one religion as good as another, he was sometimes regarded as narrow. But neither image is accurate. Robert Maddox commented on his acceptance of religious diversity:

"I've seen him and Rosalynn, in relationships with their families and other people, very much a 'live and let live' kind of thing. Their faith was very real to them, and he wanted you to be a person of faith, but also, if you didn't want to, it was okay." Maddox regarded this as characteristic of a highly individualistic kind of faith.

But it was more than "live and let live." Carter had a genuine respect for other religions. A case in point was his high regard for

Islam. He developed a close relationship with "my wonderful friend" President Anwar Sadat of Egypt. Of all the heads of state with whom he dealt, Sadat was the one for whom he had the highest respect and regard. They had long talks about religion, feeling that they worshiped the same God and that they had a great deal in common. Sadat, said Carter, "mentioned frequently, and almost casually, the brotherhood of Arab and Jew and how they are both the sons of Abraham." Carter also recounted extensive conversations with Saudi King Fahd, both during and after his presidency, on the role, importance, and stabilizing influence of religion in the life of the Saudi people and other Arab nations.

Former White House Chief of Staff Hamilton Jordan reports with some amusement an incident that occurred during the Iran hostage crisis, illustrating Carter's high regard for the Moslem faith. Regarding the problem of reaching the Ayatollah Khomeini, "[Carter] said that contacting Moslem religious figures was probably the best way, but perhaps the envoys should be armed with theological reasons against holding hostages. 'If Khomeini is the religious leader he purports to be,' Carter said, 'I don't see how he can condone the holding of our people. There is no recognized religious faith on earth that condones kidnapping.'

"I slipped a note to Harold Brown," said Jordan: " 'Whose side is God on?' Brown smiled, scribbled a reply, and pushed it back across the table: 'Ours, of course.' " Despite the levity of his aides, however, Carter's attention to the religious dimension was quite serious.

In his diary on November 6, 1979, two days after the hostages were seized, Carter wrote, "It's almost impossible to deal with a crazy man, except that he does have religious beliefs, and the world of Islam will be damaged if a fanatic like him should commit murder in the name of religion against sixty innocent people. I believe that's our ultimate hope for a successful resolution of this problem."

Both Carter's feeling of kinship with Judaism, and his high regard for Islam, especially evident in his search for peace in the Mideast, are important elements in an understanding of the impact of his personal Christian faith on public policy.

Carter drew a distinction between what was essential to his own personal faith and world view and the religious basis of a pluralistic society. His own values were explicitly based on biblical Christianity. But asked by this interviewer if he saw the Judeo-Christian tradition as an essential base for American society, he replied, "I'm reluctant to say yes. . . . I've had to face this question, at least indirectly, throughout my service as a governor and president. And I wouldn't want to say that people who don't profess belief in the New Testament or Old Testament are somehow lacking in proper citizenship motivations. I think that even if someone has a different faith, for instance a Moslem, or others, that they can indeed be good citizens. And there are moral values that apply in countries like Nepal or India; Hindu countries are religious countries that can be exemplary in shaping the personal habits or attitudes of an individual. So in a country where I profess, as a Baptist, to separation of church and state, I wouldn't want to say that the only foundation for proper moral values or citizenship values should be either Christianity or Judaism. I think it is broader than that."

Christian President and a Polarized Christianity

But though his respect for others was real, and he was able to work with people of all faiths in terms of their own religious convictions, Carter's personal position was clear. Not only did his Christian faith govern his private life, it affected all that he did as president. Here was a born-again Christian president, committed to living out his faith in the Oval Office.

Why, then, did evangelicals, who had rallied behind him and helped to elect him, desert him in droves as his presidency unfolded? The answer lies in considerable measure in the late-twentieth-century polarization of Protestant America—and, indeed, of religious America generally. Though be was authentically a conservative, Bible-believing evangelical, he parted company with many evangelicals, and most fundamentalists, as to how Christian belief is translated into public policy. They resonated to his Southern Baptist piety, but the understanding of social justice to which he was committed led him toward a different vision of the biblical mandate than that of the religious right.

The justice-centered program of Carter-style evangelicals is far closer to that of religious liberals than that of fellow evangelicals of fundamentalist persuasion. Because of his conservative religious orientation, Carter shared many of the values of his fellow evangelicals on the right, including a strong commitment to the family. His own life exemplified highly traditional family values. Early in his presidency, on a visit to the Department of Health, Education and Welfare, he spoke to its employees in terms that brought some ridicule from the sexually liberated: "Those of you who are living in sin, I hope you'll get married. Those of you who left your spouses, go home. Those of you who have forgotten your children's names, go home and get reacquainted."

Questioned once by a reporter about the living arrangements and sexual morality of some of his staff members, he answered in a somewhat jocular way that he didn't propose to do anything about the allegations except "pray for them." But though he never imposed his personal standards on others, those standards were crystal clear. He was committed to the same basic "family values" the right supported.

Carter personally opposed abortion. Asked on one occasion if he ever had to compromise his faith to carry out his duties as president, he answered, "Yes. I can only think of one issue where I had to modify my own Christian beliefs to carry out the duties of president, and that was on the subject of abortion, and this is a highly personal thing. You ask me as a human being. It is impossible for me to imagine Jesus Christ approving abortion, and my duties as a president required me to carry out the laws of our nation as interpreted by the Supreme Court, which authorized abortion, as you know, in the first three months of pregnancy if the woman and her doctor decide [to do so]. I disagreed with this, although I never failed to carry out my duty as a president. . . ."

Carter's strong commitment to freedom as a Christian value he also shared with fundamentalists and conservative evangelicals. No one, of course, opposes freedom, just as no one opposes justice. But the difference in emphasis is considerable. In the present polarized context, freedom is perceived as a major value of the religious right, and justice of the religious left. Pat Robertson's Freedom Council and Jerry Falwell's Liberty Federation would be readily recognized as organizations representing the right, just as a Mobilization for Peace and Justice would be immediately recognizable as an activity of the religious left. Carter sought as president to embody both emphases in his program, thus straddling the polarization at this particular point.

His unusual religious background was clearly reflected in his presidency: this conservative, Bible-steeped Southern Baptist who was a liberal on social issues; this naval officer/peanut farmer who led church services for sailors and went off periodically to Philadelphia or Boston on evangelistic missions; this Deep South white establishmentarian who had been a leader in the fight to gain the civil rights of blacks; this Sunday School teacher who read Niebuhr and Tillich.

In general his program was closer to that of the religious left than that of the right. His commitment to peace, justice, and compassion grew directly from his biblical frame of reference; it was the expression of his religious faith. But it was not the program of all evangelical Christians, and it was a program he shared with nonevangelical Christians as well as secular humanitarians.

Summing Up

It is easy to ascribe more significance to religion in the policy formation of the Carter years than reality would warrant. A day in the Carter Oval Office in no way resembled a prayer meeting. Presidential policy is the product of the complex interplay of numerous factors. It responds to the real needs of a nation, few of which are immediately shaped by religious considerations. It operates under a wide range of political constraints, calculated, pragmatic, and sometimes counter to religious considerations. It is developed by large numbers of people in executive departments, representing a wide range of religious views or none at all. It is fine-tuned by a presidential staff, which in Carter's case was selected without regard to religious affiliation, and included, in important policy-making positions, Catholics and Jews as well as atheists.

To label an *administration* "Christian" under these circumstances would be clearly erroneous. But a *presidency* is not the same thing as an administration. Jimmy Carter's religious faith was so central to who he was, his values and thought forms so shaped by his church, the Bible, and his personal faith, that to ignore its impact on personal conduct of the presidency would be equally a distortion.

Despite the obvious provisos, his was the presidency of a devout Christian, elected in the post-Watergate period in considerable measure *because* of his Christian morality, his positions on public issues formed out of his own biblical frame of reference, seeing his public service as a way of carrying out his Christian responsibilities. Jimmy Carter's religious faith, and the religiously derived way in which he saw the nation and its responsibilities, shaped his personal priorities, directions, and actions, and thus shaped his presidency.

Jody Powell summarized it: "There were no times when I recall that he invoked his religious beliefs as reasons for a decision, and I would have been not only surprised but shocked and put off if he had. But . . . my view of him is that his religion and his faith were so much an integral part of him, and how he viewed the world and how he viewed other people and how he viewed his responsibilities, both as a citizen and as a president, that it's a seamless thing."

Carter was a complex man, leading a complex society in a complex world. But it was no accident that his code name was "the Deacon."

Rocks and Shoals of a Religious Presidency

IN REMARKS at a National Prayer Breakfast on January 27, 1977, shortly after his inauguration, President Carter told a story that prefigured a later problem:

> The first draft of my Inaugural speech did not include the reference to Micah's admonition about justice, mercy and humility. But I had chosen instead Second Chronicles 7:14, which Congressman Wright quoted this morning: "If my people who are called by my name, shall humble themselves, and pray, and seek my face, and turn from their wicked ways; then will I hear from heaven, and will forgive their sin, and will heal their land."
>
> When my staff members read the first draft of my speech they rose up in opposition to that verse. The second time I wrote my Inaugural draft I had the same verse in it. They came to me en masse and said, "The people will not understand that verse. It is as though you, being elected president, are condemning the other people of our country, putting yourself in the position of Solomon and saying that all Americans are wicked."
>
> So, correctly or wrongly, I changed to Micah. I think this episode, which is true, is illustrative of the problems that we face. Sometimes we take for granted that an acknowledgment of sin, an acknowledgment of the need for humility, permeates the consciousness of our people. But it doesn't.

Carter was speaking at a religious gathering, to an audience that would have understood acknowledgment of sin and the need for humility, rather than the kind of general audience to which an inaugural speech is addressed. To the Prayer Breakfast audience the verse from Second Chronicles had already been quoted by Congressman James Wright of Texas.

President Ronald Reagan later quoted the same verse—also to a religious audience (the Convention of the National Association of Evangelicals)—in March 1984. Indeed, it was to this verse, heavily marked and with marginal comments in her handwriting, that his mother's Bible was opened when Reagan took the oath of office.

But the incident Carter described was significant for his presidency. The difficulty for him was that his own consciousness—indeed, his own perception of reality—was deeply permeated by an acknowledgment of sin and humility. It took two tries for his staff to convince him that, at least for purposes of an inaugural address, this seemingly sad and highly theological concept was not the right theme to proclaim. And, as indicated by his "correctly or wrongly," he still had doubts.

In many ways, despite staff warnings—and perhaps with negative political consequences—a consciousness of sin and humility did permeate the Carter presidency. So did the sacrifice theme, as we have already noted in connection with the Panama Canal treaties. A third religious characteristic which may have had negative consequences was an ethical awareness which saw the complexities of all moral decisions.

Jody Powell was pressed by this interviewer for ways in which the president's religious faith had directly affected policy, particularly when political wisdom might have clashed with his religious convictions. Reiterating once again that Carter "wasn't a Bible-thumper or a Scripture-quoter," Powell went on to say, "You can only surmise the extent to which what he did was a result of his religious beliefs. But I've always said that I think almost everything that he will be remembered fondly for by historians was contrary to the prevailing political judgment; almost everything he did that was [in this category] was something that cost him, politically."

Sin and Humility: the "Malaise" Speech

Carter's particular understanding of human reality, drawn from his Christian faith, involved a profound sense of sin—the corporate sin of all human institutions (including the United States of America) as well as personal sin. He regarded humility, public as well as personal, as a virtue in sinful human beings, institutions, and countries.

From the standpoint of traditional Christianity, Carter's theology was impeccably correct. He spelled it out to a religious audience in 1980: "[The Bible] tells us about sinful men and women, men like the Disciples—sometimes stubborn, reluctant, selfish, weak, struggling with their own fears and failures and lack of faith. Yet with God's help they were able to do great things. I am thankful that God has always done his work through imperfect human beings. . . . Only when they realized their own personal limitations could God work fully in their lives."

It is important to recognize that for a Christian of Carter's persuasion, such a view of human nature is not considered pessimistic. It is seen, rather, as profoundly optimistic, since the faith of Christianity is that sin, though universal, has been overcome by the cross and the resurrection. The habitual mode of such a believer is not one of deep gloom over sin and evil but of infectious joy over the good news of the gospel.

To outsiders, however—and to some Christians who do not share this particular biblical orientation—"all that sin talk" sounds deeply pessimistic. So does humility, a traditional Christian virtue lately largely displaced by the "proud to be me" ethic of the new narcissism in the sixties and seventies.

The politics of optimism practiced by Carter's successor, Ronald Reagan—the "morning in America" theme and the upsurge in national pride—may in part have been a reaction to the apparent gloom of the Carter years. Certainly it reflected a less critical way of looking at human nature.

In a discussion of political fallout from Christian humility in a 1987 interview, Robert Maddox offered some penetrating observations:

"Carter is an humble man in the best biblical sense," he said. "He is a very strong man, with a whole lot of pride, but there is a humility about him that I think is a genuine biblical humility. He understands that he is a man standing 'empty and undone' before God.

"But that humility translated publicly as weakness," Maddox went on to observe. "He could say, 'I made a mistake,' and feel as he would when personally confessing a sin to God. He could confess to the American people, 'I made a mistake,' but the American people perceived that as weakness and wishy-washiness. . . .

"In his personal relationships with the staff," Maddox added, "you could say, 'I made a mistake,' and he would eat you alive on it, but he was also forgiving. And maybe he thought he could do that with the American people and they would forgive him. But somehow, they didn't. His own understanding of a man before God, that was genuine humility, was perceived as weakness."

In its aftermath nothing came to symbolize the negative image widely attached to the Carter presidency as much as the television address delivered in July 1979 after a massive buildup of public expectations, which came to be known as the "malaise speech." As Jody Powell points out, that term was not actually used. But in spirit the speech was generally regarded as pointing to a widespread malaise within American society. There may have been a genuine malaise at the time (from one Christian perspective there always is). The label, however, was decidedly unpopular. And it later became symbolic shorthand for Carter's pessimistic view of the nation, in contrast with Ronald Reagan's considerably more upbeat, optimistic view.

Carter had just returned from an Economic Summit in Tokyo, in the midst of an energy crisis. He had canceled a vacation in Hawaii to prepare his fifth nationwide address on energy. His popularity in the public opinion polls was at a new low, and there was considerable evidence of malaise within the administration itself. Pat Caddell, his pollster, reported that the ratings were highly negative on the energy issue. But, as Carter later related, "Pat also seemed certain that the problem transcended the single issue of energy, and applied to the basic relationship between the people and their government. . . . Americans were losing faith in themselves and in their country." Caddell urged Carter not to focus on energy alone, but to address the more general problem.

James Wall discussed the episode in a 1987 interview: "Even though it was Caddell's idea," he said, "Carter bought in because it fit his religious framework."

The humility of that religious framework is evident in what followed—one of the most amazing episodes in the history of the

American presidency. Carter returned to Camp David for a ten-day period, during which he invited in groups of leaders from all walks of American life to advise him on what had gone wrong with America. There were representatives from business and labor, state and local governments, educators and economists, as well as political experts. And, significantly, Carter included a group of religious leaders, finding his meeting with this group, along with his meeting with state governors, "especially worthwhile." He asked for opinions about his own Cabinet and administration, as well as the state of the nation, and he listened to some sharply negative responses.

In *Keeping Faith*, Carter listed nearly two pages of comments he had written down as he listened day after day. The sheer exercise in listening, together with the apparently quiet acceptance of so much negative feedback, was an astonishing display of presidential humility. Together with the speech to the nation that reported his findings, it constituted an unprecedented national confession of sin.

Carter began with a reference to the fact that he had planned a speech on energy. But:

> It's clear that the true problems of our Nation are much deeper—deeper than gasoline lines or energy shortages, deeper even than inflation or recession. And I realize more than ever that as President I need your help. So I decided to reach out and listen to the voices of America. . . .

As the president reported on what he had heard from the voices of America, the sense of malaise was built, phrase after phrase, in terms reminiscent of a penitential litany:

> This kind of summarized a lot of other statements: "Mr. President, we are confronted with a moral and spiritual crisis." . . .
>
> These ten days [of listening] confirmed my belief in the decency and the strength and the wisdom of the American people, but it also bore out some of my longstanding concerns about our Nation's underlying problems. . . .
>
> After listening to the American people I have been reminded again that all the legislation in the world can't fix what's wrong with America.

So I want to speak to you first tonight about a fundamental threat to American democracy. . . .

It is a crisis of confidence. It is a crisis that strikes at the very heart and soul and spirit of our national will. We can see this crisis in growing doubt about the meaning of our lives and in the loss of a unity of purpose for our nation. . . .

In a nation that was proud of hard work, strong families, close-knit communities, and our faith in God, too many of us now tend to worship self-indulgence and consumption. Human identity is no longer defined by what one does, but by what one owns. But we've discovered that owning things and consuming things does not satisfy our longing for meaning. We've learned that piling up material goods cannot fill the emptiness of lives which have no confidence or purpose. The symptoms of this crisis of the American spirit are all around us.

The spiritual tone of the speech is evidenced by the repeated use of religious language: "a moral and spiritual crisis" . . . "a crisis that strikes at the very heart and soul and spirit of our national will" . . . "growing doubt about the meaning of our lives." Our "faith in God" has been replaced by a tendency "to worship self-indulgence." Symptoms of "this crisis of the American spirit are all around us."

Here was the high priest of the national faith leading the American people through an exercise strongly reminiscent in feeling of the traditional General Confession from The Book of Common Prayer: "We have left undone those things which we ought to have done; And we have done those things which we ought not to have done; And there is no health in us."

The next step, "But Thou, O Lord, have mercy upon us, miserable offenders," was omitted. It would have been in keeping with the beliefs and attitude of the president himself to include it. The human necessity for confession of sin and acceptance of pardon was inherent in his view of life.

At one point in the preparation of the speech, Robert Maddox revealed in a 1987 interview, a draft had included words to the effect that "the country is in a mess, and I am guilty; I am responsible.

"I looked at that draft," Maddox went on, "—they were all at Camp David—and I mustered great courage and put a call through to Rosalynn, and finally got her. And I said, 'He must not say that. He must not do the "I am guilty" bit, the mea culpa.' She said, 'I agree.' So they took the phrases out, but a whole lot of what the speech conveyed was not [removed]."

Spoken or unspoken, the implication of "miserable offenders" was there, and it was decisively rejected by the public at large. For many this "malaise" incident later became symbolic of what was wrong with the Carter presidency. His inaugural address advisers had been right. Acknowledgment of sin and the need for humility simply "doesn't permeate the consciousness" of most Americans as it does with devout Christians of his particular persuasion.

Jody Powell, questioned in an interview as to whether or not the "malaise" speech showed a sense of sin, was reluctant to use religious language:

"I don't know," he responded. But, he went on, "I'll say this about that speech. . . . There was in that speech, and elsewhere, too, a sense that leadership goes beyond just patting people on the back and telling them everything is fine and they're fine, and everything is going to be all right; that one of the responsibilities of leadership is to tell people and society when they're on the wrong track." And ever alert to the implication that the president was too overtly religious, Powell added, "It was the sort of thing he would never have done in a sectarian sense. He would have felt that was not the job of a political or civic leader."

The damage from the speech was probably compounded by the flurry of events surrounding it. For a president to call off a scheduled address, leave abruptly the daily responsibilities of the Oval Office and spend ten days in isolation, calling in group after group of diagnosticians of the national malaise, was a remarkable departure from normal presidential routine, inevitably tension-producing. The general negative effect was worsened by the clumsily handled replacement of several Cabinet officers in the week following. Though the speech had initially appeared to be well received, the tide quickly turned. And the symbolic significance later attached to the episode, as the word "malaise" cropped up in column after column and came to be used as media shorthand for a whole presidency, requires a deeper explanation. It constituted a wholesale rejection of leadership which saw humility and acknowledgment of error (confession of sin) as an acceptable response to what was, authentically, a crisis of the spirit.

At the heart of the whole episode was the president's religious orientation: he saw the process of self-examination and penitence as natural and desirable. But lecturing a nation on its own sin and calling for repentance and humility, while commonplace in churches, is not acceptable politically. And it is probable that this episode set a negative tone that persisted into the election year.

We have noted earlier that Carter selected a line from Reinhold Niebuhr to begin his campaign biography (and by implication, perhaps, to encapsulate the promise of his presidency): "The sad duty of politics is to establish justice in a sinful world." Did he overlook the political implications of the words "sad" and "sinful"? Probably not. Had he been forewarned that such words might constitute rocks and shoals on the navigational chart for the presidency of a devout Christian, he undoubtedly would have steamed ahead without changing course. Steeped as he was in biblical language and thought forms, the need for repentance and humility were for him simply inherent in the human condition, and he could no more have exerted his personal leadership without such concepts than without prayer.

The Call for Sacrifice

A second biblical theme that permeated the Carter presidency, perhaps with negative consequences, was that of sacrifice. The call to sacrifice is not in itself unusual in the world of politics. Presidential leadership in times of war or national crisis has frequently sounded the theme. John F. Kennedy, in the context of the Cold War, called on Americans to "bear any burden, pay any price" in the cause of freedom. Sacrifice had long been an honorable—even noble—theme in the American Judeo-Christian moral heritage.

But Carter's presidency came at a time when sacrifice was out of fashion. The seventies were the "me decade," when the self-fulfillment revolution had turned old verities upside down. An ethic of personal gratification had little room for self-imposed hardship. Nor was there a perception of national crisis demanding sacrifice. Carter's somewhat hyperbolic labeling of the energy crunch of the seventies as "the moral equivalent of war" sent no one rushing to the trenches. Gasoline lines and skyrocketing prices were not perceived by the populace at large as ennobling—only annoying.

In Carter's view the energy crisis did demand sacrifice. No return of cheaper oil was foreseen by anyone at the time, and harsh measures seemed called for. But from Carter's personal religious perspective, sacrifice was a virtue. As he said to the National Association of Religious Broadcasters in January 1980:

> Our nation is now faced with serious challenges and choices which may require sacrifice, even from those assembled here in this great hall. But it's important that we keep our perspective and realize what is truly valuable. It is not a sacrifice to give up waste. It's not a sacrifice to submit to God's will. It's not a sacrifice to care for others or to struggle for peace or to tell the truth.

Here again, his theology was impeccable. Sacrificial love, in the Christian ethic espoused by Carter, is the highest personal value, "the highest possible calling for a human being," in his words. He was aware that a nation cannot govern its affairs by the personal Christian ethic of sacrificial love. As we have seen, this was the basis on which he saw justice as the highest value for a nation. "When I was president of the United States I could not deal with foreign countries on the basis of sacrificial love. I would have been impeached had I always exhibited as president that high a standard," he said.

There is a difference, however, between sacrificing the best interests of the United States for the sake of a foreign power, which he clearly would not have done, and calling on the American people to sacrifice present advantage for the sake of long-range best interest or moral principle. This he did often.

As we have seen, the theme was a prominent one in the struggle for ratification of the Panama Canal treaties. His message to the people at that time was that it was in their long-range best interest to voluntarily give up their sovereignty over the Canal Zone and ultimately their full control over the Canal. The security of the Canal depended in the long run on friendly relations with the Panamanian people, and America's overall interests in Latin America depended on strong, democratic, and friendly Latin American nations, for all of whom the Canal Zone was a bitterly resented symbol of American imperialism. Less emphasized, but fully as important in Carter's own thinking, was the shameful (and perhaps, to a devout Christian, sinful) way in which the original treaty had been obtained. His was a call for sacrifice for the sake of moral principle. But such sacrifice does not come readily in complacent times. Far more compatible with the spirit of the people was Ronald Reagan's often-repeated line (and sure-fire applause-getter) in his 1976 Republican primary challenge to Gerald Ford: "We built it, we paid for it, it's ours, and . . . we're going to keep it!" Carter won his treaty, after a bruising battle, but he paid a heavy price.

The personal political sacrifice involved in pushing so hard for such an unpopular cause Carter accepted without hesitation. He recognized that he was asking others to make such personal sacrifices. After the battle was won he addressed a handwritten letter to each senator who had voted for ratification:

April 1987

To Senator ———

As President, I want to express my admiration for your support of the Panama Canal treaties. Rarely is a national leader called upon to act on such an important issue fraught with so much potential political sacrifice.

On behalf of the people of the United States, I thank you for your personal demonstration of statesmanship and political courage.

Sincerely,
Jimmy Carter

Devout Christianity is not the only source of the kind of courage that makes political sacrifices. John F. Kennedy's book *Profiles in Courage* detailed the stories of a number of such incidents in American political history. It might be argued that in his period, before the self-fulfillment revolution that flowered in the later sixties, the American public ethic was still one formed out of the Judeo-Christian heritage, and thus that the sacrifice theme, as Kennedy expressed it, did have Christian roots. But the point is not that a call to sacrifice can come *only* from devout Christianity—such a claim would be an obvious distortion. The point is that in Jimmy Carter, in whose life New Testament Christianity occupied a special place, it clearly did have such roots.

Ethical Complexity: the Iranian Hostages

A third aspect of Carter's faith which may have been a political liability was a Niebuhrian understanding of the complexity of all ethical issues. Wrote Niebuhr, in rejection of simplistic moralizing:

> What is lacking among all these moralists, whether religious or rational, is an understanding of the brutal character of the behavior of all human collectives, and the power of self-interest and collective egoism in all inter-group relations. . . . [T]hey do not see that the limitations of the human imagination, the easy subservience of reason to prejudice and passion, and the consequent persistence of irrational egoism, particularly in group behavior, make social conflict an inevitability in human history, probably to its very end.

Despite Carter's disclaimer of theological sophistication, it is clear both from his conversation and from his writings and public actions that he understood Niebuhr well. *Christian Century* editor James Wall, an ardent supporter and political activist, who shared Carter's Georgia background and on occasion discussed religious issues with him, said in an interview, "He understood Niebuhr's concept of irony, of ambiguity, how when we think we are absolutely right, that is the point at which we are most in danger of being wrong. He understood that even our best intentions are inevitably tainted."

And the curse of one who studies Niebuhr is the inability, thereafter, to see moral issues in simplistic, black-and-white terms.

It is quite possible that this awareness of moral complexity and ambiguity was at least one source of a widespread perception of indecisiveness, particularly during the Iran hostage affair of the last year of his presidency. Asked in an interview if his handling of the Iranian hostage crisis was directly affected by his Christian faith, Carter appeared amused. His answer, however, was straightforward: "The avoidance of violence, or the killing of innocent people, an emphasis on human life, were all compatible with Christian principles." The former president appeared to be resisting a direct connection between his handling of the crisis and his Christian faith but at the same time affirming that the Christian principles he espoused were American principles, operative in this situation in which his personal leadership loomed so large.

The restraint exercised in connection with the Iranian hostages ran counter to the expected macho response of a great power to the action of a small power. There were many pragmatic reasons for restraint: the lives of the hostages; uncertainty as to the response of the Soviet Union to American intervention in a country with which it shares a common border; the ease of escalation. For such reasons presidents who are quick to issue threatening pronouncements are sometimes considerably more restrained in backing up threats with action in response to terrorism.

But for Carter, with his deep and often-proclaimed commitment to morality in foreign policy, the fact that the right and wrong of the situation were not clear-cut was also a factor. He understood the moral ambiguities: the reality of America's past involvement with the Shah; his repressive policies and the deep resentment they had engendered; our commitment to peace and to negotiated solutions.

Robert Maddox saw in Carter's handling of the Iran hostage crisis one of the striking illustrations of his religious orientation. "If he had bombed Teheran, or if he had sent the troops into Teheran, to rescue the hostages, he probably would have been reelected; no matter what happened, he would have been reelected. But his conscience, along with his sense of public policy, would not allow him to do that."

Carter's final comment in response to this interviewer's question about the impact of his faith on his handling of the hostage crisis was revealing: "I guess you might add parenthetically, a long-suffering patience was also compatible with Christian principles." "Long-suffering" is an adjective with positive connotations in traditional Christian circles, and Carter, whose vocabulary has been shaped by his Christian background, so used it. Not so with the public at large. That long-suffering patience was widely interpreted as indecisiveness, the dillydallying of a political wimp.

Initially the restraint was widely supported. But particularly in retrospect, as the interminable crisis ran on month after month, with the not-so-long-suffering patience of the public long since exhausted, the image of impotence and indecisiveness took a devastating hold in the minds of voters. And not only was Carter defeated for reelection. Together with the negative impact of the "malaise" incident, this image of indecisiveness did much to shape the widely held retrospective opinion that his had been a "failed presidency."

It came not so much from any evaluation of accomplishments as from the personal quality that Carter himself considered "long-suffering patience."

Since the Carter years, terrorism—especially terrorism associated with the Middle East—has escalated. No Western government has mastered the formula for dealing firmly and decisively with terrorists in such a way as to demonstrate that violence will not be tolerated while at the same time protecting the lives of all innocent hostages or victims. It remains one of the most intractable problems of foreign policy. The Iranian hostage affair, the first major incident of Middle Eastern terrorism with which modern American presidents have had to deal, left no one satisfied and clearly did much to sink Carter's hopes of reelection.

The former president himself remains convinced that his patient handling of the crisis was what brought the hostages home alive, and that his course was the right one. In an extremely complex situation, no value was higher for him than the saving of the lives of the hostages. His last official visitor in the Oval Office was Veterans Affairs Administrator Max Cleland, a triple-amputee Vietnam veteran, who brought him a plaque with a quotation from Thomas Jefferson:

I HAVE THE CONSOLATION TO REFLECT
THAT DURING THE PERIOD OF MY
ADMINISTRATION NOT A DROP
OF THE BLOOD OF A SINGLE CITIZEN
WAS SHED BY THE SWORD OF WAR

"This is something I shall always cherish," wrote Carter in his diary for that last day in office.

Did the Religious Rocks and Shoals Sink Him?

It is not the purpose of this book to evaluate any presidency but rather to examine the role of presidential religion in a period in which successive presidencies have been significantly affected by a variety of religious influences. In Carter's case, however, his religious faith may have played an important part in creating a widespread public impression of presidential failure.

There were successes, from a religious viewpoint. The Panama

Canal treaties, the changed attitudes in the Third World, the justice theme in women's and minority rights and the worldwide progress in human rights, the peace initiatives and particularly the Camp David accords—all these, to many who looked at national issues from a mainstream religious perspective, constituted a considerable measure of success. And most significant of all, perhaps, was the overall moral tone, both in policy and in standards of honesty and integrity in government. Yet even from the religious perspective there was not a sense of wholeness of accomplishment.

Said Baptist minister and Carter White House staffer Robert Maddox, "The fault of the president was that he did not have a large . . . world view. He had a whole bunch of things he wanted to accomplish, all of which were very important. But there was no string to tie them together. . . . Somehow in my mind, I've always connected that with his understanding of individual faith, individual relationships. He was not able to convey a whole out of what he was trying to do. With all of Reagan's faults, he's able to do that. He's got two or three things that he pushes, and they all connect. . . . President Carter had a lot of individual things he wanted to do, but he did not convey a sense of the wholeness of those things."

To what extent is the popular perception of a failed presidency a result of Carter's religious faith? Indeed, the question must be raised as to what extent it is possible for a deeply committed Christian with a strong sense of national sin and need for humility, a belief in the rightness and necessity of sacrifice, and a sense of the complexity of ethical issues to be a politically successful president.

The religious community is the natural constituency of a presidency envisioned in such explicitly religious terms. The ambivalence—and in some sectors downright hostility—of the American religious community toward Carter clearly played a role in the reelection failure. He was to some extent caught in a tide of massive religious change, supported politically by the declining religious left (but without enthusiasm because of his evangelical piety) and rejected politically by the rapidly growing religious right (to which he was closest in evangelical spirit, but not in public priorities). He was in a no-win situation.

"We probably got the negatives on both sides in the '80 campaign," said former Carter aide Jody Powell, in answer to a question about political impact on religious constituencies. "The people that were suspicious because he was religious, we lost on that side. And then we had Falwell and that crowd, who had a secular agenda cloaked in religious terms, who would have us believe that the Bible has a position on the Panama Canal treaties, and that hurt, too." His estimate of the dual effect, with losses both on the Christian left and the Christian right, is shared by religious analysts. And, indeed, unless a period of broad consensus returns at some time in the future, no political program is likely to unite the seriously polarized American Christian community.

Carter also lost a significant portion of the Jewish constituency, prior to that time loyally Democratic. What was intended as an even-handed Middle Eastern policy was regarded by some as not sufficiently pro-Israel. The achievement of the Camp David accords was widely admired in Israel. Carter is personally liked there. Said James Wall, following a 1987 visit to that country, "In Israel, even those who don't like Carter like him." But politically, Carter was too sympathetic to the Arab cause for many Israelis, and for many American Jewish voters. This most religious of all modern presidents was, at the end of his term, by no means supported by all major religious constituencies.

Certainly many other factors contributed to the reelection defeat. It would be obviously false to suggest that Carter's religion was the sole or even major reason for his rejection for a second term. The collapse of the mid-century Democratic coalition, with a general loss of faith in New Deal/Fair Deal programs, has bedeviled every recent Democratic presidential contender. The conservative tide that Reagan rode to the White House was broad and deep, transforming many areas of American life, social and religious as well as political. The revolution of self-fulfillment, symbolized by the "me decade," was still strong enough to swamp Carter's call for sacrifice and service in the tide of this social movement. The Iranian hostage crisis, which dominated the election year (in part because Carter himself made it a central preoccupation), was such a frustrating experience for the public that it might have done in any incumbent president.

Yet underneath all these factors the theological and philosophical question is still relevant: Can a devoutly religious president, his inner being formed by the conviction that themes like sin and sacrifice are at the heart of human reality, succeed politically? Is awareness of ethical complexity a disabling handicap in an arena where the black-and-white simplicity of popular political slogans usually triumphs?

James MacGregor Burns, perhaps the foremost contemporary analyst of American political leadership, is an academic rather than a religionist. His judgments are based on secular criteria. Yet his somewhat ambivalent evaluation of the Carter presidency shows an awareness that the religious dimension is essential to understanding Carter.

His 1984 book, *The Power to Lead: The Crisis of the American Presidency*, found the roots of presidential dysfunctionality in the political system and the kind of leadership the system produces rather than in personal presidential failure. He proposed sweeping systemic changes. In establishing his case he examined in some detail three recent presidencies, those of Kennedy, Carter, and Reagan.

Regarding Carter, Burns cited approvingly his Niebuhrian cast of thought: "He was a man who read Reinhold Niebuhr and appreciated the great theologian's hard-headed view of political morality, his ironic conception of American history, and his 'Christian realism' that recognized the evil—the greed, selfishness, injustice—as well as the good in humankind."

In examining Carter's "failure to live up to his own high promise" and the public's expectations, Burns weighed personal and situational factors: "I would lean far more toward the 'impossible situation' theory in measuring the Carter presidency than toward the 'personal failure' interpretation. But Carter, bringing to the presidency a combination of high moral purpose and an engineer's grasp of details, failed to bring the two together with a clear ordering of priorities," he said. The result was policy zigzagging.

Carter preferred to rise above the level of party politics, said Burns. "He wanted to be a teaching president, as Wilson and FDR had been, a preaching president who set the tone of moral uplift so clearly that it would guide his Administration and impress his adversaries, perhaps even Congress." In the background, behind this secular analysis, the rocks and shoals of a Christian presidency can be clearly perceived.

Jimmy Carter's evangelical Christian faith was central to who he was. It helped to elect him in the post-Watergate period of moral disillusionment. It shaped his presidency in significant ways as he put his faith into action. But it had its down side as well, and it may have helped to defeat him at the end of one term.

9

The Religious Right and Ronald Reagan

IT WAS the religious right that did Jimmy Carter in, at least in part. And it was Jimmy Carter who had helped bring the religious right into being. An important aspect of the rise of Ronald Reagan can only be understood against the background of the disillusionment of conservative Christians with Carter and their determination to try again.

Carter had been elected with significant support from the burgeoning conservative movement in American Christianity. Rising concern about the moral crisis—the value vacuum at the national heart, of which Watergate was only the most visible evidence—was being articulated most strongly by these religious conservatives. They were the natural custodians of traditional values, which appeared to be crumbling under the onslaught of the social revolution of the sixties. Historically the president had been the symbol of the national faith, the high priest of the civil religion. And Americans had always regarded moral values as closely related to religious faith. Surely an evangelical Christian president offered the most lively possibility of turning the moral tide. So the hopes of evangelicals were riding expectantly on the shoulders of born-again, Sunday School-teaching, morally impeccable Jimmy Carter.

But those hopes were quickly dashed.

The Path to Political Activism

The troubled path that had led the religious right into organized political activism was described by Carl A. Anderson, former Special Assistant to President Reagan for Public Liaison (with responsibility for religious liaison), in a 1987 White House interview. Himself a Roman Catholic with a broad understanding of Protestant evangelicalism, Anderson is an excellent example of the coming together of Catholic and Protestant concerns in contemporary conservative religious movements. He described the way "some of us here [in the Reagan White House] might place it in context."

Citing the writings of John Courtney Murray, he referred to the convergence in the 1950s of a broad spectrum of Christianity, Catholic and Protestant alike, and the American democratic system, a "real meshing" of national and religious perspectives.

"In the sixties," he said, "you see that disintegrate. You see it disintegrate in Vietnam. I think you also see it disintegrate in terms of some of the things the Supreme Court started doing, like school prayer. You can argue about the substance of the [school prayer] decision, whether it was right or wrong. Or you can argue whether everybody obeys it, or whether there was much prayer in schools going on out there. But for a lot of Christians, that was sort of a signal that there was something wrong—something happening in the public consciousness that was like striking 'In God We Trust' off the coins. . . . I think that was a very important decision, particularly for Protestant evangelical Christians. . . ." A whole series of court decisions, said Anderson, reflected a widening gap between "Christian America" and what America was becoming.

"Christian America during the sixties," he said, "was undergoing the beginning of an awakening, a restoration. The Second Vatican Council was weaving together a lot of dynamics within the Catholic community. Then there was a reawakening in the Protestant evangelical community. . . . So you've got that building in one direction. And [in the other direction] you've got the secularization of the schools, and you've got all sorts of [court] decisions coming out: Eisenstat *v.* Baird, which says the states can't regulate distinctions between nonmarried couples and married couples, in terms of a lot of important family distinctions and moral relationships between the sexes that matter to Christians. I think it culminates in Roe *v.* Wade [legalizing abortion].

"You really have a divergence from what I would argue is a fundamental Christian view of life. . . . A Christian view of morality is repudiated, and repudiated in a very fundamental sense. Not only does the Supreme Court tolerate abortion, but it asserts abortion is a fundamental constitutional right. So what Christianity had looked at for two thousand years as evil now is not just permissible, but it's a basic civil right.

"All this, in a sense, brought a moral awakening, in terms of the necessity for Christians to become active. Those are some of the social developments I would cite, along with Watergate in the early seventies, that add up in my mind to the kind of things Jimmy Carter was talking about: a return to Christian morality, which he not only stated as such, but which was projected by the image of the Carter candidacy. You don't have to say the words to project the image that the community perceives. . . . I think that's the message a lot of Christians got from Carter, particularly focused on the family."

Anderson's view was widely shared in the evangelical community at the time of Carter's election, and expectations of a renewal of traditional Christian morality were high.

Disenchantment Sets In

Evangelical disenchantment with Carter came quickly. And perhaps because hopes had been so high, it engendered a sense of betrayal. The religious right became not just disillusioned but actively hostile to Carter.

The first signals were present even before he took office. It had long been assumed by many conservative Christians that the most direct road to change lay in the placing of Christian people in positions of leadership and power. The presidency was indeed a "bully pulpit," but preaching from that pulpit would not be enough to do the job. The levers of power would have to be held by Christians. Thus Pat Robertson, already in 1976 one of the major spokespersons for the religious right through his widely watched *700 Club*, asked candidate Carter in an interview on that program:

"Would you anticipate as president that you would bring godly men into your inner councils or into the Cabinet to advise you?"

"I think if would be a mistake for me to define the qualifications of a public servant according to what kind of a church they attend or what their denomination is," Carter replied. "Obviously a commitment to the principles expressed to us by God would be an important prerequisite. I think those are shared by many people who happen not to be Baptists or not to be Christians. The ethical commitments of our lives—unselfishness, truthfulness, honor, a sense of compassion and understanding of other people, a sense of integrity, those principles given to us by God and natural in so many people's lives—would certainly be prerequisites of my selection of anyone to serve in government."

The "principles . . . natural in so many people's lives" did not, in all probability, constitute the kind of criteria Robertson was seeking.

A symbolic turning point in the relationship between Carter and the evangelical community came early in the administration with the White House Conference on the Family. Evangelicals, who regarded traditional family values as being at the heart of the moral renewal for which they were calling, saw this conference as critically important.

Carter's personal commitment to family values was similar to their own, and it is probable that his original intention was, like theirs, focused on emphasizing traditional values. The conference, however, brought them into confrontation with the values of various Democratic party special-interest groups that had helped to elect him. The feminist perspective was committed to full legitimation of nontraditional families—single-parent households and cohabitation without marriage—that had become so much a part of the American scene. Gay activists sought the end of legal and social sanctions on homosexual relationships. And the White House Conference on the Family provided a forum for all of them.

Evangelicals found the new President's position, in the face of this unexpected confrontation, "entirely pusillanimous." A place was made for all the divergent views, the name of the gathering being broadened to White House Conference on Families. Anderson, who had summarized the moral hope of the Carter election as being focused on family values, attached great significance to the event. He called it a "reneging on the family promise." The family, as treated by the conference, "encompassed homosexual living arrangements, and things like that.

"I don't think the shock waves in the evangelical community

can be underestimated," he said. "There was a real awakening there, as to what they thought they were getting in '76, and what they ended up getting."

Richard John Neuhaus also emphasizes this conference as a turning point for those who became disillusioned with Carter. Earlier a supporter, Carter had appointed him a delegate to the conference, which he later labeled a complete debacle. "At what points," he asked, "did Carter ever have the courage to challenge the established definitions of justice in the interest groups that constituted the party on which he was politically dependent?"

A second factor in the disillusionment of religious conservatives with the Carter presidency, and a key factor in galvanizing the religious right into political activism, was the pressure placed on the proliferating Christian school movement by the Internal Revenue Service early in the administration. While Carter people saw civil rights as the motivation, Christian school activists saw it as antireligious. Carl Anderson, in the White House interview mentioned above, went on to elaborate:

"In addition," he said, "there came the IRS-Christian school fight, in terms of the supervision and regulation of [schools] by the Internal Revenue Service. Under the guise of getting at segregation academies, the IRS started using strong-arm tactics to get at a very minuscule number of segregation academies, with a very clear policy that First Amendment rights simply didn't matter very much. And we're not just talking Bob Jones University, we're talking about any serious kind of Christian ministry through church-affiliated schools. And I think that had a very big message for evangelical Christians.

"In 1962 [in the school prayer decision] the Supreme Court said that there must be a 'naked public square,' that you had to have separation of church and state [in public life], but within the sphere of church you had liberty and independence and autonomy. By the end of the seventies, I think the IRS-school problem telegraphed a new message to this community that said, 'No, that's not right. You can run but you can't hide. The reach of government is going to find you. No matter how intimately you view this as part of your ministry, you will be supervised by government.' So that, I think, sent a message: you cannot withdraw; you cannot go into a monastery. . . . Some of the fundamentalist and Baptist churches [with their Christian schools] are monastic in the sense that they, like monasteries, withdraw from society, and set up their own culture. Their social life revolves around their church, and their children revolve around their church. They don't participate in movies and dances and things like that in the broader society; they don't watch television. But the broader community wasn't going to let them withdraw. And I see that as part of the reason the presidency has become a focus [of conservative Christian attention]."

The generally liberal cast of Carter administration programs confirmed the disillusionment initiated by the White House Conference on the Family and the perceived IRS attack on Christian schools. Why, conservatives asked, if Carter personally opposed abortion, did he not work harder to change the law he felt constrained to enforce? No one is more bitter than a lover who feels betrayed, and the religious right's full entry into presidential politics, in the 1980 election campaign, was at least in part a response to Carter administration programs and policies.

Initially the finality of the break was not fully apparent to Carterites. As the reelection campaign began in late 1979, Robert Maddox invited a group of leaders of the emerging religious right to the White House for a meeting with Carter. In a preliminary staff memo he had said:

> If I am a judge they are Republican in sentiment but so far no Republican has emerged whom they could freely support.
>
> Even though they have serious reservations about the President—SALT, Prayer in Public Schools, Panama Canal, etc.—my feeling is they would like to be able to support the President.
>
> They have no question about his character and Christian faith. Religion for religion they are near the President's own faith—personal, experiential, politically involved. Issue for issue, they are conservative-right.

Jerry Falwell, Oral Roberts, Rex Humbard, and Jim Bakker, among others, attended the meeting. But Maddox's estimate that there was still a chance of winning their support was probably wrong. It was already far too late.

In the course of the campaign year, Maddox engineered several further attempts to reach them. Other White House briefings were arranged. Carter, who earlier had repeatedly refused to address the annual meeting of the Association of Religious Broadcasters, was persuaded to do so in 1980. But it was a lost cause.

In a 1987 interview Maddox ascribed his own efforts along this line to his newness in the position and political inexperience: "It bothered me to think that fifty or sixty million evangelical Christians might rise up and vote against him—and in the event, *did* vote against him."

In time, he said, people in the White House "pointed out to me the truism that you don't make friends out of enemies. And these were natural enemies of the president—of the Democratic party and of Jimmy Carter." A determination to *defeat* Carter was precisely the reason—or at least one of the reasons—the religious right was being forged into a formidable political instrument.

The Religious Right as a Political Movement

The religious right was certainly not solely an anti-Carter movement. Though Carter was a symbol for many, its concerns were far broader. These concerns encompassed a whole spectrum of perceived attacks on what they regarded as basic social and religious structures, attacks coming not just from the presidency but from political liberals generally, from the "secular humanist" mass media and educational establishment, and especially from the courts.

The rise of the religious right was a reaction to these forces. Social analyst Nathan Glazer suggests that the political successes of secular and liberal forces occasioned the rise and strength of contemporary fundamentalism:

> Abortion was not a national issue until the Supreme Court, in Roe *v.* Wade, set national standards for state laws. Abortion did *not* become an issue because Fundamentalists wanted to *strengthen* prohibitions against abortion, but because liberals wanted to abolish them. Equal rights for women did *not* become an issue because Fundamentalists wanted to *limit* women's rights, but because the proposed Equal Rights Amendment raised fears, both rational and irrational, that all traditional distinctions between men's and women's roles would be overturned. (That these fears were not so irrational is evidenced by the litigation against a military draft for men only.) Pornography in the 1980s did *not* become an issue because Fundamentalists wanted

to *ban* D. H. Lawrence, James Joyce, or even Henry Miller, but because, in the 1960s and 1970s, under-the-table pornography moved to the top of the newsstands. Prayer in the schools did *not* become an issue because Fundamentalists wanted to *introduce* new prayers or sectarian prayers but because the Supreme Court ruled against all prayers. Freedom for religious schools became an issue *not* because of any legal effort to expand their scope, but because the Internal Revenue Service and various state authorities tried to impose restrictions on them that private schools had not faced before. (Only tuition credits, it can be argued, is a case of an aggressive attempt to overthrow an old arrangement—but tuition tax credits are less a concern of Fundamentalists than of Catholics and conservative Protestants and Jews.)

Secular activists of the new right played an important role in the politicization of the fundamentalist movement. Paul Weyrich, of the Committee for the Survival of a Free Congress, and Howard Phillips, of the Conservative Caucus, were particularly helpful. Neither was part of the evangelical Protestant community: Weyrich is a Catholic and Phillips a Jew. But Weyrich helped Robert J. Billings, who had long been active in the Christian school movement (and who had run unsuccessfully for Congress in Indiana in 1976), to found the National Christian Action Coalition, to lobby for legislation relevant to the schools. Billings, in turn, brought Weyrich together with Jerry Falwell, whom the two of them persuaded, in 1979, to found The Moral Majority, Inc. (with Falwell as president and Billings as the first executive director).

Christian Voice had been founded in 1978 by the Reverend Robert Grant, in Pasadena, and it became strong in the West and Southwest. It depended heavily, however, on Pat Robertson's Virginia-based Christian Broadcasting Network. Robertson featured Christian Voice on his *700 Club* and provided access to the hundred or more stations of CBN.

Religious Roundtable was founded by Edward McAteer, a layman with wide contacts among evangelical preachers, and Texas evangelist Jim Robison, with the help of Howard Phillips, who had earlier recruited McAteer to be field director for the Conservative Caucus.

All this represented a stunning turnaround for politically conservative evangelical and fundamentalist Christians, who had earlier been most sharply distinguished from social activist Christians, whether liberal or evangelical in theological orientation, by their firm conviction that "religion and politics don't mix."

Jerry Falwell, whose Moral Majority became the best known and most durable of the new Christian right organizations and who became, in the public mind, the prime symbol of the movement, was quite frank in a 1980 interview for *Eternity* magazine:

"Back in the sixties I was criticizing pastors who were taking time out of their pulpit to involve themselves in the Civil Rights Movement or any other political venture. I said you're wasting your time from what you're called to do. Now I find myself doing the same thing and for the same reasons they did. Things began to happen. The invasion of humanism into the public school system began to alarm us back in the sixties. Then the Roe *v.* Wade Supreme Court decision of 1973 and abortion on demand shook me up. Then adding to that the gradual regulation of various things it became very apparent the federal government was going in the wrong direction, and if allowed would be harassing non-public schools, of which I have one of 16,000 right now. So step by step we became convinced we must get involved if we're going to continue what we're doing inside the church building."

Ronald Reagan: Candidate of the Christian Right

Ronald Reagan was not the first choice for president of most of the Christian right leaders in 1980. He was not the kind of church-related, tithing, actively involved Christian to whom they would ordinarily have been attracted.

He had had a devoutly Christian childhood. His mother, Nelle Reagan—the strongest religious influence in his life—was of Scottish Presbyterian background and had attended a Methodist Episcopal church during her youth. A conventional Protestant, she had married Jack Reagan, a conventional Catholic, and to avoid a breach with his church had promised to have their children baptized and educated as Catholics. She kept the promise with their first child, Neil, who was baptized at St. Mary's Catholic Church in Tampico, Illinois.

But before the birth of her second son, Ronald, Nelle underwent a conversion experience. She was baptized into the Disciples of Christ (Christian) church, by total immersion, on Easter Day, May 29, 1910. The conversion was a profound one, and Nelle Reagan remained a pious, deeply committed, hardworking churchwoman for the rest of her life. She had her son, Neil, rebaptized into the Disciples of Christ church when he was fourteen (though later, against his mother's will, he returned to the Catholic Church of his father).

In Tampico, and then in other Illinois towns in which the family lived—Galesburg, Monmouth, and especially Dixon—Nelle Reagan was a pillar of the church. She tended the sick and took food to the hungry; she taught Sunday School and Bible School, passed out tracts in prisons, and put on plays and skits which she herself wrote. For a period she wrote weekly church notes for the newspaper. A major interest was the Missionary Society, of which she was elected president.

Ronald Reagan's early life was therefore centered in the Disciples of Christ church. He was baptized into full church membership at the age of eleven. He acted in his mother's plays and skits; he cleaned the church; he gave dramatic recitations. In 1926 he led the congregation's Easter sunrise service. He joined his mother in a monthly church-sponsored program to entertain patients at the Dixon State Hospital. He went to a Disciples of Christ college (Eureka), and he socialized with students from another Disciples college (Drake) during his radio days. Says Garry Wills, in a 1986 article on Reagan's religious background:

> He was as close to being a "preacher's kid" as one can be without actually moving into the parsonage. In Dixon the Rev. Ben Cleaver was a father figure to Reagan; he advised him, helped him get into college, even taught him to drive. Reagan dated his daughter, Margaret, for eight years. "Reagan was in our house all the time," recalls Helen Cleaver, Margaret's sister.

Ronald Reagan's father, Jack, a traveling salesman with a history of heavy drinking and a "tendency to wander," was a considerably less important influence religiously. He was, however, a positive influence in other ways, particularly in matters of religious and racial prejudice. President Reagan remembers an incident when the elder Reagan, traveling as a shoe salesman, stopped at a small-town hotel.

"You'll like it here, Reagan," said the desk clerk. "We don't let Jews in here."

Reagan picked up his bag and stormed out. "If you won't let Jews in, the next thing, you won't let Catholics in, and I'm a Catholic." He spent the night in his car, and as a result, as his son remembered it, he contracted pneumonia.

The impression on the younger Reagan was profound. Traveling later with the Eureka College football team, which had three black players, he encountered a similar incidence of prejudice. A hotel refused rooms to the three black players. The coach was furious. He wanted the entire team to spend the night on the bus. Reagan, however, took the three to his home, which was nearby, as overnight guests. As president, Reagan has appeared to be deeply resentful of charges that his administration has failed to support full equality for minorities.

But whatever the influence of his father, he learned church life from his mother. Ronald Reagan was actively involved with the Disciples of Christ church throughout his childhood, youth, and early manhood. The time and place—the 1920s and 1930s in the small-town Midwest—reflected classic Protestant evangelicalism, what the Reverend Donn D. Moomaw, later his pastor, calls "good, down-home, mid-American piety." At the very least this background has given him an ease and familiarity in dealing with contemporary evangelicals. He knows the language, and he knows the thought forms.

But in a more profound sense, Reagan himself has pointed to the formative influence of his mother. "I believe very deeply in something I was raised to believe by my mother," he later said. "I now seem to have her faith that there is a divine plan, and that while we may not be able to see the reason for something at the time, things do happen for a reason and for the best."

The Adult Years

Ronald Reagan joined Beverly Christian Church (Disciples of Christ) after he went to Hollywood. Religion was not, however, a major factor in Reagan family life during much of the Hollywood period.

It was relatively late in life, as his early political liberalism gave way to a newly discovered conservatism, that religious interest, too, was rekindled.

Reagan's major active church involvement in more recent years has been with the Bel Air Presbyterian Church in Los Angeles. Its minister, the Reverend Dr. Donn D. Moomaw, he has continued to refer to as "my pastor." The Reagans began attending the Bel Air church, which was close to their home, in 1963. According to Moomaw, they were regular churchgoers, often accompanied by their two younger children. After Reagan was elected governor of California, they continued to attend whenever they were at their Los Angeles home.

Moomaw was asked in a 1987 interview about the accuracy of a story that they had sought to join the church but had not been allowed to do so because of a requirement that all prospective members participate in a ten-week membership class. The pastor explained that "we are in a celebrity-centered area, and if we began making exceptions it would not be fair. So we just don't."

Moomaw acknowledged that the Reagans had inquired about membership on one occasion. "I told them about the requirements," he said, "of the ten weeks. And they were the ones who didn't want any exceptions to be made. It wasn't necessarily a matter of my saying 'Because of that you cannot,' but they said, 'No, we don't want any exceptions. We will keep Bel Air as our church home, and perhaps some time it will be possible for us to become members like everyone else.' "

Moomaw said the Reagans had always been insistent that they did not want special treatment. Even when he was governor, more often than not they would drive their own car, mingle with other worshipers, and leave with little inconvenience to anyone.

"They usually came to church early enough to sit wherever they wanted to," he said. "They sat in the same place every Sunday. One Sunday they were a little late, and one of our very zealous ushers took them down to where they usually sat and asked the two men seated there if they would move and let the governor and his wife sit there. I saw it and got up from my seat behind the communion table, made a beeline for the two men, and said, 'As long as I'm pastor of this church that will never happen again . . .' And the governor afterwards agreed that he never wanted a seat saved for him."

Moomaw's pastoral relationship with the Reagan family became quite close, and continued so after Reagan became president. He delivered the invocation at both inaugurals, and contact has been maintained at fairly frequent intervals. Occasionally the president sends him letters written in longhand, he says.

"We have, I think, the kind of relationship that we have gone through some very 'dark moments of the soul' that would bind us together as friends and Christian brothers. . . . It's a deep loyalty, and I love him very much."

Upon hearing of the 1981 assassination attempt, Moomaw went immediately to Washington. "I went to the White House. . . . Nancy asked Carolyn and me if we would accompany her that evening to the hospital. . . . I went in expecting to see a very ill man, and he was . . . but he was like resilient steel. He wanted to talk about the church. He was very open to talk about the faith. So open that I said to him, 'Ron . . . are you ready to meet God?'

"He said, 'No. I have a lot more I want to accomplish before I meet God.'

"I said, 'Oh, no. That's not what I mean. If the bullet had taken you, would you have been okay with God?'

"And after he thought, he said, 'Yes.' And I said to him—to the dismay of my wife that I was pushing so hard—I said, 'How do you know?'

"I expected that he would probably give me an answer on the basis of some works, [that] the plus side of what he had done was winning. He didn't. He looked me in the eye and he said, 'I have a Savior.'

"You can say a lot of other things," Moomaw said to this interviewer, "but if you don't say that you don't have the first clue. A profound understanding of salvation."

The President's Private Christianity

The Bel Air period of church-centered religious activity has not, however, been the normative adult pattern. The sporadic nature of Reagan's adult church life, his nonattendance while president (he has probably attended church less frequently than any president in recent history), and the paucity of financial contributions to any church as revealed by tax returns made public (although Moomaw says he has continued to contribute to Bel Air Presbyterian each year) fit uncomfortably with the expected pattern for a church-oriented Christian.

Because of Reagan's strong identification with the religious right, a number of apologists have grappled publicly with these issues, stressing his many statements about his personal faith. The usual explanation for nonchurch attendance is his reluctance, as president, to burden a congregation with the heavy security precautions that accompany a president's public appearances in our times.

One book, *In God I Trust*, published under Reagan's name, consists of excerpts from a number of presidential addresses, proclamations, responses to questions, and other public statements, all dealing with the president's faith in God and the religious dimensions of public life. Its editor, David R. Shepherd, confronting the issue of nonchurch attendance directly in his introductory chapters, quotes the president himself, in response to a March 1984 question from a reporter:

"Are you going to church this Sunday, sir? The Democrats say you talk about religion but you don't go to church."

"Yes, I've noticed that," the president answered. "I haven't bothered to check on their attendance, but I think they must be aware of why I have not been attending. . . . I represent too much of a threat to too many other people for me to be able to go to church. And frankly, I miss it very much."

Undoubtedly he does miss it, since his relationship with Donn Moomaw and Bel Air Presbyterian Church in the years prior to his coming to Washington was an important one to him. There is evidence that the proliferation of security precautions following the March 1981 assassination attempt has, indeed, been a factor. Prior to that time the Reagans had attended National Presbyterian Church on occasion (though not frequently). Following the assassination attempt, such attendance ceased.

White House spokesman Carl Anderson recalled an example of the problems raised by security concerns. "Early on in the presidency, he went to church in Georgetown. The Secret Service went out there and insisted that for security purposes they cut down a tree that had been there a good number of years and was an historical landmark." Such extreme measures would obviously have a moderating effect on presidential churchgoing.

Donn Moomaw, from the pastor's standpoint, agrees with the president's decision. "It's become such an inconvenience for the people," he told this interviewer. "They have to go through metal detectors. It's just an unnatural atmosphere, with twenty motorcycles and twenty security cars, and counter-sniper squads up on the roof, and preparations two or three weeks in advance of his coming. . . ."

"[But] I wish they were able to worship more," Moomaw said later in the interview, "and to nurture [their] faith. I wish he could avail himself of some people around him that could give him more support spiritually. But I do, too, know the difficulty of that."

"A Self-taught Christian"

Given the record of the years prior to the Bel Air involvement, the ready acceptance of nonmember status there, and the apparent willingness with which churchgoing has ceased, there is some reason to conclude that the Reagans are basically nonchurch-oriented Christians—a not uncommon American phenomenon.

"The president doesn't go to church," says his former White House director of communications, Pat Buchanan, flatly. "He says he doesn't go to church because he can't upset the entire congregation.

"I don't know exactly how to read that," he continued a little later in the interview. ". . . As a practical matter he cannot be a churchgoer without taking over the church. You know, a Secret Service movement like that is an extraordinarily complex movement for the president nowadays. And I think his reasoning is okay. But I don't know how to take the fact that he's not close to any religious men. I think he's a very simple Christian in the sense that he sees himself as having a personal relationship with God. And I don't know how to judge motivation there, or why, or whether."

Buchanan, himself a devout Catholic, is somewhat baffled by this highly Protestant attitude. "It's a different tradition than the one I come out of. If I didn't go to church, I'd be a citizen under suspicion!"

In another part of the interview, however, he put his finger on what is probably the key to Reagan's largely nonchurched Christianity. "I think the president is something of a self-taught Christian," he said, "who has come later and later in life to become more and more an outspoken believer in God. He talks often about it. He is persuaded that he was saved from that assassin's bullet with the Lord's help, and that whatever time he has left belongs to Him. He told that to Cardinal Cooke. Even though he doesn't belong to any denomination, even though he is not churchgoing, he is unembarrassed by public professions of belief in God."

Reagan's pastor, Moomaw, agreed that "self-taught" was a fair description: "He has a deep private faith that has not been instructed too much by Bible classes, prayer meetings, or worship services. He does read the Bible, he does pray, and he does worship, but it has not been a regular experience for him. He has not ever, as far as I know, been in a small . . . covenant group that would nurture his spiritual life. . . ." His faith, Moomaw felt, is "more experiential than intellectual."

Secretary of the Interior Donald Hodel is a less direct observer since he lacks the continual contact of former White House staffer Buchanan, but an interested one, himself an evangelical Christian. "President Reagan has not been a visibly religious president," he said in a 1987 interview. "By that I mean he has not attended church services regularly in the public arena where his attendance record can be kept. On the other hand," he went on to say, "my sense is that he has been the most outspoken president on the subject of the importance of the Deity in recent times."

Hodel considers this nondenominational, nonchurched religion appropriate to the presidency. "He does not 'denominationalize'—if I can make up that word—his statements. He does not flaunt his Christianity. But I would commend to your attention his statement at the Baldridge funeral, his eulogy for Mac Baldridge [Secretary of Commerce Malcolm Baldridge, who had died in an accident the week prior to the interview], because in that statement he made it very plain that he believes in salvation and eternal life. Now he didn't get into a theologically definitive discussion of who does and who doesn't get into heaven. And for a president to do that would be wrong, because that would polarize people and it would bring all the wrong elements of the debate public. So I think the president's approach is the right one. I look back at the founders of this country—Jefferson and Washington and Adams—all have great quotes about the Deity and the Almighty, though they don't come through as publicly Christians. I think that's in the grand tradition of this nation.

"I have no idea what the details of the president's theology are," Hodel continued, later in the interview. "And, in a sense, I guess I'm pleased about that. . . . He does not come through as a Catholic or a Protestant of a particular stripe. He says faith in God is important. He is a model for all of us to be concerned about the Deity. . . . And I don't have a clear picture of what his personal theology is."

Several who were interviewed about President Reagan's religion were asked whether the nonchurchgoing and strict privacy surrounding his personal religious practices might have been a deliberate reaction to the highly public churchgoing and Sunday School teaching of the Carter years. Responses varied.

Buchanan was dubious. "No. I think Reagan is really his own man. He has always been very comfortable with himself. I think he was comfortable with himself before Carter came in, and he's comfortable now. So I don't think it's a reaction on the president's part. That's certainly not his style."

Carl Anderson, however, who had spoken at some length on Carter's relationship to the evangelical community, did see a contrast with Carter in Reagan's attitude. "He's very private about [his personal religion]," he said, "and I think it's a result of a dichotomy with Carter. He's been very sensitive to appearing to politicize religion. And I think that's been of great benefit to what he's trying to do, because I think this is really a problem a lot of religious leaders have to work on. That is, in a democracy, when we make a moral claim or an ethical claim, we can be consistent with Scripture, but it has to be grounded in natural law, or some kind of a natural argument, or a reasonable argument. . . . All people, whether they're believers or not, are obligated to respect the president. . . . That's been a very important part of his presidency, and I think it's one that has been conscious: not to let his own personal religious beliefs or behavior reflect on his public leadership."

That privacy has been exhibited in a variety of ways. Secretary Hodel told of an occasion when someone suggested to the president that Cabinet meetings be opened with prayer. "I do," replied Reagan. His implication that private, personal prayer on the part of individuals is the appropriate way to start such meetings settled the matter.

Whatever may have been the roots of Reagan's nonchurchgoing and the privacy surrounding his personal religious practices, he has, as Buchanan noted, been quite comfortable and unembarrassed about discussing his religion publicly. His frequent addresses to religious groups—such as the National Association of Evangelicals, the Association of Religious Broadcasters, and the annual National Prayer Breakfast—and his remarks in connection with religious events and commemorations, have contained numerous references to his personal religion (although usually in general terms). Evangelical Christian friends and associates, such as Pat Boone and his wife, Shirley, and Senator and Mrs. Roger Jepson, have quoted him as talking quite freely about his faith in personal conversations. Helene Von Damm, his personal secretary for many years, and later his Ambassador to Austria, has said, "He has a strong belief that the Lord's will plays a part in the affairs of men and that faith in the Lord is essential." This appears to summarize the generalized convictions that interviews with associates as well as biographers ascribe to him.

A belief in the will of God as Divine Planner is a particularly prominent theme in his comments on his personal faith. In a letter to a woman with a handicapped son he wrote, "I find myself believing very deeply that God has a plan for each one of us. Some with little faith and even less testing seem to miss in their mission, or else we perhaps fail to see their imprint on the lives of others. But bearing what we cannot change and going on with what God has given us, confident there is a destiny, somehow seems to bring a reward we wouldn't exchange for any other."

This is the conviction, with regard to his own life, that he expressed at the time of his election to the presidency, and that he conveyed in his oft-quoted remark to Cardinal Cooke following the 1981 assassination attempt. He took particular delight in the fact that presumed-atheist Soviet leader Gorbachev, in connection with the quest for peace, said at the Geneva summit meeting, "God will not forgive us if we fail." The remark accorded well with his own beliefs.

Reagan has actively explored particular religious subjects that have captured his interest. Said Pat Buchanan, "He's very interested in the Shroud of Turin. He's also interested in Creationism. The Shroud of Turin, I know, because he called a friend of mine, Ann Higgins, who's a very devout Catholic. She said [something about it] in a book. He was very interested in it, and he talked to her about it. And Stan Evans wrote a column on Creationism, on the proofs that Darwinism, or evolution, is false. He read the column in *Human Events*, and he went looking for the book. These subjects have always interested him."

Donn Moomaw's experience confirmed the impression: "He would call me after a sermon and would say, 'You know, I thought of another thing when you were speaking this morning. The other side of that might be so and so.' He listens to the sermon with sharp attention, and he's not cool about what he's hearing. You know that he is involved. . . . [Sometimes] he would send me an article the next week, cut out of a paper: 'Donn, I just wondered if you had gotten this article. . . . Put it in your file.' "

The picture that emerges is of a deeply held faith in God, on a rather generalized Judeo-Christian level, without much theological specificity. There is, however, a strong sense of a personal relationship to God. It is a faith that has not, since childhood, been closely associated with the institutional church (except for the period of churchgoing at Bel Air Presbyterian in Los Angeles, which appears to have been more the product of a personal relationship with an individual minister than commitment to the church as such). It is coupled with an active interest in particular religious subjects and is accompanied by a strong commitment to traditional values (particularly family values) usually associated with religion. There is an easy and natural feeling of compatibility (perhaps derived from childhood training) with contemporary evangelical Christianity.

The absence of regular churchgoing gives no reason to doubt the authenticity of this particular kind of personal religious faith. Highly individualistic (and often nonchurch-related) personal religion is common in modern America, as detailed in the widely read 1985 book by sociologist Robert Bellah and others, *Habits of the Heart: Individualism and Commitment in American Life*. Individualistic religion is perhaps particularly associated with the Reagans' home state of California, as Bellah suggests.

Nor is such religious individualism limited to the New Age religions and unfettered life-styles sometimes identified with the California spirit. Modern evangelicalism and fundamentalism have reflected a strong nonchurched dimension, as evidenced by the large number of independent parachurch organizations (such as Young Life, Campus Crusade, InterVarsity, the Navigators; a variety of television ministries, and a host of nonchurch-related mission agencies) that have been major bearers of the contemporary evangelical renewal. The political activism of the religious right has not been channeled through churches but through independent organizations.

Nor is historical precedent for Reagan's nonchurched Christianity lacking. As we have noted earlier, Abraham Lincoln, perhaps the most profound religious thinker among pre-modern presidents (particularly with regard to the relationship of religion to national life), was not only an irregular churchgoer, he never joined a church. It appears that Ronald Reagan is not a conventional institutionally centered, churchgoing, income-tithing Christian. But there is no reason to doubt that on his own terms he is a deeply convinced Christian whose religious faith is quite genuine.

The Marriage of Reagan and the Religious Right

"If the evangelicals were really looking for a born-again Christian candidate in the 1980 campaign, they had only one choice—Jimmy Carter," said James Wall in an interview. "If they were looking for ideology, their choice was Reagan."

Though his opinion was undoubtedly influenced by his high regard for Carter and his personal commitment to an activist, socially involved brand of Christianity, there is a measure of accuracy in the observation. Carter certainly fit the usual pattern of a born-again Christian, while Reagan's religious history left noticeable deficits from the conventional Christian perspective. Yet Carter had been rejected by the religious right precisely because of the political ideology into which his own kind of born-again Christianity had led him, while Reagan's ideology, like theirs, was based on a commonly held religious perspective. Though not a churchman, Reagan was clearly a soul mate.

Was it a marriage of political convenience? Research for this book began with an inquiry into the nature of the relationship and influence of the religious right in the Reagan presidency. In a number of interviews, both with persons holding high positions in the Reagan White House or administration and with observers familiar with the religious right, the issue was explored. How much contact was there between Reagan and religious right leadership? Was there evidence that the Reagan social agenda—abortion, school prayer, family values—widely attributed to the religious right, actually came from this source? Has there been, as opponents charge, religious influence (or an antiabortion litmus test) in the selection of judges and Supreme Court nominees? Did the conspicuous presence of Jerry Falwell and the Moral Majority at the 1984 Republican National Convention (particularly in shaping the platform) carry over into the councils of the administration?

It quickly became apparent that Ronald Reagan had seen very little of Jerry Falwell—or any other leader of the religious right—except as part of the religious groups he has frequently addressed and with which he has sometimes met. Jerry Falwell was by no means a latter-day Billy Graham in terms of intimate access to the White House. Indeed, Michael Deaver, a top White House adviser in Reagan's first term, was quoted as having said publicly that the Reverend Jerry Falwell was welcome to visit the White House, provided that he came in the back door.

Nor are the religious right groups in any sense collective advisers to the Reagan presidency. It began to appear that the wrong questions were being asked. What has happened has not been a matter of strong influence on a presidency by one particular special interest group. Rather the religious issues so prominent in the Reagan years reflect the president's own beliefs and are inherent in the kind of conservatism the Reagan presidency represents.

Asked about the influence of the religious right on Reagan, White House staffer Carl Anderson talked about the convergence of its interests and those of the president. "I think you have to start with the premise that the president is an evangelical Christian," he said. "You can quibble over definitions of what that means, but in one sense what it means is that the president perceives himself to be that; he identifies with that [evangelical] constituency. That constituency, broadly constituted, has influence in the sense that he's a member of it.

"In '81 when [Reagan] came into office it was clear where he was on abortion; it was clear where he was on school prayer, on tuition tax credits for attendance at private schools. Name all the real 'hot button' issues for that constituency; he had already staked out his positions. I don't think any of them were contrary to what Jerry Falwell or Pat Robertson or any of them really felt.

"In '84 the left tried to paint—you read those ads about Jerry Falwell picking the next Supreme Court, and stuff like that. Well, you don't need Jerry Falwell to pick the next Supreme Court. Because you don't have that kind of difference, fundamentally, in terms of what ought to be done."

Michael Cromartie, a neoconservative analyst of current religious trends who is a research associate with the Washington-based Ethics and Public Policy Center, made the same point. Reagan is on the same wavelength with the religious right, he said. "I think deep in his heart he's sort of a traditional-values American who believes in freedom of speech and freedom of religion, and strong family values. I think in his heart of hearts, despite his background in Hollywood and all the friends he has out there, his own conservative politics most easily converge with that sort of 'Norman Rockwell' view of America. He is in agreement with them [the evangelicals] that something terribly bad has gone wrong, within the last thirty or forty years, and we need to get it right. His view of that converges very nicely with the Moral Majority's platform."

Reagan, then, is a symbol of the way the causes and concerns of traditional secular conservatism and of the new religious right have been joined together. It is not a matter of one influencing the other; the Reagan presidency is a result of the two having become a single movement.

Two conservative writers, E. Clifton White and William J. Gill, in a 1981 book called *Why Reagan Won*, elaborate this conclusion: "Three fundamental issues," they say, "have carried conservatism from a minority status to what I believe is today an overwhelming majority position in the United States":

(1) That belief in God is necessary to freedom, and to a proper respect for our fellow man.

(2) That totalitarianism must be resisted.

(3) That the federal government interferes coercively in our lives.

The first point is not tacked on as a concession to a special-interest group. What these authors appear to be suggesting is that the religious dimension is inherent in the kind of contemporary conservatism the Reagan presidency represents. The religious right is not a separate group seeking to influence policy; its concerns have been incorporated into the modern conservative movement.

Amherst College sociologist Jerome L. Himmelstein offers a similar analysis in an essay on "The New Right." Three sets of themes define the New Right, he says:

(1) Economic libertarianism: freedom and individualism.

(2) Social traditionalism: concern focused on the breakdown of the family, the community, religion, and traditional morality.

(3) Militant anticommunism.

His "social traditionalism" encompasses the program of the religious right as represented by the Moral Majority and similar conservative religious activist groups. "American conservative ideology captures the libertarian emphasis on material progress," he says, "but envelops these within an appeal to divine providence, transcendent values, and collective social bonds":

> The preference of American conservatism for a religious, rather than a secular, justification of capitalism is reflected most clearly in George Gilder's *Wealth and Poverty* (1981), a book much favored by the New Right, and treated as a veritable bible by the Reagan administration. Gilder's work eschews the standard arguments that justify capitalism merely as technically efficient and materially productive in favor of a broader argument that capitalism is also built upon transcendent moral values and divine inspiration.

Paul Weyrich, a central figure in the new conservative coalition, compares the potential power and influence of the religious right with that of labor unions in the Democratic party. "Conservatives have no comparable group," he says. "The closest to the unions in size and potential influence are the fundamentalists and evangelicals. It was their move into the political process in the late 1970s that gave Reagan and the Republicans their significant moment in history in 1980."

Will It Last?

Whether or not the marriage will permanently endure is another question. James MacGregor Burns, in his analysis of the Reagan presidency, uses the term "Moralistic Right" to describe the movement most often (as here) referred to as the religious right. The Moralistic Right covers a wide range of groups united by four basic "moral principles," according to Burns: groups that are pro-life, pro-traditional family, "pro-moral" (on issues such as pornography and drugs), and pro-America (for a strong national defense). He gives Reagan much of the credit for welding this group together with traditional free enterprise conservatism, which he labels the "Market Right."

Says Burns, "Certainly [Reagan] has transformed the Republican Party, remaking it in his own image. Having officiated at the marriage of the "Market Right" and the "Moralistic Right" within the Republican church, he has so far kept the skittish couple together. Now he must bring them more firmly into the church itself—he must bring these powerful movements into the structure of the GOP."

Clearly there have been tensions between classic libertarian, free enterprise conservativism, and the new religious right. In some localities the religious activists have been accused of trying to "take over" the Republican party. The Moral Majority dominated the Alaska delegation to the 1980 National Convention. In Fairfax County, Virginia, just outside Washington, at the time of the 1984 election the Christian right was perceived as having "purged" mainstream Republicans from the party's governing committee. It was offering seminars in "Christians in the electoral process" and "getting godly candidates." By late 1987, however, after a long struggle, the traditional Republicans were back in control. In 1987 a coalition of religious rightists gained control of the Michigan Republican state committee and challenges were mounted in South Carolina and Louisiana.

The Pat Robertson candidacy for the 1988 Republican nomination, despite efforts of the candidate to distance himself from his ministerial status and position himself in the mainstream, was supported primarily by the Christian right within the party (and not by all of the Christian right, since some fundamentalists would have no part of a charismatic candidate). It therefore resulted in some polarization during the primary period.

In the long run, however, it is unlikely that the religious right will withdraw from political activism. And they have nowhere else to go, except the Republican party.

"The religious right will not go away when Reagan leaves," says Michael Cromartie of the Ethics and Public Policy Center. "[They] have gotten a taste for politics. They have said, for instance, 'We're tired of these porn districts in our neighborhoods; we're going to get them out.' And they've been able to see, through citizen action, and petitioning, that they can have an effect. On the grass-roots level there's more involvement. . . . They may get less press attention. But in New Hampshire, and Virginia, and Georgia, ministers from now on will say, for example, 'We want to vote for the mayor. We think the mayor of Birmingham should be a God-fearing man.' There's a new political consciousness. They're going to continue to be concerned about sorting out relationships between morality and politics.

"The next ten years," he continued, "evangelicals and fundamentalists need to learn about the art of political compromise: that they're not ushering in utopia, they just want a few things done differently. But many of them are so impatient that they don't make very good political people.

"I don't think the influence is going to wane," he concluded. "I think it's going to level out, and the present tension will be less. . . . But I think they represent a large coalition of voters."

Regardless of the future of the convergence of traditional conservatism with a religiously based social agenda, its reality in the Reagan presidency has been undeniable. Religious concerns are inherent in the new right conservatism that brought the Reagan revolution to power. Though Ronald Reagan is not a regular churchgoer, and though his faith in God is somewhat vague and general, lacking an identifiable theology, it is real and personal. Through his presidency the religious right has come into its own.

One of Reagan's major achievements, says Carl Anderson, has been the "mainstreaming" of evangelical Christianity. If the standards of a society are set by its elites, "the fact that you've got a president, very articulate, very outspoken, moving the society in this particular area—you can't do better in terms of elites than the presidency.

"It's significant," he continued a little later in the interview, "that people who on the record have been outspoken on these issues [such as Secretary of Education Bennett, Surgeon General Koop, and former Interior Secretary Watt] are not disqualified from holding significant positions in an administration. . . ."

Secretary of the Interior Hodel and his wife, both evangelical

Christians, made the same point. "The president . . . has made it possible for people like us to go out and give our Christian testimony, and not be concerned about being vilified, which I think would have happened in prior administrations."

Reagan's, as surely as Carter's, has been a religious presidency. A different constituency, a different agenda, different ground rules, clearly. The new religious right, whose concerns it bears, comes from the opposite side of America's contemporary religious polarization from that of the backers of Carter programs. It has been, however, another serious attempt to fill the naked public square with a religiously based public philosophy.

10

God in the Reagan White House

IN 1987 the cluster of events which came to be known as the Iran/Contra affair brought into question, in the minds of many Americans, the moral authority of the Reagan presidency. The hearings, conducted by a joint Senate-House Committee, had an inconclusive outcome. Former National Security Council official Oliver North, with his beribboned Marine uniform, his boyish good looks, his captivating smile, his articulate answers to questions, and his impassioned defense of the rightness of his cause, became an instant hero to many. But to others his admissions of lying to Congress and his superiors, his 3:00 A.M. shredding of official records of his activities, and his duplicity in trying to conceal his acceptance of a home security system were reminiscent of the morality of the Watergate period. So was what many regarded as the selective memory, under oath, of his boss, Vice Admiral John Poindexter, National Security Advisor. Both were later targets of criminal investigations. And worst of all, the president himself, though no evidence of his knowledge of the diversion of funds from Iranian arms sales to the support of the Nicaraguan Contras was ever offered, was nevertheless believed by a majority of the American people (according to public opinion polls) to have been lying about it.

Yet, ironically, these activities had been carried out in behalf of one of the religiously based moral imperatives of the Reagan presidency—the cause of freedom. The participants routinely spoke of the Contras as "Freedom Fighters." North was—and is—a devout evangelical Christian, a regular worshiper at Fairfax, Virginia's, rapidly growing, charismatic Church of the Apostles (Episcopal). Throughout the period of his legal and political problems, a prayer support group met at his home every Wednesday evening. Admiral Poindexter, too, is a practicing Christian, his wife an ordained Episcopal priest who serves as associate pastor in a suburban Washington congregation. Both North and Poindexter clearly felt that they were involved not just in political operations but in a highly moral undertaking.

The zeal of these two reflected the climate of the White House in which they worked. The Reagan presidency has assumed the aspect of a moral crusade. This has been true in two respects: its commitment to freedom, symbolized by the "Reagan doctrine," which promised support to freedom movements (defined as movements opposing Marxist regimes) anywhere in the world, and its social agenda, focused on opposition to legalized abortion and on support of prayer and traditional values in public schools as well as tuition credits for private schools—a program associated with the goals of the new religious right. In a 1983 speech to the National Association of Evangelicals, Reagan described the defense of freedom against the Marxist-Leninists as a struggle for morality against "the focus of evil in the modern world." And he said the abortion and school prayer agenda reflected a "spiritual awakening and a moral renewal" sweeping the nation.

The speech brought a flurry of headlines. A *Washington Post* article described "an intriguing subplot of the Reagan administration, a debate between the president and his critics over the morality and spirituality of his policies.

"Not since the Vietnam war and the civil rights movement have churchmen been so involved or played such a key role in the dialogue over public policy," the writer continued.

Said historian Henry Steele Commager with "new class" disdain, "It was the worst presidential speech in American history, and I've read them all. No other presidential speech has ever so flagrantly allied government with religion. It was a gross appeal to religious prejudice."

In an address to the same group one year later, Reagan spelled out his national goals, placing them in a religious context. After a recital of ways in which America, in recent years, had seemed "to lose her religious and moral bearings, to forget that faith and values are what made us good and great," Reagan continued:

"But the Almighty who gave us this great land also gave us free will, the power under God to choose our own destiny. The American people decided to put a stop to that long decline, and today our country is seeing a rebirth of freedom and faith, a great national renewal." The renewal is more than material, he went on to say. "America has begun a spiritual awakening. Faith and hope are being restored. Americans are turning back to God."

Within this context the president set out his goals: "In foreign affairs," he said, "I believe there are two fundamental tasks that we must perform. First, we must make certain our own country is strong, so we can go on holding out the hope of freedom for all the world. . . .

"Second . . . we must keep telling the truth, including the truth about the difference between free and totalitarian societies." This he went on to interpret in terms of opposition to the Sandinista regime in Nicaragua and support for freedom in Central America.

"Here at home," Reagan said, "I believe there are three basic tasks that we must accomplish. First, we must . . . find positive solutions to the tragedy of abortion.

"Second, we must restore education in basic values to America's schools. . . . We must make certain that we not only improve instruction in math and science, but in justice, religion, discipline, and liberty. . . ." He went on to interpret this as including tuition tax credits, enabling parents to choose their children's schools.

"And third, school prayer. . . . I firmly believe that the loving God who has blessed our land and made us a good and caring people should never have been expelled from America's classrooms. . . ."

Freedom as a Religious and Moral Value

Should this be dismissed as rhetoric cloaked in religious language for the benefit of a special-interest audience? To do so would be a serious misreading of the Reagan presidency. The emphasis on freedom as a religiously derived value has restored to prominence a central theme long inherent in the American proposition but somewhat dormant in recent years.

The "liberty and justice for all" of the Pledge of Allegiance reflected two aspects of the original American dream. Both were, at least in part, religiously based. As we have seen in earlier chapters, biblical concepts of freedom and justice undergirded the values of the new republic, and separation of church and state was never intended to imply a divorce between religion and American values.

Liberty and justice are by no means antithetical, but a certain tension has marked their historical relationship. Liberty has tended to be emphasized at the conservative end of the political spectrum and justice at the liberal end.

During the period of liberal ascendency, which stretched from the New Deal to the Great Society, justice was the reigning social value. And as justice came to be understood more and more in economic terms—justice for the poor, justice for the ethnic underclasses, justice for women in the workplace—Marxist analyses of the economic situation, while never adopted as normative by any significant groups in American society, were studied with some measure of sympathy. The liberation theologies of the Third World, for the most part strongly Marxist in orientation, were received with friendly understanding by religious liberals (though never really accepted as appropriate to the American situation). The absence of freedom in Marxist societies was seen by many as less significant than the gains in economic justice.

The conservative tide on which Ronald Reagan rode to power shifted attention back to the freedom side of the equation. Justice—even economic justice—was not disavowed, but freedom was the major theme. Economic freedom (free enterprise) and political freedom (democracy, support of which has been seen as implying anticommunism in today's world) were viewed as growing from the same roots. And secular as well as religious libertarians, joined together in the new right, saw those roots as being at least partly religious.

The rise of evangelicalism and fundamentalism in American Christianity brought a major change of focus on the religious scene. The old coalitions devoted to justice causes were joined by a cluster of new groups focused on freedom and democracy. The most conspicuous of these was the Washington-based Institute on Religion and Democracy (IRD), which quickly jumped to prominence in religious circles in the early eighties and became the bane of mainline religious liberals.

Established in 1981 largely by lay people, many of them former liberals (and some left-wing radicals) who had since become neoconservatives, IRD was intended as a way of focusing attention on the positive relationship between democratic values and Judeo-Christian religion. Intellectuals Peter Berger, Richard John Neuhaus, and Michael Novak associated themselves prominently with the new organization.

In January 1983 an article in *Reader's Digest*, and later that same month an unusual full-hour segment on the top-rated prime-time television program *60 Minutes* (usually three segments per hour), charged that funds given by mainline churches to the National Council of Churches and World Council of Churches are sometimes used to support organizations that are Marxist, either explicitly or in ideological orientation. The National Council, supported by mainline church leadership, accused the IRD of instigating the article and program, thus bestowing on it instant public prominence.

The IRD that year had been sponsoring a series of regional seminars aimed at demonstrating the moral failure of Marxism, the futility of Christian support for Marxist groups and strategies in the Third World, and the positive relationship between Christianity and democratic institutions. Clearly it had been raising the questions that *Reader's Digest* and *60 Minutes* were addressing. It had provided information and resources for both. But "instigating" probably overstates the organization's role.

Diane Knippers, present IRD deputy director, in a 1987 telephone interview, recalled being part of a group that watched with some trepidation the *60 Minutes* program, to which they had contributed. "We didn't know what they were going to do until we saw it," she said. "For all we knew, it could have turned into an attack on us."

While indicating that IRD considered the facts as presented by the *Reader's Digest* article and *60 Minutes* program to be accurate, Knippers added that "neither of them was our style. For that reason, we moved quickly, within six months, to publish our own 'A Time for Candor,' putting the issues in our terms." The National Council charges were probably exaggerated, but the resulting national publicity greatly increased the status of IRD, particularly in conservative circles.

Though it has at times tended to expend its energies negatively, on anti-Marxist and anti-mainline Protestant activism, rather than positively on the promotion of freedom and democracy as religious values, the Institute on Religion and Democracy has become the flagship religious organization in the growing emphasis on the freedom side of the freedom-justice dialectic. It has been instrumental in establishing organizations with similar goals within several mainline Protestant denominations, including Presbyterians for Democracy and Religious Freedom, United Methodists for Religious Liberty and Human Rights, and the Episcopal Committee on Religion and Freedom. (The Presbyterian and Methodist organizations are no longer directly related to IRD, having become independent groups within their own denominational systems. The Episcopal committee retains an IRD connection.) Lutherans for Religious and Political Freedom, while established independently, has been part of the same movement.

Conservative "think tanks" with religious connections, such as the Washington-based Ethics and Public Policy Center, were established in the same period. The center has no organizational connection with IRD other than a few directors who serve on both boards. But all these organizations have been part of a growing emphasis on freedom as a religious value, both supporting and intellectually undergirding the Reagan presidency in this regard.

Charles Krauthammer of the *New Republic*, in a paper presented to a Conference on Moral Purpose and American Foreign Policy held in Washington in early 1987, put the case for freedom as a moral value:

> The American imperium is about power, but power in the service of certain values. These values we hold, domestically, to be not only good but self-evidently good. And as we have gone abroad, we have spread them. In Europe, the line where American armies stopped at the end of World War II marks the limits of free, self-governing societies. Every inch of soil that lies behind American lines is now a liberal democracy. And elsewhere, where liberal democracy is not achieved, American-made or American-supported frontiers—the DMZ in Korea, the Strait of Formosa, the Thai-Cambodian border—divide more free from less free.
>
> The American conflict with the Soviet Union is not simply the blind struggle of two imperialisms, but a struggle with a moral meaning and purpose. . . . If Americans are going to intervene in the world, it has

to be for something more than just interest defined as power. It is interest defined as values.

We have looked earlier at the religious roots of this basic American value. It is by no means solely a religious value, and many of those who promote freedom, at home and abroad, do so for nonreligious reasons. Just as religiously motivated liberal activists have long made common cause with nonreligious fellow citizens in the quest for social justice, so the religious right has joined with secular freedom-promoters in the renewed emphasis on democracy as a moral value.

But Ronald Reagan voices a religious conviction which is pivotal for his presidency when he says, "I've always believed that we were put here for a reason, that there is a path somehow, a divine plan for all of us and for each one of us. And I've also always believed that America was set apart in a special way, that it was put here between the oceans to be found by a certain kind of people, based on a quality that these people had in that they came from every corner of the world. And a country then was created by men and women who came not for gold but mainly in search of God. They would be a free people, living under the law, their faith in their Maker and in their future."

Whether or not these remarks were originally written by a speech-writer, Ronald Reagan made them his own. He has repeated them, in almost identical form, to a number of other audiences. In common with the religious constituency groups that have become part of the new right and have provided basic themes for his presidency, Reagan has been deeply persuaded that freedom is a religious value and that its promotion worldwide by the United States is consistent with the will of God for America.

In 1987, President Reagan became concerned about stands taken by the Presbyterian church on his Nicaragua policy. He invited his pastor, Donn Moomaw, to bring a group of denominational leaders to the White House for discussions. Regarding that meeting, Moomaw said later to this interviewer, "[The President] has such a high view of freedom that he'll do anything to get it or promote it. . . . I think he does what he does in foreign countries because of his deep commitment to freedom."

The achievements of the Reagan presidency in promoting freedom abroad are, from the perspective of his religious supporters, formidable. They point to Argentina, the Philippines, and Korea, in which, by general agreement, American influence has played a significant role in replacing repressive regimes with more democratic ones. Haiti, El Salvador, and other Central and South American countries are less unambiguously liberated but are on the administration's roll of democratization. Instances of armed intervention or support of armed insurgencies in Grenada, Afghanistan, and Nicaragua have been controversial but are considered by the administration as part of the same freedom-promoting impulse, which is regarded as a moral imperative. However explained, during the Reagan years there has without question been a worldwide shift in Third World nations in the direction of more democratic regimes.

The Social Agenda

Much has been said earlier in this book about the social agenda of the religious right. Not so much by political pressure as by incorporation into contemporary conservatism, it has also been the social agenda of the Reagan presidency. The centerpiece has been opposition to legalized abortion.

Nearly every person interviewed in connection with either the Reagan presidency or the religious right pointed to the 1973 Supreme Court decision Roe *v.* Wade as a major trigger point that catapulted conservative religious constituencies into political activism. There may be some divergences with regard to feminism, gay rights, pornography—issues around which many are mobilized—or even school prayer, the other central issue. The entire religious right, however, is united in opposing abortion on demand.

President Reagan's personal opposition to abortion has never been in question; he has spoken out on many occasions. It is widely believed, however, that his administration, led by a succession of White House chiefs of staff—James Baker, Donald Regan, and Howard Baker—has relegated this and other social issues to the back burner.

Whether a front burner would have brought more tangible results can be debated. The administration has originated and supported an antiabortion constitutional amendment and is accused of not having pushed it vigorously. The hurdle faced by all remedies involving legislation or constitutional change, however, is the absence of a strong public consensus against abortion. Attempts in the Congress to repeal Title X of the Public Health Service Act, which establishes the government's family planning services, have repeatedly failed. A 1985 bill that would have banned abortion counseling was killed by a House of Representatives subcommittee. Some presidentially backed restrictions on the use of federal funds have, however, been incorporated into law.

While accepting what is probably the reality with regard to congressional prohibition of abortion or constitutional amendment, the Reagan presidency has produced substantial results in two other arenas, administrative and judicial. The back-door approach has produced a number of administrative regulations that restrict abortions. These regulations, together with those legislative restrictions accepted by the Congress, mean it is now the rule that federal funds may not be used for abortions unless the mother's life is in danger. Legal Aid lawyers are not permitted to give legal assistance for nontherapeutic abortions. Private employers are not obligated to provide health insurance benefits for abortions (again, unless the mother's life is endangered). And private organizations lose federal funding if they engage in abortion-related activities abroad.

In 1987 the executive branch, on direct orders from the president, initiated additional administrative rules governing Title X services, forbidding the use of federal funds for "any program that encourages, promotes or advocates abortion," forbidding the mention of abortion or referral to abortion providers by federally funded family planning counselors, and requiring that organizations (such as Planned Parenthood) that provide family planning services with federal funds and abortions with private funds must do so at separate locations. The regulations were subject to being blocked by Congress.

Reshaping the Judiciary

It may be that in the long run the most effective action out of the Reagan presidency will come through judicial channels. The changes in federal law that originally legalized abortion came not through congressional action or constitutional change but through the courts. Utilizing the resources of the Justice Department, the Reagan administration has entered far more aggressively into the judicial process than have previous administrations. In 1985 the solicitor general filed an *amicus curiae* brief in connection with two pending cases dealing with the constitutionality of state laws regulating abortion. In it he argued that the Court should return the law to the condition in which it was before the Roe *v.* Wade decision in 1973. This has been followed by a number of other *amicus* briefs placing the Reagan administration's views on cases dealing with social policy before the Court. Few if any decisions appear to have been affected by these actions of the solicitor general, although conservative members of the Court have welcomed and cited the opinions. It does, however, represent a new form of judicial activism on the part of a presidency.

Perhaps the major long-range strategy has been the appointment of federal judges who may, eventually, bring a reversal by the same mechanism that originally legalized abortions. Secretary of Interior Hodel, in a 1987 interview, cited an analysis by the attorney general holding that Roe *v.* Wade was "a judge-made rule when it was improperly made, ten years ago, [and] there's nothing wrong with reversing it now," without violating judicial restraint.

Opponents of Reagan and the religious right have long charged that opposition to legalized abortion has been a litmus test for judicial appointments. Carl Anderson, then Presidential Religious Liaison official, was asked in a 1987 interview whether or not this had been the case:

"It is if you understand it in the correct way," he answered. "I don't think there's anybody around here that feels more strongly about it than I do, for example. But it's meaningless to me whether somebody supports abortion or opposes abortion. That's a personal matter. What I'd like to know: Do they think Roe *v.* Wade was a good exercise of the judicial function in a democracy? If they think it is, then there's a question of their fitness to be on the Supreme Court. That's more the kind of requirement that goes on in the Department of Justice. It's a delicate matter, but from what I know, they're not asking how someone feels about abortion. They're asking what they think about certain decisions, and about their philosophy of judicial review."

The 1987 replacement of retiring Supreme Court Justice Lewis Powell was regarded as a particularly important step in the judicial strategy. It was seen as an opportunity to tilt the Court in a conservative direction for many years to come. The unexpectedly bitter battle over Senate confirmation, leading to the rejection of the first nominee and withdrawal of the second, was a severe blow. However, by the end of the administration more than half of all federal judges will have been appointed during the Reagan years. Whether or not a conservative majority on the Supreme Court is firmly in place by the end of his presidency, Reagan's appointments have clearly changed the overall ideological complexion of the federal judiciary. It may be that in the long run, social changes which the presidency has been unable to bring about through legislation will come through court decisions.

Traditional Values

The ideological balance of the court system will have a long-range effect on other aspects of the Reagan/religious right social agenda, as well as the abortion issue. The second point in Reagan's social program, as outlined in his 1984 speech to the National Association of Evangelicals, was the restoring of education in values to the public school system. In a sense this touches on the heart of the evangelical concern. The charge, not only from the religious right but from a far broader spectrum of religious people, is that a kind of overzealous secularization of the culture has largely stripped the society of the value system it received from its religious faiths.

One of the major functions of schools, in the view of religious parents, is that of passing on society's values (perceived as religious) to the next generation. And for this there is venerable precedent. The two hundredth anniversary of the Northwest Ordinance of 1787 (passed by the Continental Congress to govern the settling of the Northwest Territory, that huge area between the Mississippi River and the Great Lakes) was celebrated, along with that of the Constitution, in 1987. The intention of the founders was made clear in Article III: "Religion, morality and knowledge being necessary to good government and the happiness of mankind, schools and the means of education shall forever be encouraged."

The fundamentalist wing of American Protestantism has to a considerable extent opted out of the public education system. Racial discrimination, on the basis of which the IRS, during the Carter presidency, challenged the Christian school system, was a real issue during the civil rights revolution when a number of "segregation academies" were established. Further, it is true that white fundamentalists have not been notably liberal in racial attitudes. But to the extent that it ever was, segregation has long since ceased to be a major issue in the Christian school movement. This rapidly growing school system exists for the purpose of providing an education centered in conservative Christian values, often in a closed environment sharply separated from the rest of society, for a constituency which has written off the American public school system as "godless."

"Secular humanism" has long been a code word for conservative Christians, symbolizing a philosophy that seeks to establish a culture without religion or religious values. Public schools have been the primary arena in which battles over the influence of secular humanism have been fought. More moderate conservatives, put off by the fundamentalist conviction that secular humanism is a conspiracy aimed at taking over the schools, have preferred to avoid the term. The demands of a pluralistic society, in which each religion objects to having its children taught the tenets of any other religion, have placed public education in a no-win position. Textbook publishers, afraid Christians will be offended if Judaism is mentioned, and vice versa, have almost totally eliminated religious references from schoolbooks.

The issue of values education in a pluralistic society has been an extremely knotty one. Various experiments in "values clarification," or teaching morality divorced from religion, have met with mixed success at best. For most Americans, values are still authenticated religiously.

There are rapidly growing signs that the extremes of a culture without religion are being reversed. Significantly, the Association for Supervision and Curriculum Development, a professional group of 80,000 public school teachers, principals, and other curriculum specialists, cried "enough" in the summer of 1987. The schools must do more to teach about the world's religions, they said in their report on "Religion in the Curriculum."

The report said, "An elementary student can come away from a textbook account of the Crusades with the notion that these wars to win the Holy Land for Christendom were little more than exotic shopping expeditions." It noted the absence of the role of religion in shaping the United States or in explaining current Middle East tension.

"We can't wait for textbook publishers to change their books," said an association spokesperson. "We are encouraging people who make curriculum decisions to take action now."

But teaching "about religion," while essential to accurate portrayal of American and world history and culture, will not solve the values problem. The 1987 decision of Alabama Federal Judge Brevard Hand that secular humanism was, indeed, a religion, as fundamentalist parents had claimed, and that textbooks supporting it had to be removed from the schools, has not stood up under appeal. But the concern is a basic one for the Reagan presidency. Ultimate answers will probably have to come primarily through the court system, since a legislative or administrative solution to the values crisis is not readily apparent.

Reagan has, however, raised the problem to a high level of visibility and has given it new respectability. Where middle-of-the-road Americans earlier ascribed talk about secular humanism to a fundamentalist fringe and dismissed it as the ravings of fanatics, Reagan has, to use Carl Anderson's term, "mainstreamed" the concern. Further, Reagan's appointment of William Bennett to head the U.S. Department of Education (a Cabinet department he had earlier intended to eliminate) has given a highly visible platform to a religious conservative who is not at all reluctant to champion loud and long before the educational establishment the cause of religiously based values.

School Prayer

The final social goal outlined by the president to the National Association of Evangelicals in 1984 was school prayer. Liberals are sometimes baffled by the tenacity with which conservatives battle to keep prayer in public schools, since such prayer, at best, is likely to be nothing more than an ill-defined "moment of silence." But the significance for conservatives goes deeper than prayer itself. The religious right, and many moderates as well, are convinced that moral values are derived primarily if not solely from religion. The school-prayer issue, therefore, is closely related to the values issue. It symbolizes the larger absence of religion from public education.

School prayer is a complex issue. On the one hand it is deeply enmeshed with the problem of religious pluralism; all agree that freedom of religion means a Buddhist child cannot be forced to pray to a Judeo-Christian God. But on the other hand it is equally intertwined with the issue of public morality, for that very freedom of religion is a moral value. And morality is not produced in a vacuum. It is rooted in beliefs about ultimate reality. The real issue is not school prayer itself but the absence from public education of religious assumptions of which prayer is a symbol—those religious assumptions on which basic values such as freedom of religion are based.

Some of the Christian right is calling for a return to the Protestant culture of the nineteenth century, with America seen as a "Christian nation." Most, however, are aware that this is neither possible nor desirable. A far broader constituency is convinced that the civil religion of the Judeo-Christian tradition, the basis of the ordering of American society for nearly two hundred years until the upheavals of the sixties, can still perform that function. Harvard Professor Mark Silk, in a 1988 book called *Spiritual Politics: Religion and America Since World War II*, maintains, from a Jewish perspective, that the Judeo-Christian consensus is still intact and inherent in American culture.

Is there in modern American society a sufficiently broad consensus about ultimate reality to undergird an American value system? This is the underlying question. The Reagan presidency answered it with a forthright yes. After decades of doubt about the consensus, of a growing perception that religious belief had become so diverse that no common ground was possible, of a gradual stripping away from public education of all evidences of the religious dimension of American history and culture, the Reagan presidency called for a reversal.

It was a presidency that produced some memorable slogans: "It's morning in America," "the pride is back," "America is standing tall again." It was accused of fostering an emotional kind of patriotism, even jingoism. Opponents charged that these slogans papered over a failure to address deep economic and social problems. Yet there was an authentic connection between the renewed patriotism and the hospitality to traditional religious values. The eclipse of those values had left the society without a public philosophy, without a moral basis for public life. Prayer in schools may not be the answer. Clearly the religious pluralism of the society cannot be ignored and the rights of religious and nonreligious minorities cannot be disregarded. But the religious basis for a moral consensus, of which school prayer is a symbol, was seen by the Reagan presidency as a critical issue for America.

Has the paucity of legislative and constitutional change, with regard to the originally announced social goals of the Reagan presidency, brought disillusionment on the part of the religious right, with which these goals are identified? Says Paul Weyrich, who was instrumental in originally bringing those social goals into the Republican coalition, "Almost everything that President Reagan has accomplished can be swiftly undone by a single session of a heavily Democratic Congress, or by the stroke of a pen from a new Democratic President himself."

Weyrich assigns a considerable measure of responsibility to the religious right itself, in its failure to assert its power: "In 1981 I urged Falwell to send the Republicans a strong signal that they could not take the religious right for granted. A good opportunity, I suggested, would be to endorse Chuck Robb, a Democrat, over Marshall Coleman, a Republican, in the Virginia gubernatorial elections that year. Robb wanted Falwell's support, and he was no worse than Coleman on social issues, but Falwell backed off and ended up with a last-minute endorsement of Coleman. Coleman lost. Robb won without Falwell. The GOP got the message that you can do anything to the religious right and they will still support Republicans.

"Most leaders of the religious right behaved the same way as Falwell. They were so happy, after years of isolation, to get invited to state dinners at the White House that many forgot what had moved them to get into politics in the first place."

White House Religious Liaison official Carl Anderson, however, took a more positive view. He felt that the leadership of the religious right, if not the rank and file, understood the obstacles presented by a Congress controlled by the Democrats and that support for Reagan remained strong.

Personal Morality in High Places in the Reagan Years

The Iran/Contra affair of the closing years of the Reagan presidency focused attention on a final aspect of public morality—perhaps the aspect that looms largest in the minds of ordinary citizens and is most closely identified with religion by the public. Adherence to basic standards of right and wrong, in the personal behavior of public officials, is a high priority for the American people. How did the Reagan presidency, in its alliance with rigid morality of the religious right, meet this elemental test?

The high number of administration officials investigated by special prosecutors, including such figures as Attorney General Meese as well as the principals in the Iran/Contra affair, National Security Advisor Poindexter and Assistant Oliver North, together with former White House officials, such as former Reagan intimates Lyn Nofziger and Michael Deaver, indicted for influence-peddling after leaving office, has been unsettling to many.

The president himself, however, was long immune to any fallout damage from charges of moral lapses on the part of his subordinates. The phrase "Teflon presidency" described a situation in which no scandal, no political error, no moral failure in the administration seemed to stick to the president personally. This Teflon factor was variously ascribed to Ronald Reagan's skill as a communicator, his ability to relate directly to the American people, the fact that he was widely thought of as a father figure or a kindly uncle. It was, however, in considerable measure simply a matter of trust. The American people had confidence in Reagan's honesty and integrity. He might be old, he might be detached from day-to-day governmental business, he might have memory problems, he might be the recipient of bad advice, he might be poorly served by subordinates, he might even be lazy, but they trusted him. This aura of trustworthiness and integrity was an immensely valuable resource.

Donn Moomaw, the president's pastor, is convinced that Reagan's moral rectitude is unsullied: "He called me right after the Nicaragua-Contra situation was made public—the diversion of funds," said Moomaw. "And I asked him very frankly, 'Will you ever be embarrassed? Will anything come out to reveal that you have not told the truth?'

"He said, 'What you know is what I know. I have said everything.'

"I really went for the jugular," Moomaw continued. "I said, 'Are you sleeping well at night?'

"He said, 'Well, I get nervous about a lot of the problems of our world. But as far as my own conscience is concerned, I'm up to date.'

"That's about all you can ask. . . . I thank God for a man like that," Moomaw said.

"Lying is not his style. Cheating is not his style. He's a trustworthy man. When he gives his word, I know it's going to be done."

His pastor believes in him deeply.

Whether or not the trust of the public at large has been permanently dissipated by the uncertainties of the Iran/Contra affair will be the judgment of history. From the perspective of the moral and religious dimension of the modern presidency, it is a critically important judgment. That a majority of the American people, long after the evidence was presumably all in, persisted in believing the president had been lying about his knowledge and role in connection with the diversion of funds from Iranian arms sales to the support of the Contras was an ominous sign.

Former President Carter, commenting in an interview on the moral issues surrounding the Iran/Contra affair, suggested that the public had no stomach for another impeachment. "There is no inclination on the part of the American people to punish President Reagan," he said. He was undoubtedly right. Even the discovery by investigators of a "smoking gun" in the form of incontrovertible evidence that the president had indeed known of the diversion probably would have brought no move in the direction of impeachment.

But from the moral perspective, that is beside the point. It was the moral disillusionment of Watergate, with Vietnam and the turmoil of the sixties in the background, that brought renewed interest in the religious dimension of the presidency. It is against this background that the significance of the quiet but staunch Episcopalianism of Gerald Ford, the highly public Southern Baptist evangelicalism of Jimmy Carter, and the heartfelt embrace by Ronald Reagan of the religious right must be seen. Seeking a recovery of public morality, Americans have looked to presidents who offered not only moral rectitude but the kind of religious undergirding on which they believe public morality must rest.

Reactions to the moral question marks surrounding the final years of the Reagan presidency have been sharply polarized—as was the response to the crisis that ended the Nixon presidency. Predictably, the division has followed the fault lines dividing left from right in the polarized ideological and religious arenas. The religious right is deeply committed—and on religious grounds—to the cause in which, as Oliver North's secretary, Fawn Hall, aptly put it in the Iran/Contra hearings, it had been "sometimes necessary to go above the written law." It has, by and large, been willing to excuse whatever duplicity may have been required by covert operations. Its belief in the president's rectitude has apparently remained firm.

The religious left has unabashedly and explicitly opposed the Reagan revolution from the beginning. As one observer put it, "The program of the Methodist Board of Global Ministries is indistinguishable from that of the left wing of the Democratic party." Never in sympathy with his goals, and rejecting the fundamentalism of the religious right with which he has been identified, the left has gleefully seized upon the Iran/Contra affair as confirmation of the moral shortcomings it saw all along.

But in a larger sense, increasingly the underlying moral issue transcends the ideological polarization. Growing numbers of moderates and liberals share with worried conservatives a mounting concern over the loss of moral fiber in public life. Ultimately the judgment of the American people on the moral dimension of the Reagan presidency is likely to be one of the potent factors in determining his place in history.

Former President Gerald Ford, in a 1987 interview, ascribed the vastly heightened interest in religion in post-Watergate presidencies to the media. Said he, "Certainly the press has focused on that issue to a far greater degree. I guess you could go back to the press interest in . . . the Kennedy issue about Catholicism. Ever since then there has been a growing press interest in the religious beliefs of candidates and the president himself. I suspect the press will continue to focus on issues of morality in candidates—the Gary Hart incident being the most recent. And I can't imagine the press being less interested in the future—probably more so. Whether that's right or wrong, it's a fact of life, and all candidates had better expect it."

No doubt the media have been a significant factor, as with most public events in the electronic age. Certainly President Jimmy Carter's evangelicalism was a major media theme, as was the rise of the religious right and its prominent role in the presidency of Ronald Reagan. Ford himself succeeded in keeping his own religious life relatively private, but public awareness of his reputation for morality and integrity helped put him into the Oval Office.

Vietnam and Watergate, in the wake of the turmoil of the sixties, brought American society into its greatest internal moral crisis of the century. In the years following, more than the media has pushed religion to a position of prominence in three successive presidencies.

This book has treated those three presidencies in the context of the nation's historic commitment to separation of church and state. With Ford no question arose, but always in the background, as the strong religious dimensions of the Carter and Reagan presidencies were examined, has been the implicit question: Has this basic American principle been violated? In the next chapter that issue will be addressed directly.

11

Church and State and the Oval Office

AMERICA has entered a new era of president-as-pastor, said presidential historian Henry F. Graff of Columbia University in 1987. Referring to President Reagan's eulogy in May of that year at memorial services for thirty-seven Navy men killed in an Iraqi attack on the U.S.S. *Stark*, and to his earlier participation in similar services for Marines slain in Beirut, for those killed in the Grenada invasion, and for soldiers who died in an air crash in Newfoundland, Graff viewed the president's pastoral role in such services with dismay. "Presumably inhibited by the constitutional requirement of church-state separation, and wary of assuming clerical functions, historically Presidents have acted gingerly in discussing the Deity," Graff said.

No more. In this period in which successive presidencies have been deeply influenced in different ways by religion, charges have proliferated that the principle of separation of church and state has been endangered.

Former President Carter, in several public statements, has suggested that evangelists in politics (such as Pat Robertson) and the organizations of the religious right, politically promoting a religious agenda, are infringing on the separation principle. Yet Carter, whose religious faith and practices were highly public during his White House years, was himself sometimes accused of endangering that same principle. Hugh Sidey, noted columnist on the presidency, said late in 1986, "I feel more comfortable with a Pat Robertson, who I am sure will ultimately be laughed off the stage with his religious vaudeville, than with Jimmy Carter, who practices it in musty closets and makes political decisions on the results without telling anyone."

His point, said Mr. Sidey, was "that wise Americans should hold all these 'religious professionals' at arm's length":

> I simply don't want Mormons, or Episcopalians, or Jews or Adventists running this nation. It is surely okay to have American politicians who happen to be Mormons, or Episcopalians, or Jews or Adventists. I would like a president who, when he feels his pancreas jump, consults his physician and not his archbishop.

Is this alarm about overly religious approaches to the presidency justified? Specifically, has Carter's White House religiosity, or has the influence of the religious right on the Reagan presidency, crossed the line that traditionally separates church and state?

Only the court system gives definitive church-state rulings in specific instances, when legal action is brought. But in ordinary human judgments as to where the line between church and state should be drawn, the eye of the beholder tends to shape the vision. Secularists want a high wall, with no religious influence at all on organs of government. Some religionists tend to be less worried about separation—as long as the religion enjoying a cozy relationship with the state is their own. But (as with Carter viewing the religious right, and Sidey viewing Carter) most people tend to be highly suspicious of influence by religions or religious groups of which they disapprove.

As we have noted earlier, the pluralism of the Congress (the only branch of government actually mentioned in the First Amendment) has been a safeguard against undue influence on government, or violation of the rights of particular religions, through congressional action. Too many denominations are represented in the halls of Congress, and no one denomination has ever commanded a majority.

But the presidency is a different matter. The institutional loyalty of a religiously committed president is necessarily denominational, and a president's personal religious convictions may be uniquely shaped by its particular tradition. Here denominational influence might conceivably be significant.

Catholicism and Today's Presidency

The longtime bar to Roman Catholics in the presidency reflected a fear of such influence, and before asking how separation of church and state has fared in modern presidencies, a look at the present status of the Catholic issue is appropriate. There was a considerable measure of anti-Catholic prejudice in the barrier that long existed, evident in such things as the Know-Nothingism of the nineteenth century. But the claim of the pre-Vatican II Catholic Church to be the only true church was a substantive roadblock for Protestants. And its longtime assertion of the right to a preferred status where a government was controlled by Catholics gave rise to seemingly justified suspicions as to how the separation principle would fare under a Catholic president. So did the opposition of the church to private judgment in matters of conscience and its insistence on the church's right to form the conscience of Catholic believers. Especially was this the case with regard to issues such as the legality of birth control, in which public opinion generally was at odds with the official Catholic position.

In reality, American Catholics were moving away from strict adherence to the church's classic position on these issues, and adapting wholeheartedly to the American system of pluralism, long before the church itself, in Vatican II, made it permissible. Yet the question remained a difficult one until the combination of John F. Kennedy's forthright pledge to adhere to the separation principle, and the fresh winds of the pontificate of Pope John XXIII, laid it to rest.

In the mid-eighties, public clashes between Cardinal John J. O'Connor, archbishop of New York, and two of New York's most famous Catholics in politics—1984 Democratic vice presidential candidate Geraldine Ferraro and New York Governor Mario Cuomo—briefly threatened to reopen the issue. The authority of the church to speak to the position of a Catholic public official on abortion was the point of contention. Both Ferraro and Cuomo made clear their own independence in taking public policy positions, while at the same time affirming their loyalty to the church.

In this they were representative of most contemporary American

Catholics. The church hierarchy has shown no signs of modifying official Catholic positions, nor is it likely to do so. The 1987 visit of Pope John Paul II to the United States confirmed once more his intention of holding the line. But by that time 93 percent of American Catholics believed that they could disagree with official church positions and still be good Catholics. A survey for *Time* magazine just prior to the papal visit showed surprisingly little difference between Protestants and Catholics on issues once regarded as litmus tests of Catholic loyalty to the church. American Catholics are used to thinking for themselves, says the Reverend Richard McBrien, chairman of the theology department at the University of Notre Dame. "They simply accept as basic what any American citizen accepts as basic—due process, freedom of expression, all those things we identify with the Bill of Rights."

The papal visit highlighted the contest of wills between an independent-minded American laity, thoroughly committed to freedom of conscience and determined to think for itself, and an authoritative Vatican, staunchly upholding traditional Catholic teachings and giving not an inch to the demands of individualism.

American bishops, who form the bridge joining the two forces, have performed their function well. The perceived clash between the Vatican and American laity, despite the apparently irreconcilable differences and the vigor of the debate, probably signals a strength of the church rather than a weakness. For the firm, consistent, and unyielding quality of official church positions speaks powerfully to a near-rootless and valueless society. It is precisely the combination of full commitment to American freedoms, together with a consistent and authoritative moral position, that has created what Richard John Neuhaus, in a 1987 book, calls "the Catholic moment" in American history.

The recovery of the moral consistency of biblical authority within the Protestant majority has enabled evangelicalism to speak strongly to contemporary America. The traditional ecclesiastical authority in Catholicism is similarly consistent. And the convergence of Protestant and Catholic concerns about the moral vacuum has made them allies in the public square.

It is apparent that Catholicism is no longer a special case where the presidency is concerned. The principle of separation of church and state could conceivably be violated by a president who belonged to any church, if he or she were deeply committed to denominational beliefs not shared by the country at large. But in the context of modern lay Catholicism, this is no more likely to be the case with a Catholic president than with one of any other denomination. And the strong influence of some organized parachurch religious group, to which a president might give allegiance, could bring an equally serious threat. Indeed, the question of church-state infringement has arisen in the late twentieth century, not in connection with Roman Catholic John F. Kennedy, but with Protestants Jimmy Carter and Ronald Reagan.

Is "Moderation" Necessary?

Kennedy continued the tradition of "gentlemanly moderation" which kept presidential religion from becoming an issue. But is moderation on the part of presidents necessary? The American system of religious pluralism has never required indifference. Indeed, the moral vigor of the American people historically has come from a kind of diversity in which adherents of various faiths have taken their own beliefs extremely seriously. Authentic American civil religion has not been a watered-down faith on which everyone could agree because no one cared much. It has depended, rather, on the difference between a "saving faith" (of which there are many) for the governing of lives and an "ordering faith" (on which there has been general agreement) for the governing of society. The vitality of the latter depends on the vigor of the former—on a system of lively denominational religions in which people deeply believe, for the salvation of their souls and the enriching of their faith communities and personal lives. Public morality is grounded not solely in the common agreement of the ordering faith but also in the spiritual power of the saving faith. It requires a populace with strong commitment to the differing beliefs of its different religions.

But is such strong commitment inappropriate for presidents, who symbolize the unity of the civil religion? The religious presidencies of the post-Watergate era have provided a testing ground.

Clearly, in the case of President Ford, the answer was no. His deep religious commitment provided the assurance of honesty and integrity his moment in history demanded. But he adhered to the traditional presidential pattern of distinguishing sharply between the public and the private, with religion limited to the private sphere of life. His strong conservative belief that organized religion should stay out of organized government provided an additional safeguard. It was Jimmy Carter who broke the pattern.

Separation of Church and State in the Carter Presidency

Can a president be too religious? This is the underlying question of the Carter presidency, for some have suggested that his deep and evident piety was itself a violation of separation of church and state. Clearly Carter saw no limits placed by his office on how religious, or how publicly religious, a president can be. He tried, insofar as possible, to live what was for him a normal church life, which involved a level of activity far beyond regular churchgoing. As one who believed (in full accord with the tenets of his denomination) in sharing his faith with others, he saw no bar to witnessing to those with whom his official duties brought him into contact, even, on occasion, foreign heads of state. He talked openly and frequently about his church, his Christian life, and his personal faith. As we have seen, his actions and decisions as president were significantly affected by that personal faith, which was central to his being.

Yet he had a sense of constitutional limitations on the place of religion in his presidential role. In September 1978 he received a letter from Robert Maddox, later to become a White House Religious Liaison official, but then serving as a pastor in Georgia. Said Maddox:

> . . . It occurs to me that the nations of the world need a pastor. Surely our own country needs a pastor. . . . Without ever using the word "pastor" you can speak to that gnawing hunger in the American and international spirit by carefully making evident and living out who, in fact, you are. . . . There are no easy, slick ways to pastor this nation. . . . Mr. President, make more evident that spiritual dimension of your leadership. Be the spiritual catalyst. Call us to greatness. . . .

In his reply, Carter (who had rejected the routine acknowledgment first presented by the White House staff for his signature) gently disavowed the "pastor to the nation" role, pointing to constitutional limitations:

> . . . You and I both subscribe to the doctrine of separation of church and state, and I trust that you and others who are not restrained by Constitutional limitations will continue to provide leadership in spiritual affairs.
>
> It goes without saying that I will continue to make my personal witness. With your prayers, and with the prayers of the American people, I know that we will accomplish much by example as well as by precept.

That deep and frequently reiterated commitment to separation of church and state was a traditional emphasis of Southern Baptists. Strongly aware of the constitutional principle, Carter obviously saw no violation of that principle in the role his own religion played in his presidency.

When Maddox was asked in a 1987 interview, after his White House service, if Carter had felt that as a Christian president he had to walk a fine line relative to the separation of church and state, he answered negatively:

"No. I don't think he struggled with that. He realized that certain matters of faith spilled over into public policy—that justice and human rights, these kinds of things, had biblical roots. But they translated on the larger stage, and so there was no sense of conflict there. On the narrow things of abortion, and student prayer, and parochial [school] aid, he invoked the doctrine of separation of church and state. . . . He was a religious man in politics, and being in politics did not keep him from expressing his faith. But he also had a sense of the separation of church and state which kept him from promoting [aspects of] individual faith that would have required government support to carry them on."

Carter sought to be scrupulously impartial in dealing with all organized churches and religious bodies. His record of respect and support for non-Christian religions, particularly Judaism and Islam, as demonstrated in his close relationships with Israeli Prime Minister Begin and Egyptian President Sadat, bears out a judgment that the impartiality was real.

Curiously, the major exchange over church-state separation preserved in the presidential files in the Carter Library was not a charge of Southern Baptist influence on the government but of presidential influence on the Southern Baptists. It was raised in a letter to the president from his friend Jack Harwell, editor of a Baptist paper, *The Christian Index*. Harwell wrote of his grave concern "about the fact that you invited ten of the leading employees of the Southern Baptist Convention to the White House for a conference to plot denominational strategy. And a week later the Southern Baptist Convention adopted that strategy as its policy and mission program for the next five years. This raises in my mind some extremely serious church-state problems."

The president was obviously disturbed. In his two-page handwritten reply, he spoke of the fact that the White House was his current home, in which he had felt free as a Baptist to discuss religious matters with other Baptists. He went on to give one of his most compelling statements regarding his own commitment to separation of church and state and his awareness of the fine line a president must walk in preserving it:

> As you know, as Governor and as President I have taught Sunday School and on occasions have addressed congregations and convention audiences which were religious in nature—[Protestants], Jews and Catholics. I believe in the separation of church and state and would not use my authority to violate this principle in any way. You refer to the President "setting denominational policy." I did encourage the Convention to emphasize a strong mission program, but feel that this has always been the policy of the Southern Baptists. Obviously, I realize that I, as President, have a special influence.
>
> Jack, I trust your judgment about matters such as this and will be careful and will consult with my pastor and others to be sure that Baptists have no reason to be concerned about my actions in the future.

This and other evidences point to a strong awareness on the part of President Carter of the importance of separation of church and state in the American system, a conscious effort to preserve it and a conviction that his own religious faith and active church life in no way constituted a church-state infringement. Asked about this in an interview, Jody Powell confirmed that it was an area in which Carter had been extremely careful.

But with a chuckle to indicate how farfetched he considered the idea, he said, "He didn't, nor did I, ever imagine that the separation of church and state could be construed as prohibiting a president from the free exercise of religion." Carter did not believe that the separation principle requires a lukewarm presidential religion.

His presidency demonstrated that he was right. The country has nothing to fear from a president with strong religious convictions and an active church life as long as he or she allows no denominational tenets which are not part of the American consensus to become government policy, is fully respectful of other religions, and is carefully impartial in dealing with them.

Perhaps the best evidence that the Carter presidency did not violate separation of church and state lies in the fact that it was not an issue in his reelection campaign. We have earlier noted ways in which his religious convictions may have contributed subtly to the perception that he was an inept president. Conclusions as to the reason for his 1980 defeat are perhaps best left to the political scientists and historians. But no one has suggested religion itself as a reason. There is no evidence at all that it was because he was perceived by the public as "too religious" or because of church-state considerations.

Danger Point

There is a danger in conspicuous presidential religion, however, not to the principle of separation of church and state, but in the more subtle realm of the president's symbolic unifying role in a multifaith society. Modern presidents live in a fishbowl, and all aspects of their lives and activities are regarded as legitimate grist for the media mill. If a president is known to be devoutly religious, public attention will inevitably be centered on this aspect of his or her life. There is no way a presidential family can live a fully "normal" church life, taking a covered dish to the potluck supper, participating in a small covenant group, volunteering for the church's drug-counseling program. The very "normality" of such participation in the life of the religious community becomes "abnormal" in the presidential context.

Certain aspects of President Carter's religious life which were entirely normal for him as an active Baptist layman before and after the White House years—his Sunday School teaching, his witnessing to foreign dignitaries—were public "curiosities" in terms of presidential expectations. It could be imagined that he might have chosen, during a presidential vacation period, to participate in a week of the kind of house-to-house evangelistic visitation in which he had engaged earlier. He might have reasoned that the power of example, the good done in terms of his Christian conviction about the salvation of souls, and the vitality of such person-to-person contact, would outweigh such considerations as presidential dignity or the unconscious comedy of door-to-door evangelistic calling amid a coterie of TV cameras and gun-toting Secret Service agents. Had he done so, however, or had he participated in a hammer-wielding week of volunteer work for Habitat for Humanity, as he has done several times since, the "curiosity" factor would have been even greater.

President Carter, making his personal judgment as to the appropriateness of each, drew the line at the latter kinds of activity, which symbolically would have sent a highly public message. But he continued to participate in the former kinds (Sunday School teaching and personal witnessing to individuals), which he presumably regarded as private. Each president is entitled to make such decisions. But since very little that a president does is really private, the sectarian image is easy to acquire. Carter might have chosen, with no compromise of piety or principle, to forgo temporarily even such commonplace Baptist activities as Sunday School teaching and witnessing to those he encountered (particularly if they were foreign heads of state) in order to relate to a wider range of religious constituencies. The avoidance of such denominational activities could make it easier for a president to symbolize the unity of all American religions in the moral and spiritual undergirding of national life.

Reagan, the Religious Right, and Church-State Issues

From what could hardly be called a nonpartisan perspective, former Carter Press Secretary Jody Powell, in response to questions during a 1987 interview, gave his views on the new religious right and its close relationship to the Reagan administration. He was less than complimentary.

"The net result, I fear, is going to be . . . significant damage to people's confidence in, and thus to the legitimacy of, both government and religion. I think that is almost inevitably the case. Historically, when religion and government get all wrapped up together, what you get is a bastard child that combines the worst elements of both." Similar views have been expressed by other Carter partisans.

Questions from the church-state standpoint about the relationship of the organized religious right to the Reagan presidency, however, do not come exclusively from the political opposition. From a perspective quite sympathetic to the Reagan presidency, former President Gerald Ford expressed in an interview strong reservations about the relationship. Believing deeply that organized religion should not get involved with organized government, he considers the Moral Majority and similar groups, though not churches, to be "organized religion." Asked if this is a separation of the church-and-state issue, he said that it is very fundamentally so.

If the Carter presidency, then, raised a church-state question having to do with the effect on public policy of a devoutly religious president's personal faith, the Reagan presidency raises a different issue, having to do with the effect of influential religious constituency groups. Does the strong voice of the religious right violate separation of church and state?

The fact that the organizations known as the religious right are not churches but are independent parachurch groups is important here. The Liberty Federation (formerly Moral Majority), long associated with Jerry Falwell, claims both Roman Catholic and Jewish as well as Protestant members. Said he, "Moral Majority is a political organization, and is not based on theological considerations. . . . [It] strongly supports pluralistic America. While we believe that this nation was founded upon the Judeo-Christian ethic by men and women who were strongly influenced by biblical moral principles, we are committed to the separation of church and state."

It is, of course, made up predominantly of fundamentalist Protestants and has been closely associated with Falwell's other ministries. But his claim to broader representation was legitimate. We have noted earlier that Paul Weyrich, who was instrumental in persuading Falwell to start it, is Roman Catholic, and that Howard Phillips, who helped to establish the Religious Roundtable, is Jewish.

But even if the organizations were solely Protestant, or even solely Baptist, in membership, they are still not churches. Parachurch groups, independent of church control, have been the traditional channels through which conservative Christians, believing churches should stay out of politics, have worked to influence political processes. Organizing for political purposes is quintessentially American, and the fact that the common interest uniting the members of such a political organization is religious makes it no less legitimate than if that common interest were feminism, or concern about the welfare system, or opposition to capital punishment.

The Church "Lobbies"

Many Americans, from both the religious and the political perspective, would go a step beyond this and maintain that it is entirely legitimate for churches, as churches, to seek directly to influence political processes. This has long been the position of mainline Protestant as well as Roman Catholic church leadership. Most of the major denominations maintain Washington offices, funded from official denominational budgets, for the purpose of influencing government. Their staffs are, in effect, church-supported lobbyists, and they are quite active on a broad range of political issues.

Conservatives within these denominations have a long record of opposing such lobbying by official church agencies, which they regard as a violation of the principle of separation of church and state. Perhaps equally persuasive is the fact that the lobbyists generally support the liberal side of controversial issues, which conservatives within the denominations oppose. But repeated efforts through church governing bodies to close down the Washington offices have met with consistent failure. The liberal bureaucracies of these denominations are in firm control.

From the political side there have from time to time been challenges to the tax-exempt status of church organizations that engage in political activity. The most lively current challenge to such political activity on the part of churches comes not from the right but from the left. Proabortion groups have sought to examine Roman Catholic church financial records to determine the level of official church funding of antiabortion political activity. This demand the church hierarchy has firmly resisted, despite the threat of heavy fines. The ultimate outcome of such court tests remains to be seen. On the basis of current practice, however, it appears that officially funded political activity on the part of institutional churches is generally accepted. Conservative opponents to such activity, whether within the churches or from the political side, have so far not carried the day. Even the Southern Baptists, with their strong tradition of separation of church and state, help to support a joint Baptist office in Washington.

We have noted earlier that the influence of the religious right on the Reagan presidency has been more a matter of convergence of interests than of organized group pressure. But however exercised, it would be hard to sustain the claim that the relationship of this presidency to the religious right violates the principle of separation of church and state. Like Carter's personal religiosity, the influence of this constituency group is well within the allowable pattern of church-state relationship.

Danger Area for the Reagan Presidency

But just as the Carter presidency focused attention on a potential danger point in a level of denominational religious activity that might handicap a president's symbolic unifying role, so the Reagan presidency, too, encounters a danger point. The social agenda of Reagan and the religious right does not command the kind of overwhelming consensus that unites a society behind particular policies or laws.

Abortion, for instance, is a highly controversial issue. The administration has not been able to muster a reliable majority in Congress to do away with legal abortions by legislative action. Public opinion on the issue is divided. A majority of Americans oppose abortion on demand but believe abortions should be available under some circumstances. (The justifiable circumstances vary with different people.) Protestants and Catholics, incidentally, are surprisingly close together in their views. A mid-1987 Yankelovich Clancy Shulman poll for *Time* magazine indicated that 27 percent of U.S. Catholics and 34 percent of Protestants believe women should have the right to abortion on demand; 57 percent of Catholics and 52 percent of Protestants believe it should be available under certain conditions. Only 14 percent of Catholics and 12 percent of Protestants believe abortion should always be illegal. The poll did not measure the level of commitment, which may be considerably deeper for Catholic opponents of abortion than for Protestants, but it gave a clear picture of the divided state of public opinion.

Abortion is a political issue with especially strong religious implications. Many would argue that opposition to abortion is by no means exclusively dependent on religious judgment. Catholics, particularly, point to reason and natural law as prudential grounds for prohibiting abortion, available to all, quite apart from revealed religion. Many Protestants would agree. Clearly there are secular opponents of abortion who do not base their opposition on religious grounds at all. But opposition to abortion is, nevertheless, an issue with strong religious undergirding, the major constituency being conservative Catholics and Protestants. Other elements of the Reagan social agenda, such as school prayer, are even more explicitly religious.

The church-state danger lies in the imposition by administrative regulation of religiously motivated restrictions that cannot be legislatively enacted because of the absence of a sufficiently strong consensus. To the extent that pro-choice constituencies, who are not themselves persuaded by reason or natural law that abortion is always evil, see the Reagan presidency as administering Title X of the Public Health Service Act according to the tenets of one particular religious group, their case has some legitimacy. Indeed, if the same administrative changes had come from a Catholic president (whose church would almost certainly be regarded as the source of the antiabortion convictions) cries of violation of church-state separation would probably be loud and strong.

Because the religious right is not made up of churches as such, and because the Protestant churches do not have a clear position on abortion, such a charge against the Reagan presidency cannot be sustained. As a matter of fact, the official positions of the two denominations with which President Reagan has some identification (Disciples of Christ and Presbyterian) are closer to pro-choice than pro-life. But use of the office of the presidency to promote within the government policies, whatever their source, that are regarded by most people as religiously inspired, does lead a president into dangerous church-state territory.

"What Falwell and company really want is state-sponsored religion," said Robert Maddox, executive director of Americans United for Separation of Church and State in commenting on the influence of the religious right.

"They really want some kind of official Christian-Jewish government religion. They would deny that, but you begin to read what they say, what they are emphasizing, and you have to come out with the conclusion that they want state-sponsored religion . . . . much more government support of religious activities. And therein lies the danger, not only to [the] state but to the church." Maddox was careful to say, however, that these groups "have every right to be involved" in political processes.

Summing It Up: the Church-State Question

Ford, Carter, and Reagan, in quite different ways, have all presided over far more religious presidencies than was the norm before the collapse of the national moral consensus associated with Vietnam, Watergate, and the upheavals of the sixties. Because Ford maintained a sharp line between his personal religion and his public life, church-state questions did not arise during his presidency. With both Carter and Reagan, such questions have been raised: with Carter in connection with his unusually devout and highly public personal religious faith; with Reagan in connection with the influence of the religious right. But charges of violations cannot be sustained. Upon careful examination it appears that neither presidency has actually infringed on the traditional separation of church and state. Carter was not "too religious" to conform to the principle, nor has there been anything illegitimate about Reagan's relationship with and the influence of the organizations of the religious right. Both presidencies, however, have pointed to possible danger areas in the relationship of religion to the presidency.

The Preacher Candidates: Jackson and Robertson

The era of moral uncertainty that led Nixon and the Congress to select the impeccably "clean" Episcopalian Gerald Ford, and led the electorate successively to Southern Baptist evangelical Jimmy Carter and religious rightist Ronald Reagan, is not over. It can hardly be regarded as coincidental that for the first time in history each of the major political parties, as the 1988 election approached, had among its candidates for nomination a Christian minister.

Liberal Democrat Jesse Jackson and conservative Republican Pat Robertson presented intriguing parallels. Each was a Baptist minister, but each sought to downplay the ministerial image in favor of a broader identification, with Robertson resigning from the ministry when he formally entered the race. Each represented a special constituency within his party, the loyalty of which party leaders considered essential. Each, in the course of the campaign, was the object of charges or innuendos of moral shortcomings, but each retained the loyalty of his own constituency. Neither was regarded by political pros as having any real chance of winning the nomination. Each, however, had an excellant chance of winning enough convention delegates to influence the party's choice if no one candidate achieved a pre-convention majority. At the very minimum, each would be in a position to influence the party's platform and directions. Both, in the primary contests did far better than traditional politicians had expected making it clear that the role of religion in presidential politics was by no means at an end.

Jesse Jackson and the Democrats

To consider Jesse Jackson primarily as a religious figure might be regarded as questionable. His basic constituency is not determined religiously but racially. He is, in the words of one journalist, "the President of black America." A former aide of Martin Luther King, Jr., he was an alumnus of the civil rights movement of the sixties. His base in the years following (he has held no elective office) was the Chicago-based black self-help organization "Operation Push."

Jackson became a candidate for the 1984 presidential nomination of the Democratic party in a move that may have been partially rooted in resentment. According to some accounts, the party's two leading liberals, Walter Mondale and Edward Kennedy, had both refused to support Harold Washington, insurgent black candidate in Chicago's mayoral contest, and had backed white candidates instead. Along with other factors, this led Jackson to a decision that a black should run nationally as a protest to the party's white establishment.

For the 1988 campaign, however, he adopted a far more positive strategy, seeking to run as a mainstream candidate. Espousing the cause of a wide range of the disadvantaged—women, farmers, Hispanics, poor and blue-collar whites as well as blacks—he sought to build a coalition of those on the fringes of economic and political life. He is clearly an urbanite, but he made a serious effort in rural Iowa, site of the first caucuses on the long road to the Democratic nomination. Yet despite some success with whites, his constituency remained overwhelmingly black.

This being the case, was Jackson's status as a minister irrelevant to his candidacy? Not at all. In reality it was a major factor. The black churches—evangelical in theology and predominantly Baptist—have long been the focal point of political life in the black community. A Reagan White House insider has been quoted as saying black churches are "the single most underestimated political force in the country." Black evangelicals espoused political activism long before white evangelicals did. The civil rights revolution was charted and led from the pulpit. And though lay power is growing, ministers still have an active political leadership role in the black community. It was "Daddy King," father of Martin Luther King, Jr., and other preachers who mobilized blacks behind the Carter candidacy in 1976. Jackson, carrying on in this tradition, preached in various churches regularly on Sunday mornings. Black churches raised funds and organized voter turnout. His political themes and goals—though more economic and social than biblical—were probably as central to the concerns of black American Christianity as Pat Robertson's were to those of the religious right.

Pat Robertson and the Republicans

For political purposes, Pat Robertson played down his ministerial status, identifying himself as having been a "professional broadcaster" for twenty-seven years. A few days before formally announcing his candidacy in October 1987 he resigned from the Southern Baptist ministry. But unlike Jesse Jackson's, Pat Robertson's constituency within the Republican party *was* delineated religiously. He was the candidate of the religious right, or at least of a major part of the religious right.

As the campaign for the party's nomination unfolded, the strength of the Robertson effort surprised many. It was, however, the culmination of a long process. In 1981 he had founded a tax-exempt educational organization called the Freedom Council, with the stated goals of organizing members to pray for national leaders, educating Christians about religious freedom, and getting them involved in politics at all levels. It had received substantial donations of money from the Christian Broadcasting Network, also controlled by Robertson at that time.

An early success in Michigan in 1986 startled the nation. As the campaign moved on he shaked the Republicans repeatedly with successes in precinct meetings, caucuses, and primaries in South Carolina, Florida, Georgia, Hawaii, North Carolina, Iowa, and elsewhere. His powerbase appeared formidable. With the extensive contacts provided by his TV background, he proved more successful at fund-raising than most other Republican aspirants for the nomination in the early stages of the campaign. Conventional wisdom had predicted that the scandals and quarrels among TV evangelists, would seriously damage his candidacy. As headlines faded, however, Robertson emerged relatively unscathed. His campaign demonstrated a mastery of political processes and a remarkable ability to mobilize the religious right around his banner.

Robertson called for a return to the Judeo-Christian heritage, and his effort was not exclusively Christian. Ben Waldman, who headed a Jewish group supporting the 1984 Reagan campaign, had resigned as associate director of personnel at the White House to work for Americans for Robertson. The candidate was careful to declare his support of religious liberty for all. During the October 1986 Washington rally at which he called for petitions signed by three million supporters, he had said, "The atheists among us should have every right of citizenship—the right to print, to broadcast, to speak, to persuade, to own businesses, to organize politically, to run for office."

But Robertson added that the remaining 94 percent of Americans who believe in God, according to a Gallup poll, do not have to "dismantle our entire public affirmation of faith in God just to please a tiny minority who don't believe in anything." Clearly his was primarily a fundamentalist Christian effort. After his early tactical victory in Michigan, he sent out a fund-raising letter announcing, "The Christians have won," and this was the distinctive mark of the Robertson candidacy. He later campaigned with some success as a conservative, saying little or nothing about religion, but his image was indelibly fixed and his basic constituency remained unchanged.

It was the religious cast of the candidacy that frightened the traditional wing of the party. Former Republican National Chairman Mary Louise Smith accused Robertson and his followers of using the GOP "as a vehicle for institutionalizing their religious views."

"If the Republican Party lets itself be taken over by fundamentalist religious views and it becomes almost exclusively that," she said, "it will survive for a little while and then self destruct, because it won't provide a foundation of a party."

By no stretch of the imagination was the Robertson candidacy supported by all evangelicals. Many moderates in the evangelical camp rejected him as an extremist. Not even all of the fundamentalists supported him. A significant number of conservative Christians still adhere to the classic position that "religion and politics don't mix."

Yet Robertson made considerable progress in positioning himself as the candidate of the religious right, and while it was clear that the movement would never be completely united behind him, his breadth of support was impressive. He acquired endorsements from two former presidents of the Southern Baptist Convention, from the presiding bishop of the Church of God in Christ and from several fellow TV evangelists. The major holdout, Jerry Falwell, who had earlier endorsed George Bush, late in 1987 resigned his chairmanship of the Liberty Federation and announced that he was withdrawing from direct political activity. This left the political field largely to Robertson.

Both George Bush and Jack Kemp placed on their campaign staffs liaison persons for the religious community. Kemp, long an actively involved evangelical Christian, had excellent credentials within the community. But to the extent that the religious right united behind any one candidate, Robertson was that candidate. He had positioned himself to become a major factor in the future of the Republican Party.

Testing the Limits

Robert Maddox, of Americans United for Separation of Church and State, indicated in a 1987 interview that he saw in the Robertson candidacy real danger to the separation principle. As he had observed about the religious right generally, he maintained that what Robertson was seeking was a form of state-sponsored religion.

"He really does want a church-state," said Maddox, who was also alarmed by Robertson's personal sense of receiving directives from God. "If God could tell him to go off and leave his wife when she was about to have a baby, God could tell him to have a war. . . . He is a frightening man."

Maddox also saw church-state dangers in Robertson's campaigning methods. "When Pat Robertson goes to Foursquare Churches and groups like that . . . and asks them to help him organize—they did that in Michigan—he's putting those churches at risk. He's putting their tax-exempt status at risk, he is putting their overall ministry at risk." Maddox added, in response to a question, that he would say the same thing, and had frequently done so, about Jackson and the black churches.

Whether or not one agrees with this spokesperson for the organization that seeks to be the watchdog of church-state separation, there are question marks in the Robertson candidacy. His constituency is essentially the same religious right that backed Ronald Reagan, and his social program is a strengthened version of that of the Reagan presidency. But he goes considerably further than Reagan—and much further than Carter—in identifying America's interests with those of the religious perspective he represents. His 1986 book, *America's Dates with Destiny*, presumably written for campaign purposes, was a religious interpretation of the nation's history and destiny, designed "to call America once again to its spiritual heritage":

> What will happen to America and to the world if the people of this generation rediscover our spiritual heritage and commit their lives and the life of the nation to it? I have written *America's Dates with Destiny* to help bring us one step closer to that great goal.

We noted earlier in this chapter that Carter signaled a possible church-state danger with a highly denominational style. He did not violate the separation principle. But he raised questions for some as to whether he could symbolize the unity of the civil religion, which provides the common "ordering faith" for this diverse society.

Robertson, while not strongly identified with a particular denomination, has a pentecostal image based on many years with the *700 Club*, which is much further from the customary norm than was Carter's. That image is buttressed by well-documented incidents such as his claim to have diverted a hurricane from striking his hometown of Virginia Beach, Virginia, through prayer. While clearly there is no constitutional bar nor any technical danger to separation of church and state from one whose personal religion is so far from the mainstream, there is a serious question related to the delicate balance on which this multifaith society rests.

Similarly, we noted a danger point in Reagan's attempts to give governmental authority to religiously based policies not consensually supported by most Americans. While here, too, there is no question of violation of law or abridgment of constitutional principle, the program of Robertson's religious constituency, with which he has long been identified, appears to go much further in this direction and thus tests the limits of the system.

Success of the Robertson candidacy for the Republican nomination would have significantly reshaped the Republican party, signaling a victory of the religious right over the market right for control, and transforming it, in considerable measure, into a "religious party." Success in the election campaign would have marked the first time the candidate of a "religious party" had won the presidency.

A Pat Robertson could probably serve as president without technically violating the principle of separation of church and state. Indeed, the strength of the society's commitment to church-state separation is such that in all probability no president, no matter how committed to a religious view of public life, would be allowed to get away with overt and obvious violations. The frequency and fervency with which Robertson declared his loyalty to the separation principle were evidence of the seriousness of the public concern about what he would do and the importance he attached to that concern.

But from the perspective of that principle, the Robertson candidacy aroused anxiety. The central question, perhaps, is not whether there would have been technical violations in a Robertson presidency, but whether he has the religiously based respect for other religions that the delicate balance of a multifaith society requires. The real significance of the Robertson candidacy—far more than was the case with Jackson, whose program was well within the bounds of tradition—is that of testing the limits of religious influence on the presidency. There is every evidence that Ford, Carter, and Reagan have all been well within the limits that the doctrine of separation of church and state allows. But there is some reason to believe that a Robertson presidency would exceed those limits.

12

Conclusion: the Presidency and the Public Square

WHILE separation of church and state is a basic issue for religious presidencies, there are other questions that must be examined as conclusions are drawn. A persistent puzzle, throughout this study of the prominent role of religion in recent presidencies, has been whether or not devout presidential faith is a disadvantage—to presidents or to the country. Was the old gentleman's agreement, after all, justified?

The Pros and Cons of a Religious Presidency

In looking at the downside of the Carter presidency in an earlier chapter, we examined in some detail those religious attitudes and themes, such as sin, humility, and sacrifice, that may not have "played well" politically and may have been related to some of the perceived failures of his presidency. There are other possible negatives as well.

During a 1987 interview on Carter's presidency Robert Maddox pointed to a second downside factor: "Because he was seen as religious, a lot of people all over the country kept saying, 'He's too good to be president.' " But what they really meant, Maddox continued, was "He's too naive to be president. You have to be mean, and Machiavellian, and sinister, to be president."

The charge of softness or naiveté was not made against Reagan. Indeed, among religious constituencies it has been new right advocates of religious realism, of the morality of "realpolitik," who have welcomed the firmness of Reagan's anticommunism and regarded Carter as lacking in toughness.

Carter explicitly rejected "realpolitik." In 1986 remarks at Messiah College he talked about this approach to foreign policy: "It means, in effect, doing what is best for us regardless of the effect on others—at times using strength to force our way on others. I think there can be a higher calling for a nation than that."

Yet he would have rejected the charge that this constituted softness. He considered morality in foreign policy to be an expression of the essential character of this nation, not a weakness. He felt that ability to make hard decisions was a basic requirement for presidents. Jody Powell, in a 1987 interview, recalled a conversation on what is for many the ultimate test of toughness, the presidential finger on the nuclear button. "I remember him talking one time, as he was deciding to run for president, considering the starkest question, 'Could you as president, in effect, destroy the world?' And [he said] if you don't believe you can do it, you ought not to run for president."

Even though the charges were not made against Reagan, they are in a sense inherent in the public perception of devout religiosity on the one hand and of the requirements of the presidency on the other. As Powell put it a little later in the same interview, "It is one thing to say that as an individual you should go the second mile, turn the other cheek, and in a sense put the welfare of others before your own. It is quite another thing to say that you as a president would do that with regard to . . . the country. It is an age-old paradox, and also one that is still real." There is a sense in which any presidency perceived as devoutly religious is likely to face this question.

Another quandary, for presidents whose religion is more than a conventional affiliation, is the necessity for political compromise. Here an inherent contradiction must be faced.

Politics, in a democratic system, is the art of compromise. Even the most homogeneous of political parties is made up of various constituencies whose differing and sometimes conflicting interests must be reconciled. In particular the Democratic party in modern times has been regarded as a collection of special-interest groups: labor unions, ethnic minorities, feminists, gays, the poor, and the disadvantaged. But the Republican party, too, as we have seen in connection with the religious right and the market right, is made up of interest groups. As it has broadened its appeal in the Reagan years to Yuppies and blue-collar ethnics, the number of special interests has grown. In any such party, compromise is a necessity. And beyond the intraparty compromise on which the political system is based, a president in office, more often than not in our times, must deal with one or both houses of Congress under the control of the other party. The system simply does not work without meeting opponents halfway, moderating demands, striking deals—in other words, compromise. And this is not merely a quirk of today's politics. It is inherent in democratic rather than authoritarian government.

In religious circles, however, compromise has a bad odor. The adjective "uncompromising" tends to be regarded as complimentary. Numerous typologies of religious groups, from the classic delineation of Max Weber and Ernst Troelsch between "church" and "sect," to the widely influential cultural delineation of H. Richard Niebuhr (from opposition to accommodation to the culture) illustrate the point. At one end of the religious spectrum are the purists (sects), who separate themselves from the secular culture, demanding rigid conformity from believers and refusing to compromise with "the world." At the other end are those who accommodate to the culture, who make themselves at home in the world, who are perceived by the purists as "compromisers."

Contemporary evangelical movements, with their emphasis on biblical authority, have tended to shift the center of gravity in American religion toward the more conservative, sectarian, uncompromising end of the scale. It is worth noting, however, that the modern-day religious polarization has also brought into play a group of activist liberal church leaders who have been equally uncompromising in their insistence on particular programs of social and political action. They have, indeed, sought to lead mainline churches into radical positions of no compromise on such issues as opposition to nuclear weapons, the sanctuary movement, or support for Nicaraguan Sandinistas. From both ends of the political spectrum, then, and in the very period when religion has entered most vigorously into public affairs, compromise has been in ill repute.

The religious presidencies examined in this book have obviously compromised on a multitude of issues. No president can exercise leadership in a democracy without doing so. And vast numbers of middle-of-the-road religious people recognize the necessity. But activists at either end of the spectrum, who have opposed a particular president from the beginning, or have come to oppose him, or to support him less than wholeheartedly, have found the charge of "compromising principle" a convenient hook on which to hang opposition.

To the religious right, Carter's compromise in broadening the White House Conference on the Family to a White House Conference on Families, by responding to pressure from feminist and gay Democratic party constituency groups, was unacceptable. His compromise on abortion, which he personally opposed but presidentially supported in administering the law, was even more abhorrent. To some his appointments of large numbers of women and blacks to high positions was regarded as a compromise of quality to meet racial or gender quotas.

To the religious left, the climate of the Reagan presidency, in which end runs around congressional intent were encouraged in order to keep the cause of the Nicaraguan Contras alive, was a compromise of principle. And to the religious right—particularly the extremists—the slow progress of the pro-life, school-prayer social agenda reflected unacceptable compromise with moderates. It is precisely as a practitioner of the art of compromise that the influence of Chief of Staff Howard Baker was anathema to some of the Reagan revolution's most ardent supporters.

Beyond the perception of religious constituencies, Carter's use of the powers of incumbency for political purposes in his losing battle for reelection, and Reagan's use of the powers of office in circumventing law on behalf of the Nicaraguan Contras—to cite two common accusations—may have represented, even to nonreligionists, instances of compromise of moral principle. The question of how far to go in practicing the art of compromise in order to govern well—or succumbing to the temptation to compromise for political advantage—will always be a particularly acute one for religious presidents. Retaining the support of religious constituencies is a key issue for such presidents, and true believers (the religionists most likely to be motivated to political action) will always be keeping a sharp eye open for "compromise of principle."

Examination of the post-Watergate religious presidencies, then, has pointed to a number of "rocks and shoals." One is the danger that the convictions of a devoutly Christian president such as Carter, about such matters as sin, repentance, or sacrifice, might lead to politically negative consequences in a nation not generally so theologically oriented. Another concern is the question, raised about Carter but not about Reagan, as to whether a religious president can be "tough enough" to make the hard choices sometimes demanded. Another, applicable to all religious presidencies, relates to the question of compromise of principle.

No evidence has been discovered anywhere in this study that any of these is a disqualifying danger or concern. The personal beliefs and the ideological orientation of any president, whether religious or nonreligious, constitute an element in his or her qualifications, on the basis of which judgments will be made—by the electorate in advance and by history in retrospect. Based on an examination of the post-Watergate presidencies, the question as to whether strong personal religious conviction or strong influence from religious groups makes a presidency overly vulnerable to any of these dangers must be answered negatively. Even though the dangers are real, the strength or weakness of such presidencies must be found in their achievements, seen within the context of their times.

Similar Beliefs, Opposite Policies: the Polarization Factor

An intriguing puzzle is why Jimmy Carter and Ronald Reagan, both conscientious Christians, both evangelicals, presumably sharing much of the same basic belief structure, came out in such radically different places politically. Why did public policy, under these two religious presidencies, reflect opposite extremes of belief as to what is "right" for America?

All three of the post-Watergate presidents have been identified with the evangelical wing of Christianity. They have not been asked, nor should they be, to spell out in detail their personal religious creeds. But assuming that they accept classic evangelical Christian beliefs (as there is every evidence that they do), all three believe in a provident God who governs a moral universe. All three accept Jesus Christ as the Son of God and claim a personal relationship to him as "Savior." All three believe that God, as the Holy Spirit, is present and active in the world. All three regard the Bible as the "word of God" in the traditional Christian sense, authoritative in matters of faith and practice. All three accept the biblical imperative to obey the two "great commandments," to love God and fellow human beings. On these essentials of Christian belief, they probably differ very little.

The question of the relationship between such beliefs and public policy was not raised by the presidency of Gerald Ford, whose faith was intensely private and who was not publicly perceived as being particularly religious; he insisted that religion should stay out of government. But the contrast between the presidencies of Jimmy Carter and Ronald Reagan raises the question sharply. The back-to-back presidencies of liberal (in many ways) Democrat Carter and conservative Republican Reagan demonstrate that *social and political applications of religious belief systems are highly personal.* Even when motivated by deep religious convictions, they are still personal judgments as to the social and political implications. And even when backed by large religious constituencies, or embodied in majority votes by denominational conventions, they still represent nothing more than the collective religiously based personal judgments of the people making up those particular constituencies or denominations. Trouble arises with the certainty that particular political or social policies are God's will. Trouble is compounded when such certainty is used to justify trampling roughshod over the contrary convictions of others. Certainty about basic biblical or theological truths cannot be translated into certainty about human applications in the modern political and social arena.

There is simply no agreed-on "Christian position" or "Judeo-Christian position" or "religious position" on issues of modern public policy, except in the most general terms. Nearly all religious people can agree on the advocacy of peace, or justice, or freedom, but when it comes to specific implementing policies, disagreement is almost certain. This is a source of serious problems, in terms of the goal of contributing as religious persons to public discourse and policy. Contributions can be made from various religious perspectives to public discourse. But contributing to policy formulation requires broad consensus.

In American history there have been periods of widespread consensus which led to general agreement among most religious people regarding particular policies. But such a consensus is likely to be fragile (as was that which brought about Prohibition in 1919) or the product of a bitter struggle (as was the eventual consensus on the abolition of slavery). In periods of polarization, like the present, there is little or no religious consensus on matters of public policy.

A religious presidency in our times, then, may not be expected to bring a particular set of policies that will be supported by all religious Americans. Neither the insistently private faith of Ford, nor the highly public faith of Carter, nor the Reagan alliance with the religious right has rallied the American public to a single banner. And the reason lies not so much in the presidency as in religion itself. From the standpoint of some segment of the American religious community, each of these religious presidencies has not only been a failure but a mortal danger to "sound" religion. The quietism of the Ford approach, the unwillingness to have organized religion involved with organized government, is roundly denounced by most religious liberals. They consider the application of one's faith in the world, through seeking change in the social, economic, and political realm, to be the test of whether or not that faith is authentic and to be taken seriously. And they believe such application must be organized to be effective. "Private" religion, from their perspective, is a failure. In our times they have been increasingly joined in this latter conviction by religious conservatives.

But the special combination of theological conservatism and political liberalism that marked the Carter approach fared even worse with religious constituencies. Conservatives regarded him as a traitor. Particularly on the abortion issue but on other aspects of the conservative social agenda as well, he was viewed as weak and wishy-washy. Yet religious liberals, many of whose public policy positions he adopted, were put off by his evangelicalism and supported him lukewarmly. In the end he had the worst of both worlds in terms of meeting the expectations of religious constituencies in this polarized era.

The Reagan presidency's marriage of religious conservatism to the political right has brought the most direct and forceful entry of organized religious groups into the political arena in recent history. But it has brought angry reactions, not only from religious liberals, who reject the policies, but also from a number of conservatives, who still adhere to the strict separation position articulated so clearly by President Ford.

It has also revealed the minority status of the Moral "Majority." The religious right is a potent political force, but it does not have behind it the kind of general consensus that will enact its program into social policy for the nation.

Mainline religion, though beleaguered and declining, comes out of what was once a mainstream tradition. Some of the positions taken by its present bureaucratic leadership are on the fringes of political reality, marginal to today's mainstream concerns. It has within it moderating forces that may, in time, bring it back toward the center, where the American mainstream—politically, socially, and religiously—has historically found itself most comfortable. Meanwhile, however, the two wings are bitterly divided. A *New York Times* columnist in 1987 likened dialogue between polarized churches and church groups today to "a conversation between people speaking different languages and sitting in different rooms."

Hardly anyone of any religion, then, has supported all three recent religious presidencies. Those who have liked the religious style and the religiously motivated policies of one have rejected the others. But the failure of Ford, Carter, and Reagan to unite religious America for moral and spiritual renewal does not mean failure for the basic thrust. On the contrary. The fact that each partial failure has been followed by a fresh attempt from a new direction is a powerful indicator of the strength of the impulse.

The Morality Factor

Despite the polarization, there is a reasonable level of agreement on the need for moral renewal. Religious America—liberal mainline, evangelical, fundamentalist, Catholic, Protestant, Jewish, even Moslem and Moonie—is largely united in its awareness that the emptiness of the public square needs to be filled. And religious America is America. This country remains, as foreign observers and internal analysts agree, the most incorrigibly religious of nations, with astounding numbers of churchgoers, with moralists on every street corner, and with overwhelming majorities who believe in God and the Ten Commandments.

And despite many differences, there is much agreement across the religious spectrum on the kind of personal morality that ought to be exemplified in public life—a Ten Commandments kind of honesty, integrity, fidelity, and respect for life and property. It is in this realm that the effect of religion on recent presidencies can be most clearly seen.

It was a moral question that in the summer of 1987 ended Democratic front-runner Gary Hart's chances of winning his party's presidential nomination. His dalliance with model Donna Rice (who later capitalized on the affair with a series of blatant TV commercials for a product called No Excuses), their overnight trip to the Bahamas on a yacht incredibly named *Monkey Business*, the staked-out tryst in his Washington apartment while his wife was home in Colorado—all this was the stuff of soap opera.

When Hart dropped out of the presidential race at the time of the incident, during his months on the sidelines, and when he reentered the race at year's end, he maintained repeatedly that the affair was "not relevant" to his qualifications for the presidency. Those qualifications otherwise included undoubted intellectual brilliance, carefully worked-out positions on a number of major national issues, extensive political experience, and a claim to fresh ideas. He apparently hoped that the affair would blow over, maintaining that the morality of his personal life was no one else's business.

But he was probably wrong. If there was ever a time when the moral character, integrity, and basic fidelity of a candidate were "not relevant" to presidential qualifications, that time was not the last quarter of the twentieth century. The public has on occasion forgiven the peccadillos (which have usually come to light long after the fact) of presidents already elected—especially if the president's place in public affection was already firmly fixed. But it has not readily overlooked questionable conduct on the part of as-yet-unelected candidates. As Senator Edward Kennedy has had reason to conclude, the electorate has a long memory when it comes to incidents related to the personal morality of potential presidents. This is a period when personal and public probity are far more pervasive underlying concerns—especially with reference to the presidency—than conventional analyses of political and public life have generally recognized.

In the end no issue is more central to the presidential role, in the complex relationship of church and state, and of religion and society, than that of presidential character. In the fall of 1987, following the temporary departure of former Senator Gary Hart from the ranks of Democratic presidential contenders over the question of his "womanizing," and that of Senator Joseph Biden following charges of plagiarism in speeches and falsification of his academic record, "the character issue" became a media cliché.

Wrote *Washington Post* columnist Jonathan Yardley, "Washington has discovered 'character' much as Sutter discovered gold: Eureka! From every nook and cranny prospectors now emerge, each determined to stake his or her claim on the politically vendible product called 'character.' " Yardley's treatment of the newly popular character issue was somewhat cynical. "It is no oversimplification," he went on, "to say that in Washington or wherever else two or more politicians may gather together, he who does not get caught has 'character' and he who gets caught has none." He was right, however, in identifying it as a striking phenomenon of the early stages of the 1988 presidential campaign.

Commentators at the time tended to regard the character issue as a creation of the media. Most political pundits appeared to assume that failings like those of Hart and Biden were common to all political figures, and that it was only the media attention and the temporary popularity of the character issue that had trapped the two. Hart's political difficulties were blamed on *Miami Herald* reporters who staked out his Washington town house while he entertained model Donna Rice there. Scapegoats for the Biden fall were two members of the campaign staff of Massachusetts Governor Michael Dukakis, who had distributed video clips to newspapers and a TV network. Media analysts engaged in endless navel-gazing over whether discovering and reporting such candidate lapses was "responsible journalism."

The media furor seemed to bear out the prescient observation of Duke University Professor James David Barber regarding the post-Watergate climate: "If enough people become moralistic enough, the President-choosing process can transform itself into a national goodness contest, in which the political meanings fade out as the electoral light searches for a spotless lamb."

Those of the media and the "new class" who seized on the emergence of the character issue in the 1988 campaign as the latest seven-day wonder, underestimated its real significance. It was not a creation of the media but a deeply felt concern of the American people. It was not a product of the Hart and Biden incidents but a far deeper groundswell present as a significant undertone factor in American political life since Vietnam, Watergate, and the turmoil of the sixties. As a *New York Times* editorial pointed out, what had been spread about aspiring candidates was not vicious lies but "the vicious truth."

Further, media treatments of the character issue probably erred in the suggestion that concern about the morality of potential presidents was diverting attention from the "real issues" of political programs and philosophy. Assumptions about basic honesty, integrity, and morality—the conviction that a president can be trusted—must underlie campaign debates about policy, programs, and proposals. It is only in times when presidential character cannot be taken for granted that it rises to the surface as a subject of explicit examination. But character is the starting point in the process of president selecting.

The character issue was not, as media pundits seemed to think, a passing fad, soon to be replaced by another headline grabber. Underlying much that has happened in presidential politics since Vietnam, Watergate, and the turmoil of the sixties has been this concern. The character issue destroyed President Nixon. It was compounded by the Agnew debacle, which preceded his own resignation and pardon. But ultimately he was rejected not so much over legal technicalities of obstruction of justice as over the conclusion of the American people that he simply could not be trusted. It was the character issue, positively construed, that snatched Congressman Gerald Ford out of the quiet retirement he was then contemplating and placed him in the presidency Nixon had vacated. The character issue was a key factor in the election of Jimmy Carter. It brokered the marriage of the "Moralistic Right" and the "Market Right" (to use Burns's terms), which swept Ronald Reagan into office. It is here to stay, until the moral vacuum in public life that has so deeply disturbed Americans of all religions is filled.

The condition of moral crisis in which America has perceived itself to be since Watergate has not been resolved. President Ford clearly was a man of integrity, but he was too closely associated with his predecessor, by whom he was selected and whose pardon he granted. President Carter's moral character was unquestioned, but he was rejected by the very group calling most strongly for moral renewal—the religious right—and the image of weakness and vacillation became too strong to overcome. President Reagan, whose cause was that of the morality-conscious religious right, seemed initially to be moving the country out of its sense of moral crisis. At the end of his first term it appeared to have been countered by the widespread sense that "the pride is back." But large numbers were still concerned about the deeper moral vacuum, the nakedness of the public square. And the Wall Street scandals of the second term, the "sleaze" surrounding certain presidential subordinates that brought an unprecedented number of independent investigations, and especially the Iran/Contra affair of 1986 and 1987, brought it back.

As long as the sense of moral crisis continues, presidential character will remain a major issue in national politics. It is seldom a dominant issue, as it was in the immediate post-Watergate period. But it is a major "undertone issue," which can never in itself elect a candidate but can readily defeat one.

At the time of the Gary Hart affair, during the primary phase of the 1988 presidential campaign, a column in the *Boston Globe* was titled "The Issue Is Not Morality but Integrity." Many secular intellectuals have struggled, as did Hart himself, to separate the "integrity" of his political positions from the "morality" of his relationships with women. Similarly, when borrowed material in the speeches of Senator Joseph Biden was perceived as plagiarism, members of a television panel maintained that the plagiarism did not affect his basic "integrity." Yet the panel unanimously agreed that he was finished as a candidate—as turned out to be the case.

And for Americans, character cannot be separated from religiously grounded morality. The ubiquity of the term "moral character" in ordinary discourse indicates the extent to which "moral" and "character" go together in the American mind. Morality—which for most Americans is religiously derived—and character are inseparable.

Character is obviously a complex concept, with multiple meanings and many dimensions. Professor Barber's book on "the presidential character," mentioned above, dealt with it on a much broader basis than the moral alone. Certainly it may be understood as including various traits without direct moral implications—wisdom, courage, steadfastness, tenacity. But at its heart, in the understanding of the American people, is "*moral* character." And in the understanding of the American people, moral character is religiously formed. Surely this is the reason, at least in part, for the strong religious dimension of all post-Watergate presidents, and the reason presidential religion will continue to be a matter of considerable interest to the public.

Summarizing Some Conclusions

An examination of the religious dimension of recent presidencies points to some fairly clear conclusions:

First, the religious aspect of these presidencies can only be understood in historical context. The United States remains, as it has been from the beginning, an uncommonly religious society, but one with an uncommon level of religious diversity. It has responded by developing a unique system of separation of church and state, which has erected a legal wall between the institutional churches and official organs of government while at the same time recognizing and encouraging the special role of religion in the society, as symbolized by the motto "In God We Trust." Americans have looked in complete freedom to their various churches, faith groups, and denominations for the *saving faith* required to meet their personal and corporate needs while recognizing substantial agreement on the *ordering faith* that has undergirded national life.

Through two hundred years of history, presidents have symbolized, and in some cases defined, the civil religion or public faith that has held this diverse society together. A "gentleman's agreement" has kept the denominational religion of presidents conventionally temperate, unobtrusive, and out of the public view. But with the turbulence of the sixties and the moral crises of Vietnam and Watergate, all that changed. In post-Watergate presidencies, religion has played a highly visible and strongly influential role.

Second, the prominence of religion in recent presidencies has not been accidental. This much seems clear from our entire study. Religion has spoken to the special needs and conditions of the times. Religion itself has rarely been an object of political debate. Rather, it has been a matter of climate, of motivation, of context. But in each case the presidential religion has spoken to underlying moral factors and needs.

Religion remains a "sleeper" issue in connection with the presidency. It is seldom mentioned (except subliminally) in the TV ads or introduced as a topic for discussion. It was John Kennedy himself—not the Protestants who were concerned about it—who brought the religious issue out into the open in the 1960 campaign. No one, until Pat Robertson, ever ran as the candidate of a religious group, and he, of course, downplayed that identification. But for some time religion has been, and for the immediate future is likely to remain, a matter of major underlying concern.

And the reasons are evident. First, there is a widespread sense that secularization of the society has gone too far. Despite the veneer overlaid on American society by the dominance of the new class in the media, the arts, and the governing establishment, every empirical indicator points to continued widespread religious faith in the people as a whole. The growth of an organized religious movement on the political right has been only the tip of a far larger iceberg.

A second reason is that the moral unease brought to the forefront by the turmoil of the sixties, Vietnam, and Watergate has not subsided. The moral emphasis of the religious right is once again a signal of a far larger concern. The prominence of religion in the three most recent presidencies is but the foremost among many signs that the moral concern remains strong. The absence of a common moral foundation is widely recognized, and no one has clear answers. But America continues to seek its moral bearings, as it always has, in religion. The prominent role of religion in post-Watergate presidencies has not been accidental.

Third, the prominent role of religion in these presidencies has not violated the principle of separation of church and state. Both Carter and Reagan have skirted certain dangers. Carter, as a devout Southern Baptist evangelical seeking to live what was for him a normal church life in the White House, created a sectarian image that threatened in some quarters his unifying role as symbol of the common public faith. Reagan, in pushing to place governmental authority behind the social program of the religious right without the backing of a national consensus, came close to threatening the religious freedoms of those who oppose such policies. But neither presidency actually violated the principle, and both (particularly Carter, but Reagan to some extent) demonstrated the importance of a strong personal commitment to one of America's various saving faiths, along with the unity of the ordering faith, as a basis for moral and spiritual vitality in the public realm.

The candidacy of one clearly identified with a religious bloc of political activists, such as Pat Robertson, points to an even greater danger to the separation principle. In the event of such a presidency, separation would become a far more overt issue than has been the case thus far. Such a presidency would probably be held within technical bounds of the separation principle by the strength of American commitment to it. But the limits would be tested.

Fourth, religious presidencies have brought some minuses as well as some pluses. In certain identifiable ways Carter's presidency was probably handicapped or weakened by his deep religious faith. The sense of national malaise on the part of one who sees human sin as inevitable, and humility as the appropriate response, is theologically accurate. But it is politically treacherous, and perhaps even dangerous. Similarly, the ethical awareness which weighed carefully the moral ambiguities of policy decisions did not present what Americans usually perceive as strong and decisive leadership. But against these minuses must be weighed some morally admirable achievements, which had not come from previous, less religiously committed presidencies, and a period in which presidential moral character was above reproach.

The essentially nonchurched personal faith of Ronald Reagan is undoubtedly genuine and to be respected, as is the moral fervor of the religious right, the views of which he shares. Perhaps the major flaw in the religious dimension of his presidency was the opposite of Carter's: too little rather than too much ethical discrimination; not enough awareness of moral ambiguities. The religiously rooted commitment to freedom was deep and authentic, but it translated at times into a troublesome kind of uncritical anticommunism. The Iran/Contra affair perhaps epitomized the lack of moral sensitivity that marked certain aspects of the presidency. While Reagan himself should be taken at his word that he was personally unaware of what was going on, a White House climate that encourages deceit, falsehood, and the breaking of rules (and perhaps laws), in pursuing a *moral* crusade, was one for which the presidency itself bore ultimate responsibility. But the restoring of freedom to its historic importance in America, as a religiously derived moral value, was a significant achievement. So also, from the traditional religious perspective, was the strengthening of the public role of religious constituencies through the "mainstreaming" of conservative religion.

In neither presidency was the religious dimension an unqualified plus or minus; in both it was a major factor. There is no reason to believe that the negatives, for a religious president, outweigh the positives. And for these times, clearly the electorate has judged the positives to be more important.

Fifth, a major factor in weighing the religious dimension of contemporary presidencies is the polarized state of American religion. The anomaly of radically different religiously motivated programs led by theologically similar Christian evangelicals Carter and Reagan, and the fact that neither succeeded in mobilizing religious America behind his program, reflected no failure of intent or effort. It reflected rather the depth of division between left and right on the current religious scene. Presidents cannot impose unity of moral policy in the absence of consensus. And such consensus will continue to be elusive until religious groups themselves overcome their polarization. But the persistence of the effort bespeaks its urgency. Presidents, historically and necessarily, symbolize the unity of the ordering faith on which the nation is based, even in times when the saving faiths are bitterly divided.

Finally, the moral issues which underlay the religious dimensions of recent presidencies remain compelling. The prominence of the "character issue" in the early stages of the 1988 presidential campaign was not a media creation but a sign of the times. The nakedness of the public square is a many-faceted concern, but one inescapable dimension is a demand for a certain level of personal morality in public life. Whatever distinctions may be drawn by secularists between personal "morality" and political "integrity," the distinction is meaningless to the public. This is a period in which personal morality will continue to be a central issue—an undertone issue rather than a policy issue, true, but a central one nevertheless—in choosing and judging presidents.

As long as moral questions continue to be asked, religious answers will be sought. American society's experiments with values divorced from religion have not been encouraging. Despite the complex reasoning of secular ethicists, Americans by and large remain convinced that morality and religion are inseparable. And as long as that remains the case, religion is likely to play a continuing role in the presidency, and the presidency in religion.

Possibilities for the Future Presidential Role

It has become fashionable to speak of the rising tide of concern about the naked public square in terms of a battle between "separationists," who want to erect a high wall between church and state, and "accommodationists," who are portrayed as seeking to breach such a wall by allowing certain relationships and accommodations between church and state. Such labels, which tend to come from the secular new class, obscure the basic issue.

Separation of institutional church from institutional state is a firmly established principle, accepted by all. But the late twentieth-century tendency to broaden the principle of separation of church and state, to include the separation of religion and society as well, is a new constitutional reading. It is this reinterpretation of traditional separationism that those concerned with the moral undergirding of society are questioning.

The presidency has rightly become a focal point of this struggle, for the changes sought are not legislative. They are changes in symbol, in tone, in moral context. Neither the Ford nor the Carter nor the Reagan presidency has succeeded in bringing divided religious America together and reestablishing a common moral foundation. Yet the quest remains a promising one. The presidency continues to be the one place in which the immensely important undertone issue of religiously based public morality can have a significant effect. This is true in two ways.

First, the presidency can exhibit the vital role of the various denominational religions in American life. Moral strength comes not from watered-down general principles but from deeply held personal faith. It comes from people who are strongly committed to what they believe, even though those beliefs differ from denomination to denomination. A Gerald Ford with a lifelong loyalty to the Episcopal church and a Sunday School-teaching Southern Baptist Jimmy Carter, who at the same time demonstrate their commitment (not in addition to but as *part of* that denominational faith) to the American principle of religious freedom and mutual respect, are far better models of the traditional American system than a president to whom religion is a peripheral concern, who "happens to be" Episcopalian or Baptist.

Even a Ronald Reagan, with no particular denominational commitment and a rather generalized system of belief, comes down firmly and forthrightly on specific religious beliefs (some of them controversial) to which he is strongly committed. His is a general and nondenominational, but not a namby-pamby, faith.

It is not enough for a president to be a proponent of "civil religion." Such a position is not even true to the essence of American civil religion itself. Civil religion makes no claim to be a "religion" in the sense of meeting personal human needs. A president can authentically lead and articulate the ordering function of a civil religion—and particularly its public moral function so persistently sought today—only from the firm base of a personal faith commitment. The three religious presidencies of the post-Watergate period, and particularly the denominational commitments of Ford and Carter, have modeled well this aspect of the religious function of the presidency.

Symbol of Unity

But the presidency also symbolizes the unity which accompanies and underlies the particularity when the system is working properly. This is the civil religion role of the president. Civil religion is the bridge between an often-divided denominational society and a single, consensually supported government. Ideally the president, as the central symbol, unites all religious constituencies in their commitment to the American proposition. Said James David Barber in *The Presidential Character*, "The President is a symbolic leader, the one figure who draws together the people's hopes and fears for the political future. On top of all his routine duties he has to carry that off—or fail."

The roadblock for recent presidencies has lain not so much in personal attitudes and performance, and not even in the modest growth of that small segment of the society which lies outside the Judeo-Christian tradition, but in the religious polarization of the Judeo-Christian majority. The bitterest divisions have been within Protestantism, but each side of the Protestant polarization has found allies within the Jewish and Catholic communities.

And, ironically, the conflicting goals over which they have most bitterly divided have not been matters of faith, but the applications of faith in public life: such matters as the legalization or constitutional prohibiton of abortion, support or opposition to the Sandinista regime in Nicaragua. Religious Americans are willing to allow other denominations to follow their differing beliefs within their own faith communities, but not to seize the high ground in public life for policies with which they disagree. In matters of inner denominational faith it is "live and let live," but in the division over public policy it is a no-quarter-given struggle for victory. How much of this bloody battling for victory between different religious factions can the system of religious freedom survive? The question is an open one.

In the end it is a matter that America's religions must resolve for themselves. What is at stake for them is not just particular policies zealously advocated in the political context of the day, but the very system under which multiple religions have flourished. It has been not only their diversity, but their unity, the ability of America's religions to support a common ordering faith, that has characterized this unique system of religious liberty. Peaceful diversity requires the civility of mutual respect and support, and this the religious groups must find a way to recover.

The problem is the same one the founders faced: that of finding, in the midst of a startling diversity of saving faiths, a common ordering faith on which national life can be based. It is complicated in modern times by the fact that pluralism has become more diverse (though not as impossibly so as some have perceived it to be) while at the same time those groups that make up the Judeo-Christian core have become extraordinarily polarized. The new prominence of religion in the presidency, the symbolic heart of American public life, has reflected both the continuing concern for a common religious base and the intensified pluralism.

Today, as originally, the answer does not lie in a watered-down common religion offered in the place of multiple denominational religions. Americans take their religion, as well as their personal freedom, too seriously to be tempted by such a basically antireligious solution. The strength of the American system has been not only the mutual respect and core of agreement of its ordering faith, but the vitality of its denominational religions.

The beginning of the third century of national history brings a new set of moral challenges. Americans experience a different kind of society with an enlarged religious pluralism, and they face a future quite unlike that faced by the eighteenth-century founders. But the task is the same. A creative combination of religious diversity with an ordering unity still lies at the heart of the American experiment.

From the beginning America has welcomed and made a place for adherents of non-Judeo-Christian religions, and as well for atheists and agnostics who claim no religion at all. These few who have not shared the central religious vision have embraced the "liberty and justice for all" of the American dream on its own terms. They have adopted the society's value system even while rejecting its Judeo-Christian roots. Indeed, the recent immigration of waves of non-Judeo-Christians to the American shores has been in considerable measure a response to the beacon call of such values. Each new immigrant, gladly and voluntarily, pledges allegiance to this "one nation under God, with liberty and justice for all." The denuding of the public square destroys the very values, underlying this society, which have attracted them in such numbers.

Public attention focused on the small minority of counterculturists drawn to sects, cults, and Eastern religions in the sixties and seventies vastly exaggerated the shape of American religious pluralism. An overwhelming majority of Americans, including many who are no longer active in institutional religions but who still adhere to the values, are in the Judeo-Christian tradition. The unbelieving or dissenting minority are at home and continue to be welcome in a society which has never imposed religious tests and has always been open (and for *religious reasons*) to every variety of belief and nonbelief. But the country they have chosen is dependent on that Judeo-Christian tradition for the very openness, inclusiveness, and liberty and justice for all that attracted them. The alternative of a totally secular society, with no public philosophy ordering its values, is desired by very few.

The challenge for today's broadened pluralism is that of inviting adherents of non-Judeo-Christian religions to enter into the ongoing dialogue on the God in whom the nation trusts, the liberty and justice for all, the quest for domestic and international peace, and the personal and public morality with which that God has endowed us, enriching the Judeo-Christian base with their additional insights.

The alternative to religious freedom with which the founders flirted was a kind of multiple established church, which would have given official government support to all (or at least most) religions.

The alternative with which the contemporary new class has flirted is a totally secular society. Ruling elites of government, academia, and the media, while not "messing" with the coinage, have sought, in effect, to eliminate "In God We Trust" from its place in the national consciousness.

They have failed. The widespread turn toward more traditional values, the underlying winds of change through the religious communities, and the gathering forces of moral renewal signal a change of direction. America is not willing to become a secular society. It remains insistently religious in its outlook. And there is no surer evidence than the religious presidencies of the post-Watergate era.

Presidents today can sound the unifying themes of civil religion, as all three post-Watergate presidents, like their predecessors in office, have done. They cannot undo the divisions in present-day religious America. But as the preeminent symbol of unity, the presidency can continually demonstrate that such unity is not only compatible with, but is called for by, the denominational faiths of the republic.

Notes

In the following notes, the page on which each entry appears or begins is found preceding each entry.

Chapter 1

4 Wooten quotation: James Wooten, *Dasher: The Roots and the Rising of Jimmy Carter* (New York: Summit Books, 1978), pp. 26–27.

Chapter 2

12 Major sources for material in this chapter include Martin E. Marty, *Pilgrims in Their Own Land* (Boston: Little Brown and Co., 1984); Sidney E. Ahlstrom, *A Religious History of the American People* (New Haven: Yale University Press, 1972); A. James Reichley, *Religion in American Public Life* (Washington: The Brookings Institution, 1985); Sidney E. Mead, *The Lively Experiment: The Shaping of Christianity in America* (New York: Harper and Row, 1963); William Lee Miller, *The First Liberty: Religion and the American Republic* (New York: Alfred A. Knopf, 1986); Patricia U. Bonomi, *Under the Cope of Heaven: Religion, Society and Politics in Colonial America* (New York: Oxford University Press, 1986); John P. Diggins, *The Lost Soul of American Politics* (New York: Basic Books, Inc., 1984), and John Courtney Murray, *We Hold These Truths: Catholic Reflections on the American Proposition* (New York: Sheed and Ward, 1960).

14 Churches in the middle colonies: Bonomi, p. 81.

15 Roger Williams: Quoted by Marty, *Pilgrims in Their Own Land*, pp. 77–78.

15 Anglican rector: James de Gignillat to the Secretary, Society for the

Propagation of the Gospel, Goose Creek, S.C., July 15, 1711, quoted by Bonomi, p. 58.

16 Marty quotation: *Pilgrims in Their Own Land*, p. 109.

17 Ahlstrom quotation: *Religious History*, p. 134.

18 Niebuhr on Deism and Calvinism: Reinhold Niebuhr, *The Irony of American History* (New York: Charles Scribner's Sons, 1952), pp. 23–24; Similarly, John P. Diggins, in *The Lost Soul of American Politics*, finds the basis of American democracy in a combination of "liberalism" and Calvinism.

18 Calvinist destiny: Niebuhr, *Irony*, p. 24.

18 Early presidents and checks and balances: Diggins, pp. 7–9, 67, 71ff.

19 Jefferson quotation: From *Notes on the State of Virginia; Written in 1781 . . . [and] . . . 1782*, first published in Paris in 1785, quoted by Mead, *Lively Experiment*, p. 59.

19 Washington's prayers: Peter Marshall and David Manual, *The Light and the Glory: Did God Have a Plan for America?* (Old Tappan, N.J.: Fleming H. Revell Co., 1977), pp. 284–85.

20 John Courtney Murray: *We Hold These Truths*, p. 36.

20 Murray on pluralism: p. 27.

21 Jefferson on freedom of religion: Miller, *The First Liberty*, p. 10. Much of this account of the Virginia debates is based on Miller's treatment.

22 Taxpayer determination of denomination to support: West Germany has a somewhat similar system at the present time.

24 Miller quotation: *The First Liberty*, p. 344.

24 Marty quotation: *Pilgrims in Their Own Land*, pp. 220–21; see also Reichley, pp. 101–06, on the belief of the founding fathers that public order must be undergirded by religion.

24 Miller quotation: *The First Liberty*, p. 208.

26 Denominationalism and free enterprise: Marty, *Pilgrims in Their Own Land*, pp. 108–28, 169ff.

27 Alexis de Tocqueville, *Democracy in America*, 1835, quoted in Ahlstrom, p. 386.

28 Bellah quotation: Robert N. Bellah, "Civil Religion in America," *Daedalus*, 96:1, Winter, 1967, pp. 1–21.

28 Miller quotation: *The First Liberty*, pp. 237–38.

29 Will Herberg, *Protestant-Catholic-Jew: An Essay in American Religious Sociology* (New York: Doubleday and Company, 1955); Marty, in *Pilgrims in Their Own Land*, discusses at length the replacement of the Protestant consensus by the Protestant-Catholic-Jew paradigm, pp. 417–49.

30 For varying labels and views on civil religion, see Russell E. Ritchey and Donald G. Jones, eds., *American Civil Religion* (New York: Harper and Row, 1974); John F. Wilson, *Public Religion in American Culture* (Philadelphia: Temple University Press, 1979); Robert S. Alley, *So Help Me God* (Atlanta: John Knox Press, 1972), pp. 13–28; Sidney E. Mead, *The Nation with the Soul of a Church* (New

York: Harper and Row, 1975); Robert Booth Fowler, *Religion and Politics in American Life* (Metuchen, N.J.: The Scarecrow Press, 1985), p. 31ff.; Martin E. Marty, *The Public Church: Mainline-Evangelical-Catholic* (New York: Crossroads Publishing Co., 1981), and Richard John Neuhaus, *The Naked Public Square: Religion and Democracy in America* (Grand Rapids, Mich.: William B. Eerdmans Publishing Co., 1984), also make significant contributions to the debate.

31 Ordering faith and saving faith: Martin E. Marty, "A Sort of Republican Banquet," in Robert W. Lovin, ed., *Religion and American Public Life* (New York: Paulist Press, 1986), pp. 146–180. See also Marty's *Pilgrims in Their Own Land*, pp. 220–21.

32 Presidents and civil religion: Robert S. Alley, in *So Help Me God*, maintains that civil religion has no consistent identity except as a function of the presidential will, p. 24.

33 Presidents and religious fervor: Wilson, *Public Religion in American Culture*, p. 45.

34 Kennedy: Berton Dulce and Edward J. Richter, *Religion and the Presidency* (New York: Macmillan Publishing Co., 1962), deals with "the religious issue" (anti-Catholicism), a factor in one out of three elections throughout American history, the authors suggest, and a major factor in the Kennedy campaign.

Chapter 3

35 Motto on coins: John McCollister, "*. . . so help me God." The Faith of America's Presidents* (Bloomington, Minn.: Landmark Books, 1982), p. 122.

37 Washington to New Church: Quoted in Norman Cousins, *In God We Trust* (New York: Harper and Brothers, 1958), p. 62.

37 Washington's letters: Quoted in Cousins, pp. 56–63.

38 First inaugural: Quoted in Cousins, p. 66.

39 Jefferson's proposal of professorships for sects: Berton Dulce and Edward J. Richter, *Religion and the Presidency* (New York: Macmillan Publishing Co., 1962), p. 10, quoting from Anson Phelps Stokes, *Church and State in the United States* (New York: Harper and Brothers, 1950), p. 338.

39 Jefferson's *Life and Morals of Jesus*: Quoted in McCollister, "*. . . so help me God.*"

39 Madison and family worship: Bonomi, *Under the Cope of Heaven*, p. 101.

40 Marty quotation: *Pilgrims in Their Own Land*, p. 220.

41 Lincoln on nonchurch membership: Carl Sandburg, "Introduction," *Lincoln's Devotional* (Great Neck, N.Y.: Channel Press, 1957), p. xiii.

42 Lincoln on the Declaration of Independence: *The Collected Works of Abraham Lincoln*, Roy P. Basler, ed. (New Brunswick, N.J.:

Rutgers University Press, 1953), vol. II, p. 276; quoted by Diggins, *Lost Soul of American Politics*, p. 303.

42 Lincoln on sinful human nature: Mead, *Lively Experiment*, p. 84.

42 Original sin of slavery: Diggins, p. 296.

42 North and South, same God: Quoted by Marty, *Pilgrims*, p. 224.

43 Julia Ward Howe, *Reminiscences, 1819–1899* (Boston: 1899), pp. 269–76, stanzas 2 and 3 in original draft, quoted in Ahlstrom, *Religious History of the American People*, p. 671.

43 Lincoln on the will of God: Marty, *Pilgrims*, p. 224.

43 Alley quotation: *So Help Me God*, p. 126.

45 Mead quotation: *Lively Experiment*, p. 134.

45 Schaff quotation: "Church and State in the United States," *Papers of the American Historical Society*, vol. II, no. 4, New York, 1888, p. 6; quoted in Wilson, *Public Religion in American Culture*, p. 13.

46 Lyman Abbott: quoted by Robert T. Handy, *A Christian America: Protestant Hopes and Historical Realities* (New York: Oxford University Press, 1971), p. 190. The crusading spirit of American Protestantism is a major theme of Handy's book.

46 Wilson on sin in the world: Woodrow Wilson, "The Bible and Progress," May 7, 1911, Roy Stannard Baker and William E. Dodds, eds., *The Public Papers of Woodrow Wilson*, 6 vols., New York, 1925–27, vol. II, p. 294, quoted by Diggins, *The Lost Soul of American Politics*, p. 345.

46 Peace as triumph of right: quoted from the Letters and Papers of Woodrow Wilson, Woodrow Wilson Collection, Firestone Library, Princeton University, by Alley, *So Help Me God*, p. 33.

47 Speech to Senate: Baker and Dodds, eds., *The Public Papers of Woodrow Wilson*, vol. V, pp. 551–52, quoted by Handy, p. 185.

47 Fools resist Providence: McCollister, p. 130

48 Second disestablishment: Handy, p. 190.

49 Satolli speech: Marty, *Pilgrims*, p. 283.

50 Roosevelt quotation: *Wartime Correspondence Between President Roosevelt and Pope Pius XII*, Myron C. Taylor, ed. (New York: Macmillan Publishing Co., 1947), p. 18.

50 Truman: quoted by Alley, *So Help Me God*, pp. 78–79.

50 Eisenhower intensely religious: Marty, *Pilgrims*, p. 405.

51 William Lee Miller, *Piety Along the Potomac* (Boston: Houghton Mifflin, 1964).

51 Wilson quotation: *Public Religion in American Culture*, p. 45.

51 Marty quotation: *Pilgrims*, p. 405.

51 California billboards: Miller, *Piety Along the Potomac*, p. 19.

52 Sorensen quotation: Theodore Sorensen, *Kennedy* (New York: Harper and Row, 1965), p. 19.

52 Wicker quotation: Tom Wicker, *JFK and LBJ: The Influence of Personality upon Politics* (New York: William Morrow and Co., 1968),

p. 124. Both this observation and that of Sorensen are quoted by Alley, *So Help Me God*, pp. 95 and 101.

53 Kennedy "not the Catholic candidate": *New York Herald Tribune*, April 22, 1960, quoted by Berton Dulce and Edward J. Richter, *Religion and the Presidency*.

53 Miller quotation: William Lee Miller, *The First Liberty*, p. 286.

53 Kennedy to Texas Baptists: Quoted in McCollister, p. 166.

54 Alley quotation: *So Help Me God*, p. 94.

56 Most of the presidential religious trivia reported here comes from McCollister.

57 Fersh study: Seymour H. Fersh, *The View from the White House* (Washington, D.C.: 1961), cited in Wilson, *Public Religion*, p. 54ff.

58 Rituals of civil religion: this summary is based on Wilson, *Public Religion*, pp. 56–63, who draws heavily from *A Compilation of Messages and Papers of the Presidents*, James D. Richardson, ed., 20 vols., New York, p. 1897ff.

Chapter 4

60 Sects and cults: David G. Bromley and Anson D. Shupe, *Strange Gods: The Great American Cult Scare* (Boston: Beacon Press, 1981), provides a good overview of the cults of the period.

61 Harvey Cox: See *The Secular City* (New York: Macmillan Publishing Co., 1965).

61 Milovan Djilas, *The New Class* (New York: Praeger, 1957).

61 Herman Kahn and Anthony J. Wiener, *The Year 2000—A Framework for Speculation on the Next Thirty-three Years* (New York: Macmillan Publishing Co., 1967), p. 7 (table 1), cited by Peter L. Berger, *A Rumor of Angels* (Garden City, N.Y.: Doubleday and Co., 1969), p. 1.

61 Wilson quotation: *Public Religion in American Culture*, p. 17.

62 *New Rules*: New York: Random House, 1981.

62 *Habits of the Heart*: Berkeley, Cal.: University of California Press, 1985. The self-fulfillment value system of the "humanistic psychology" developed by Maslow, Rogers, Fromm, and others is treated in the author's doctoral dissertation, *An Examination of the Value System Reflected by the Sensitivity and Encounter Group Movement in Adult Education, 1950–1970*, The American University, Washington, D.C., 1971.

64 John J. O'Connor, *A Chaplain Looks at Vietnam* (Cleveland: World Publishing Co., 1968).

64 Dwight D. Eisenhower, *Crusade in Europe* (Garden City, N.Y.: Garden City Books, 1948), p. 60, quoted by David Eisenhower, *Eisenhower at War 1943–1945* (New York: Random House, 1986), p. 175.

68 Membership statistics from *Yearbook of American Churches*, 1969

and 1979, and *Yearbook of American and Canadian Churches*, 1986, Constant H. Jaquet, ed. (New York: National Council of Churches).

76 Public and private Protestants: Martin E. Marty, *Righteous Empire: The Protestant Experience in America* (New York: Dial Press, 1970), p. 177ff.

76 Sociopolitical involvement: See, for instance, Dean Hoge, *Division in the Protestant House* (Philadelphia: Westminister Press, 1976).

76 The contrasting "Christian programs" of right and left are discussed in the author's article "Will the Real Christian Program Please Stand Up?" *The Christian Century*, October 7, 1981, 98:31, pp. 994–97.

77 Falwell quotation: Jerry Falwell, "An Agenda for the Eighties," in Jerry Falwell, ed., with Ed Dobson and Ed Hinson, *The Fundamentalist Phenomenon: The Resurgence of Conservative Christianity* (Garden City, N.Y.: Doubleday-Galilee, 1981), p. 188.

78 Bonhoeffer quotation: Eberhard Bethge, *Dietrich Bonhoeffer*, Eric Mosbacker, trans. Erwin Robertson, ed. (New York: Harper and Row, 1970), pp. 118–19.

79 Statistics: Everett Carl Ladd, "Religious and Secular America," in Richard John Neuhaus, ed., *Unsecular America* (Grand Rapids, Mich.: Eerdmans Publishing Co., 1986), pp. 20–22 and appendix, pp. 115–58; and Fowler, *Religion and Politics*, pp. 1–4.

79 Furio Colombo, *God in America: Religion and Politics in the United States* (New York: Columbia University Press, 1984), p. ix.

Chapter 5

81 Religious inaugural observances: Niels E. Nelson, Jr., *The Religion of President Carter* (Nashville: Thomas Nelson, Inc., 1977), p. 71.

82 Buchanan quotations: Interview with Mr. Patrick J. Buchanan, June 2, 1987.

82 East Room church services: McCollister, ". . . *so help me God,*" pp. 178–79.

83 Nixon and Key Biscayne church: Interview with Dr. John Huffman, June 11, 1987.

88 Marty quotation: *Pilgrims in Their Own Land*, p. 221. This book gives an extensive account of the history of the quest.

89 Wall quotation: Interview with Dr. James M. Wall, May 15, 1987. Other quotations from Dr. Wall in this chapter come from the same interview.

90 Richard John Neuhaus, *The Naked Public Square* (Grand Rapids, Mich.: William B. Eerdmans Publishing Co., 1984).

90 A. James Reichley, *Religion in American Public Life* (Washington, D.C.: The Brookings Institution, 1985), p. 359.

90 Allan Bloom, *The Closing of the American Mind* (New York: Simon and Schuster, 1987).

92 Ford quotation: Interview with President Gerald R. Ford, Vail, Col., August 21, 1987. Quotations from President Ford in the remainder of this chapter, unless otherwise identified, are from this interview.
92 Sunday as family day: Gerald R. Ford, *A Time to Heal* (New York: Harper and Row/Reader's Digest, 1979), p. 72.
93 Prayer quotation: *A Time to Heal*, p. 10.
94 Communion quotation: *A Time to Heal*, p. 175.
94 Littlefair quotation: Sermon preached by Dr. Duncan E. Littlefair, Fountain Street Church, Grand Rapids, Mich., September 15, 1974, Gerald R. Ford Library, White House Central Files, Code JL-1/ Nixon.
95 Zeoli references: Billy Zeoli, *God's Got a Better Idea* (Old Tappan, N.J.: Fleming H. Revell Co., 1978).
95 Mr. Zeoli is a minister of the Christian Reformed Church.
96 Comment on Carter's religion: *A Time to Heal*, p. 416.
96 Zeoli quotation: *Better Idea*, p. 19.

Chapter 6

99 Carter quotation: Interview, President Jimmy Carter, May 18, 1987. Other quotations from President Carter in this chapter, unless otherwise identified, are also from this interview.
102 Powell quotation: Interview, Mr. Joseph L. (Jody) Powell, May 5, 1987.
102 Miss Lillian quotation: Interview in *MS* magazine, October 1976, p. 8, quoted in Neils C. Nelson, Jr., *The Religion of President Carter* (Nashville: Thomas Nelson, Inc., 1977), pp. 18–19.
103 Carter quotation: Jimmy Carter, *Keeping Faith: Memoirs of a President* (New York: Bantam Books, 1982), p. 48.
103 Southern Baptist Sunday School system: James C. and Marti Hefley, *The Church That Produced a President* (New York: Wyden Books, 1977), p. 9.
104 Wall quotation: Interview, James M. Wall, May 15, 1987.
106 Moral Majority: Jerry Falwell, ed., with Ed Dobson and Ed Hinson, *The Fundamentalist Phenomenon: The Resurgence of Conservative Christianity* (Garden City, N.Y.: Doubleday-Galilee, 1981).
107 Miss Lillian quotation: Wooten, *Dasher*, p. 104.
108 Comparison to Eleanor Roosevelt: Wooten, *Dasher*, p. 96.
108 Mr. Earl's philanthropy: Wooten, *Dasher*, p. 209.
108 Carter quotation on Miss Lillian: Jimmy Carter, *Why Not the Best?*, Nashville: Broadman Press, 1975, p. 72.
108 Second born-again experience: *Why Not the Best?*, pp. 131–32.
110 Maddox quotation: Interview with Robert L. Maddox, September 14, 1987.
110 Mrs. Niebuhr: Letter to Mrs. Reinhold Niebuhr, August 3, 1976, Box RM 1, White House Central Files, Subject File, Jimmy Carter Library.

111 Hypocrisy: Wooten, *Dasher*, p. 278.
111 TV interview: *Larry King Live*, Cable News Network, June 1, 1987.
112 Carters at Maranatha Baptist Church: Robert L. Maddox, *Preacher at the White House* (Nashville: Broadman Press, 1984), p. 177.
112 Carter's understanding of Niebuhr: William Lee Miller, *Yankee from Georgia: The Emergence of Jimmy Carter* (New York: Times Books, 1978), quotations from pp. 201, 212, and 216.

Chapter 7

114 Carter quotation: Interview, President Jimmy Carter, May 18, 1987. Other quotations from President Carter in this chapter, unless otherwise identified, are also from this interview.
115 Maddox quotation: Interview, September 14, 1987. Other quotations from Dr. Maddox in this chapter, unless otherwise identified, are also from this interview.
115 Powell quotation: Interview, Mr. Joseph L. (Jody) Powell, May 5, 1987. Other quotations from Mr. Powell in this chapter are also from this interview.
117 Maddox incident: *Preacher at the White House*, p. 159.
118 Carter quotation: Remarks to National Association of Religious Broadcasters, January 21, 1980, *Public Papers of the Presidents of the United States: Jimmy Carter, 1980–81*, Book 1 (Washington: U.S. Government Printing Office, 1980), pp. 180–83.
119 Interview by John Hart: NBC News, March 28, 1976, quoted in Wesley Pippert, ed., *The Spiritual Journey of Jimmy Carter* (New York: Macmillan Publishing Co., 1978), p. 101.
120 Campaign incident: Interview, James M. Wall, May 15, 1987.
121 Carter quotation, foreign policy: Address and remarks at Messiah College, February 18, 1986.
122 Panama: David McCullough, *The Path Between the Seas: The Creation of the Panama Canal, 1870–1914* (New York: Simon and Schuster, 1977), pp. 383–84. An account of the revolution and the activities of Bunau-Varilla can be found on pp. 361–402.
124 Carter quotation, injustice: *Keeping Faith*, p. 154.
124 Carter quotation, political cost: *Keeping Faith*, p. 178.
125 Carter quotation, forgiveness: *Public Papers of the Presidents of the United States: Jimmy Carter, 1977*, Book 1, January 20 to June 24, 1977 (Washington: U.S. Government Printing Office, 1977), p. 26.
126 Carter quotation, land of Bible: *Blood of Abraham*, p. 31.
127 Carter quotation, homeland ordained by God: *Keeping Faith*, p. 274.
127 Carter quotation, Jews, Moslems, and Christians: *Blood of Abraham*, p. 4.
127 Carter quotation, monotheistic religion: *Blood of Abraham*, p. 8.
128 Carter quotation, Bible to Camp David: *Keeping Faith*, p. 322.

129 Love and justice: Address by former President Jimmy Carter at Messiah College, February 18, 1986.
130 Carter quotation, Vins: *Keeping Faith*, pp. 148 and 143.
131 Sadat and Fahd: *Blood of Abraham*, p. 5 and pp. 184–85.
131 Jordan quotation: Hamilton Jordan, *Crisis: The Last Year of the Carter Presidency* (New York: G. P. Putnam's Sons, 1982), p. 51.
131 Carter quotation, Khomeini: *Keeping Faith*, p. 485.
133 Miller quotation: *Yankee from Georgia*, p. 127.
133 Abortion: Questions and answers following address at Messiah College, February 18, 1986.

Chapter 8

136 Carter quotation: *Public Papers of the Presidents of the United States: Jimmy Carter, 1977*, Book I (Washington: U.S. Government Printing Office, 1977), p. 24.
137 Reagan's quoting of Bible verse: *Public Papers of the Presidents of the United States: Ronald Reagan, 1984*, vol. 1 (Washington: U.S. Government Printing Office, 1984), p. 314.
137 Powell quotation: Interview, May 5, 1987. Other quotations from Mr. Powell in this chapter are from the same interview.
138 Carter quotation: Address to the National Association of Religious Broadcasters, January 20, 1980, *Public Papers of the Presidents of the United States: Jimmy Carter, 1980–81*, Book I, pp. 180–83.
138 Maddox quotation: Interview, September 14, 1987. Other quotations from Dr. Maddox in this chapter are from the same interview.
139 Carter quotation on Cadell: *Keeping Faith*, p. 115.
139 Wall quotation: Interview, May 15, 1987. Other quotations from Dr. Wall in this chapter are from the same interview.
140 List of comments: Carter, *Keeping Faith*, pp. 118–20.
140 Carter quotations: Speech on "Energy and National Goals," *Public Papers of the Presidents of the United States: Jimmy Carter, 1979*, Book II, June 23–December 31, 1979, pp. 1235–241.
144 Carter quotation, sacrifice: *Public Papers of the Presidents of the United States, Jimmy Carter, 1980–81*, Book I, p. 182.
144 Carter quotation, love and justice: Address on Religion and American Foreign Policy, Messiah College, February 18, 1986.
144 Panama Canal: See *Keeping Faith*, pp. 152–54.
145 Letter: *Keeping Faith*, p. 152.
146 Niebuhr quotation: Reinhold Niebuhr, *Moral Man and Immoral Society* (New York: Scribner's, 1932), p. xx.
146 Carter quotation: Interview, May 18, 1987. Other quotations from President Carter in the remainder of this chapter, unless otherwise noted, are also from this interview.
148 Plaque: Carter, *Keeping Faith*, p. 596.

151 Burns analysis and quotations: James MacGregor Burns, *The Power to Lead: The Crisis of the American Presidency* (New York: Simon and Schuster, 1984), quotations from pp. 25, 39, and 32, respectively.

Chapter 9

154 Anderson quotations: Interview, Special Assistant to the President for Public Liaison Carl Anderson, April 13, 1987. Other quotations from Anderson in this chapter are also from this interview.

155 Robertson-Carter exchange: Interview on Christian Broadcasting Network during 1976 campaign, quoted by Wesley G. Pippert, ed., *The Spiritual Journey of Jimmy Carter* (New York: Macmillan Publishing Co., 1978), p. 100.

156 Comment on Carter and White House Conference on the Family: Letter to the author from Richard John Neuhaus, July 14, 1987.

157 Neuhaus quotation: Interview, September 17, 1987.

157 On the importance of the Christian school controversy in the mobilization of the religious right, see Robert C. Liebman and Robert Wuthnow, eds., *The New Christian Right: Mobilization and Legitimation* (New York: Aldine Publishing Co., 1983), pp. 2–3, 60. Also Jerry Falwell, ed., with Ed Dobson and Ed Hinson, *The Fundamentalist Phenomenon: The Resurgence of Conservative Christianity* (Garden City, N.Y.: Doubleday-Galilee, 1981), p. 21ff.

158 Memo re: Meeting, Moral Majority Leaders, September 27, 1979, B. Maddox to Phil Wise and Anne Wexler, August 28, 1979, Box RM-1, White House Central Files, Subject File, Jimmy Carter Library. Also Robert L. Maddox, *Preacher at the White House* (Nashville: Broadman Press, 1984), p. 161–62.

159 Maddox quotation: Interview, September 14, 1987.

159 Glazer quotation: Nathan Glazer, "Fundamentalism: A Defensive Offensive," in Richard Neuhaus and Michael Cromartie, eds., *Piety and Politics: Evangelicals and Fundamentalists Confront the World* (Washington: Ethics and Public Policy Center, 1987).

160 Sketch of the major political organizations of the Christian right based on A. James Reichley, *Religion in American Public Life* (Washington: Brookings Institution, 1985), p. 319ff.; Robert Zwier, *Born Again Politics: The New Christian Right in America* (Downers Grove, Ill.: InterVarsity Press, 1982), pp. 18–34; and Falwell, *The Fundamentalist Phenomenon*.

161 Falwell quotation: William I. Peterson and Stephen Brand, "Where Is Jerry Falwell Going?" *Eternity* 31:7, July–August 1980, pp. 18–19, quoted in Falwell, *The Fundamentalist Phenomenon*, p. 144.

162 Wills quotation: Garry Wills, "Nelle's Boy: Ronald Reagan and

the Disciples of Christ," *The Christian Century*, 103:34, November 12, 1986, pp. 1001–006. Quotation from p. 1003. Most of the information on Reagan's childhood religious background is from this article.

163 Racial prejudice incident: Bob Slosser, *Reagan Inside Out* (Waco, Texas: Word Books, 1984), pp. 42–43.

163 Reagan quotation: Slosser, p. 34.

164 Moomaw quotations: Interview, Dr. Donn D. Moomaw, October 6, 1987. All quotations from Dr. Moomaw in this chapter are from this interview.

166 Reagan's remarks on church attendance: Ronald Reagan, *In God I Trust*, written and compiled by David R. Shepherd (Wheaton, Ill.: Tyndale House Publishers, 1984), p. 6. Books emphasizing Reagan's religious faith include Slosser, *Reagan Inside Out*; Frank Van der Linden, *The Real Reagan* (New York: William Morrow Co., 1981), and Helene Von Damm, ed., *Sincerely, Ronald Reagan* (Ottawa, Ill.: Green Hill Publishers, 1976).

167 Buchanan quotations: Interview with former Reagan White House Director of Communications Patrick Buchanan, June 2, 1987. All quotations from Buchanan in this chapter are from this interview.

168 Hodel quotations: Interview with Reagan administration Secretary of the Interior Donald Hodel and Mrs. Hodel, August 2, 1987. All quotations from Hodel in this chapter are from this interview.

170 References to the Boones and Jepsons: See Slosser, *Reagan Inside Out*, pp. 40, 47, 51.

170 Von Damm quotation: *Sincerely, Ronald Reagan*, p. 88.

170 Reagan letter: Von Damm, p. 93.

170 Gorbachev quotation: Buchanan interview, June 2, 1987.

171 Robert N. Bellah, et al., *Habits of the Heart: Individualism and Commitment in American Life* (Berkeley: University of California Press, 1985).

172 Wall quotation: Interview with James M. Wall, May 15, 1987.

173 Deaver remark: Paul M. Weyrich, "Reagan's Illusory Revolution," *Washington Post*, August 30, 1987, p. C2.

174 Cromartie quotation: Interview with Michael Cromartie, Center on Ethics and Public Policy, Washington, D.C., April 7, 1987. Other quotations from Cromartie in this chapter are from the interview.

174 E. Clifton White and William J. Gill, *Why Reagan Won: A Narrative History of the Conservative Movement, 1964–1981* (Chicago: Regnery Gateway, 1981), p. 30.

175 Jerome L. Himmelstein, "The New Right," in Liebman and Wuthnow, *The New Christian Right*, pp. 13–30. Quotations from p. 23.

175 Weyrich quotation: Weyrich, *Washington Post*, August 30, 1987, p. C-1.

176 Burns quotation: James MacGregor Burns, *The Power to Lead: The Crisis of the American Presidency* (New York: Simon and Schuster, 1984), pp. 46–71. Quotation from p. 71.

Chapter 10

180 Reagan quotation: *Public Papers of the Presidents of the United States: Administration of Ronald Reagan, 1983*, March 8, 1983 (Washington: U.S. Government Printing Office, 1983), pp. 359–64.
180 Commager quotation: quoted by Bill Peterson, "Reagan's Use of Moral Language to Explain Policies Draws Fire," *Washington Post*, March 23, 1983, p. A-15.
181 Reagan goals: *Public Papers of the Presidents of the United States: Administration of Ronald Reagan, 1984*, March 6, 1984 (Washington: U.S. Government Printing Office, 1984), pp. 312–17.
183 Rael Jean Isaac, "Do You Know Where Your Church Offerings Go?" *Reader's Digest*, January 1983, pp. 120–25.
183 IRD: Telephone interview with Diane Knippers, Program Director, Institute on Religion and Democracy, August 19, 1987.
184 Krauthammer quotation: Charles Krauthammer, "A Theory of Intervention: Morality, Strategy, and American Foreign Policy," paper presented to Center on Religion and Society Conference on Moral Purpose and American Foreign Policy, Washington, D.C., February 20–21, 1987, p. 3.
185 Reagan quotation: Remarks to Annual Convention of National Religious Broadcasters, February 9, 1982, *Public Papers of the Presidents of the United States: Administration of Ronald Reagan, 1982* (Washington: U.S. Government Printing Office, 1982), p. 158.
185 Similar quotations: See, for instance, his remarks to the National Religious Broadcasters the following year (February 1983) and the "Salute to Free Enterprise," January 26, 1984.
185 Moomaw quotation: Interview, October 6, 1987. Other quotations from Moomaw in this chapter are also from this interview.
187 *Amicus* briefs filed by solicitor general: Diamond *v.* Charles and Thornburgh *v.* American College of Obstetricians and Gynecologists.
188 Hodel quotation: Interview, August 2, 1987.
188 Anderson quotation: Interview, April 13, 1987.
189 Northwest Ordinance: Quoted by Martin E. Marty, "Neutrality and Religious Freedom," *The Christian Century*, 104:22, July 1–8, 1987, p. 580.
190 Religion in curriculum: Laura Sessions Stepp, "Educators Urge Wider Teaching of Religion," *Washington Post*, July 2, 1987, p. A3.
192 Mark Silk, *Spiritual Politics: Religion and America Since World War II* (New York: Simon and Schuster, 1988).
193 Paul M. Weyrich, "Reagan's Illusory Revolution," *Washington Post*, August 30, 1987, pp. C-1, 2.

196 Ford quotation: Interview, August 21, 1987.

Chapter 11

198 Graff quotation: Henry F. Graff, "Presidents Are Not Pastors," *New York Times*, May 27, 1987.

198 Sidey quotation: Letter to the editors, *Washington Post*, October 7, 1986, p. B-16.

201 Catholic statistics and McBrien quotation: "John Paul's Feisty Flock," *Time*, September 7, 1987, pp. 46–51.

201 Richard John Neuhaus, *The Catholic Moment* (New York: Harper and Row, 1987).

202 Catholic church and American freedom: See Richard P. McBrien, *Caesar's Coin: Religion and Politics in America* (New York: Macmillan Publishing Co., 1987), for an excellent contemporary treatment.

203 Letter from Dr. Robert L. Maddox, Jr., to President Jimmy Carter, September 1, 1978, and reply, October 3, 1978, Box RM 1, White House Central Files, Subject File, Jimmy Carter Library.

204 Maddox quotation: Interview, September 14, 1987.

205 Letter from Jack V. Harwell to President Jimmy Carter, June 23, 1977, and reply, August 11, 1977, Box RM 1, White House Central Files, Subject File, Jimmy Carter Library.

205 Powell quotation: Interview, May 5, 1987.

207 Powell quotation: Interview, May 5, 1987.

208 President Ford on church-state issue: Interview, August 21, 1987.

208 Falwell quotation: Jerry Falwell, "An Agenda for the Eighties," in Falwell, ed., *The Fundamentalist Phenomenon* (Garden City, N.Y.: Doubleday-Galilee, 1981), p. 188.

210 Abortion poll: *Time*, September 7, 1987, p. 48. Poll was conducted by phone, August 17–19, 1987, with 860 U.S. adults, including a special sample of 425 Catholics. Potential error: plus or minus 4 percent for all Americans surveyed, plus or minus 5 percent for Catholics.

211 Maddox quotation: Interview, September 14, 1987.

213 Jesse Jackson: Walt Harrington, "On the Road with the President of Black America," *Washington Post Magazine*, January 25, 1987, pp. 14–22, 41–44.

214 Black churches as political force: Quoted by Mary McGrory, "The Supreme Sacrifice," *Washington Post*, October 6, 1987, p. A2.

214 Pat Robertson's self-identification: Pat Robertson, *America's Dates with Destiny* (Nashville: Thomas Nelson, 1986), p. 20.

215 Robertson quotation: Beth Spring, "One Step Closer to a Bid for the Oval Office," *Christianity Today*, October 17, 1986, pp. 39, 41.

216 Smith quotation: "Robertson Followers Puzzle Iowa GOP," *Washington Post*, October 31, 1987, p. A7 (quoted from *Des Moines Register*).
217 Maddox quotation: Interview, September 14, 1987.
217 Robertson quotation: *Dates with Destiny*, p. 20.

Chapter 12

220 Maddox quotation: Interview, September 14, 1987.
221 Carter on "realpolitik": Address, Messiah College Annual Lectures on Religion and Society, February 18, 1986.
221 Powell quotation: Interview, May 5, 1987.
222 Church-sect typology: Max Weber, "The Protestant Sects and the Spirit of Capitalism," in *From Max Weber: Essays in Sociology*, Hans Gerth and C. Wright Mills, eds. (New York: Oxford University Press, 1946); Ernst Troelsch, *The Social Teachings of the Christian Churches*, Olive Wyon, trans. (New York: The Macmillan Co., 1931). Many have elaborated on this typology.
222 Cultural typology: H. Richard Niebuhr, *Christ and Culture* (New York: Harper and Brothers, 1951).
227 Religious polarization: E. J. Dionne, Jr., "Religion and Politics," *New York Times*, September 15, 1987.
229 Yardley quotation: Jonathan Yardley, "When Washington Discovers Character," *Washington Post*, September 21, 1987.
229 Barber quotation: James David Barber, *The Presidential Character*, 2nd ed. (Englewood Cliffs, N.J.: Prentice-Hall, 1977), p. vi.
230 *New York Times* editorial: October 2, 1987.
237 Barber quotation: *Presidential Character*, p. 4.
238 Challenge of the third century: These issues are dealt with extensively in Richard John Neuhaus, ed., *Unsecular America*, Encounter Series (Grand Rapids, Mich.: William B. Eerdmans Publishing Co., 1986).

Index